FAR WEST,
MISSOURI

The monument the LDS Church dedicated to Far West.

FAR WEST, MISSOURI

It Shall Be Called *Most Holy*

DAN A. *and* JANET L.
LISONBEE

CFI
Springville, Utah

ISBN 13: 978-1-59955-334-4

Published by CFI, an imprint of Cedar Fort, Inc., 2373 W. 700 S., Springville, UT 84663
Distributed by Cedar Fort, Inc., www.cedarfort.com

LIBRARY OF CONGRESS CATALOGING-IN-PUBLICATION DATA

Lisonbee, Dan A. (Dan Arthur), 1947-
  Far West, Missouri : "it shall be called most holy" / Dan A. and Janet L. Lisonbee.
    p. cm.
  ISBN 978-1-59955-334-4
  1. Far West (Mo.)--History--19th century. 2. Church of Jesus Christ of
Latter-day Saints--Missouri--History--19th century. 3. Mormon
Church--Missouri--History--19th century. 4. Missouri--Church history--19th
century. 5. Adam-Ondi-Ahman (Mo.) 6. Haun's Mill Massacre, Mo., 1838. 7.
Liberty Jail. I. Lisonbee, Janet. II. Title.

  BX8615.M8L58 2009
  289.3'77818309034--dc22

2009045370

Cover design by Megan Whittier
Cover photo by Sheli Cunningham
Cover design © 2010 by Lyle Mortimer
Edited and typeset by Kimiko Christensen Hammari

Printed in the United States of America

10 9 8 7 6 5 4 3 2 1

Printed on acid-free paper

Contents

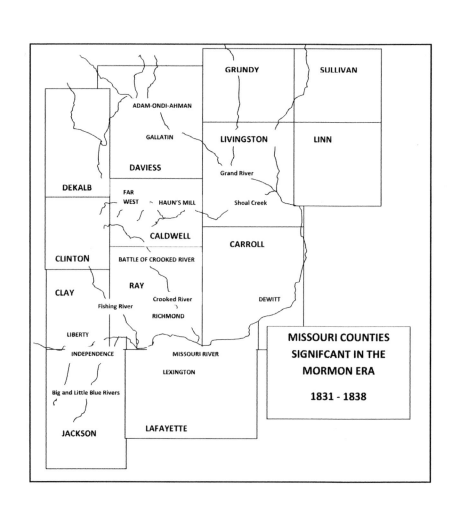

GRUNDY

SULLIVAN

ADAM-ONDI-AHMAN

GALLATIN

LIVINGSTON

LINN

DAVIESS

Grand River

DEKALB

FAR
WEST

HAUN'S MILL

Shoal Creek

CALDWELL

CLINTON

BATTLE OF CROOKED RIVER

CARROLL

CLAY

RAY

Crooked River

DEWITT

Fishing River

RICHMOND

LIBERTY

INDEPENDENCE

MISSOURI RIVER

LEXINGTON

Big and Little Blue Rivers

JACKSON

LAFAYETTE

MISSOURI COUNTIES
SIGNIFCANT IN THE
MORMON ERA

1831 - 1838

Preface

FAR WEST, MISSOURI

IN RECENT YEARS, THE CHURCH of Jesus Christ of Latter-day Saints has restored many of its historical sites to commemorate the people and events of those areas and to build testimonies of the Restoration. However, one important location in Church history remains largely undeveloped—that of Far West, Missouri.

The temple site at Far West is fenced and well maintained, with cornerstones and a plaque commemorating the principal revelations given there. But otherwise, no physical evidence remains of what was once a thriving community of more than ten thousand Saints, Church headquarters, and the home of Joseph Smith for approximately one year. Perhaps this is due to the negative events associated with the Mormon era in Far West, particularly the so-called Mormon War of 1838 that resulted in the Mormons being driven from the state of Missouri under Governor Boggs's extermination order.

However, there is more to the story of Far West than the Mormon War. This book is primarily written to tell other parts of Far West's history and significance, utilizing eyewitness accounts in the journals and personal histories of many early Mormon settlers. Of necessity, this book covers the principal events of the Mormon War because no book about Far West would be complete without a discussion of those events.

Accounts written during this era express the Saints' great optimism that they would be able to make permanent homes in the state of Missouri (which they believed to be the land of Zion) for the first time since November 1833, when they were forcibly driven from Jackson County.

Many of them made great sacrifices to go to Far West, and they worked hard to build a thriving community on the prairie, while enduring many hardships.

Joseph Smith received several important revelations in Far West, and in one of these, the early Saints learned that Far West was a holy land. They began the foundation for a temple, which they were not able to complete due to the opposition that arose against them. The Far West era was also a time of internal dissension within the Church when the local members took the highly unusual and contentious step of removing the local presidency from office.

During the past several years, members of the LDS Church have shown increased interest in the historical and spiritual significance of the Far West region. The scriptures indicate that the region will play an important role in events connected with the Second Coming of Jesus Christ. Many Church members have moved to the area or have purchased property there. Some have felt spiritual direction to move there, and others have done so in apparent recognition of the spiritual and historical significance of the area and the general belief that we are living in the last days prior to the Second Coming of Jesus Christ.

This book is also written to honor the early Mormon settlers who lived in Far West and sacrificed so much for their religious beliefs and to lay the foundations of the Church.

Chapter 1

THE SIGNIFICANCE OF FAR WEST

F ROM THE MORMON[1] TEMPLE SITE at Far West, Missouri, it is possible to look in all directions for miles. Today, the surrounding countryside is filled with beautiful rolling prairies, farms, and stands of timber. However, other than the temple site itself, there is no visible evidence that during the years 1836–39, the city of Far West was a thriving community of an estimated ten thousand Latter-day Saints.[2]

The Mormons were forced to abandon their homes in Far West in early 1839 under the extermination order issued by Missouri Governor Lilburn Boggs, which resulted from conflicts between Church members and nearby non-Mormon settlers. After the Mormons left, local farmers took the wood from their abandoned homes, or their properties deteriorated over time, and the area remains largely undeveloped farmland. The lack of remaining structures makes it difficult to visualize the once flourishing community.

The Mormon era in Far West is usually remembered for the so-called Mormon War of 1838. This conflict resulted in the Mormons being driven from the state of Missouri under Boggs's extermination order and in the incarceration of Joseph Smith and others in jails at Liberty and Richmond. It is important to remember the lessons learned from these conflicts, even though the causes of these conflicts have long since disappeared. The Mormons now live peaceably in Missouri, side by side with their neighbors. In 1976, Missouri Governor Christopher Bonds officially rescinded the Extermination Order of 1838 (see Appendix for the full text).

However, there is much more to the Far West story than the Mormon War of 1838. Along with Jackson County, Missouri, Far West played an

1

important role in the history of the Church, although the Church's presence in the area was comparatively brief in duration. Far West was a major gathering place for the Church members and also served as Church headquarters. Joseph Smith made his home there for approximately one year, and it was the only permanent residence he had in the state of Missouri.

The Mormons began to settle Caldwell County in the fall of 1836 with high hopes of making a permanent home for themselves in the state of Missouri for the first time since November 1833, when they were forcibly driven from Jackson County. The early Saints' personal accounts indicate that many of them made great sacrifices and encountered difficulties as they left their homes to go to the Far West region. Nevertheless, they went and established homes, farms, and stores and built a thriving community. After the initial Mormon settlers arrived, many other Church members began to flock to the area, and it became a major gathering place for the Church as a whole. Due to the number of members moving into the area, the Brethren soon realized that other stakes of Zion would need to be established as the habitable areas of Caldwell County began to fill up. Consequently, a community and stake were established at Adam-ondi-Ahman, twenty-five miles to the north.

When Joseph Smith moved to Far West from Kirtland in March of 1838, local Church members deemed it a privilege to have the Prophet living among them. While in Far West, Joseph Smith received several revelations now recorded in the Doctrine and Covenants, including, among others, the name of the Church and the law of tithing (D&C 113–20). Joseph also received several important revelations near the end of the Far West era while he was incarcerated in Liberty Jail (D&C 121–23).

In a revelation given to the Prophet Joseph Smith on April 26, 1838, the Lord called Far West "most holy" and directed the Mormons to gather to this land, which was to be a "refuge from the storm and from wrath when it shall be poured out without mixture upon the whole earth" (D&C 115:6–7). This revelation stated: "Let the city, Far West, be a holy and consecrated land unto me: and it shall be called most holy, for the ground upon which thou standest is holy" (D&C 115:7).

These words are reminiscent of those used long ago when God appeared to Moses on the mountain and commanded him to remove his shoes, "for the ground upon which [he stood was] holy" (Exodus 3:5). The revelation does not specify why Far West is holy ground, but Joseph Smith taught the early Mormons that the Far West region was part of the land where Adam and Eve dwelt and raised their children after they were expelled from the Garden of Eden and that the region will play a significant role during the Second Coming of Jesus Christ.[3]

The Lord directed the Saints to build a temple at Far West "for the gathering of [his] Saints, that they may worship [him]" (D&C 115:8). The Saints' optimism about their new home reached its peak at ceremonies held on July 4, 1838, when they laid the cornerstones for the temple. The foundation for this temple was dug, but the temple itself was never built due to the opposition that rose against the Church members and forced them to leave Missouri in early 1839.

The Organization of the Church and the Concept of Zion

The story of the Mormon era in Far West begins with the foundation of the Church itself. The Church was organized in Fayette, New York, on April 6, 1830, by Joseph Smith, who claimed to have had several heavenly manifestations. Young Joseph was extremely interested in finding the true church of Jesus Christ at a time when the region was filled with religious strife. While studying the Bible, he was impressed to take action by James 1:5, which says, "If any of you lack wisdom, let him ask of God, that giveth to all men liberally, and upbraideth not; and it shall be given him." To put the scripture to the test, Joseph Smith retired alone to a secluded spot in the woods not far from the family home. According to his own account, on that occasion, God the Father and his resurrected Son, Jesus Christ, appeared to Joseph and directed him to join none of the existing churches. They also told Joseph he would be the instrument though which God would restore the true church of Christ to the earth.

A little over three years later, Joseph received a second visitation, this one from an angel who identified himself as Moroni. This messenger said he was the custodian of an ancient record written on plates of gold that contained a history of the former inhabitants of the American continent (identified in the record as Nephites and Lamanites). In 1827, Joseph obtained the plates from Moroni and translated the inscriptions into English. The completed manuscript was published in 1830 as the Book of Mormon. Shortly thereafter, on April 6, 1830, the Church of Christ was organized with six official members in Fayette, New York, near Palmyra.[4]

As president of the Church, Joseph Smith received other revelations from time to time that directed him in this work of restoring the true church to the earth. In translating the Book of Mormon, he learned that a New Jerusalem, or city of Zion, would be built on the American continent (see Ether 13), and a revelation received in September 1830 said "that it is not revealed, and no man knoweth where the city Zion shall be built, but it shall be given hereafter. Behold, I say unto you that it shall be on the borders by the Lamanites" (D&C 28:9).[5] Shortly thereafter, Joseph Smith sent four men on a mission from Palmyra, New York, to the western borders of Missouri, which was on the borders by the Lamanites, or American Indians.

In early 1831, Joseph and his family moved to Kirtland, Ohio, where they would make their home until January 1838. In June 1831, he and twenty-seven other men went two by two on missions from Kirtland to Independence, Missouri. While there, Joseph declared that he had received a revelation that the area was to be the land of the Saints' inheritance and the center place of Zion: "This land, which is the land of Missouri . . . is the land which I have appointed and consecrated for the gathering of the Saints. . . . Behold the place which is now called Independence is the center place; and a spot for the temple is lying westward, upon a lot which is not far from the courthouse" (D&C 57:1, 3).

While Joseph was in Missouri, he dedicated a lot for a future temple, and a foundation stone was laid. Joseph summarized his experience in these words:

> I received, by a heavenly vision, a commandment in June follow-ing [1831], to take my journey to the western boundaries of the State of Missouri, and there designate the very spot which was to be the central place for the commencement of the gathering together of those who embrace the fullness of the everlasting Gospel. Accordingly, I under-took the journey, with certain ones of my brethren, and after a long and tedious journey, suffering many privations and hardships, arrived in Jackson County, Missouri and after viewing the country, seeking diligently at the hand of God, He manifested Himself unto us, and designated, to me and others, the very spot upon which He designed to commence the work of the gathering, and the up building of an "holy city," which should be called "Zion."[6]

Further, Joseph Smith taught that Independence and the Far West region will play a significant role in events associated with the Second Coming of Jesus Christ. There will be a gathering to the area; an important temple will be built in Independence; the city of New Jerusalem, referred to in biblical prophecies (Isaiah 2:3; Micah 4:2), will be built in Jackson County; and Jesus will reign on the earth for a thousand years, from two earthly centers—one in Jackson County and the other in Jerusalem.

Part of the Land Where Adam and Eve Dwelt

The early Mormons were also delighted when they learned that west-ern Missouri had a biblical significance as part of the land where Adam dwelt. Joseph Smith taught that the Far West region was part of the land where Adam and Eve raised their children after they were expelled from the Garden of Eden, which he said was located in Jackson County.[7] Joseph also said that Adam-ondi-Ahman means "the land where Adam dwelt."[8] Even though Joseph named a city in Daviess County Adam-ondi-Ahman, the Far West area was included in the "land where Adam dwelt" (D&C 117:8–10).[9] In addition, Joseph Smith taught that Adam-ondi-Ahman was a place where Adam was given priesthood authority (D&C 78:15–16). It was also there that Adam gave an important blessing to his posterity three years prior to his death and where the Lord appeared to them:

> Three years previous to the death of Adam, he called Seth, Enos, Cainan, Mahalaleel, Jared, Enoch, and Methuselah, who were all high priests, with the residue of his posterity who were righteous, into the valley of Adam-ondi-Ahman, and there bestowed upon them his last blessing.
>
> And the Lord appeared unto them, and they rose up and blessed Adam, and called him Michael, the prince, the archangel.
>
> And the Lord administered comfort unto Adam, and said unto him: I have set thee to be at the head; a multitude of nations shall come of thee, and thou art a prince over them forever.
>
> And Adam stood up in the midst of the congregation; and, notwithstanding he was bowed down with age, being full of the Holy Ghost, predicted whatsoever should befall his posterity unto the latest generation. (D&C 107:53–56)

Further, Joseph Smith taught that Adam-ondi-Ahman is the place that Daniel saw in a vision where Adam, the Ancient of Days, will sit in the last days (D&C 116; Daniel 7:9, 13–14). Joseph explained:

> Daniel in his seventh chapter speaks of the Ancient of Days; he means the oldest man, our father Adam, Michael; he will call his children together and hold a council with them to prepare them for the coming of the Son of Man. He (Adam) is the father of the human family and presides over the spirits of all men, and all that have had keys must stand before him in this grand council. This may take place before some of us leave this scene of action. The Son of Man stands before him (Adam), and there is given him glory and dominion. Adam delivers up his stewardship to Christ, that which was delivered to him as holding the keys of the universe, but retains his standing as head of the human family.[10]

Philo Dibble, an early Church member who lived near Far West, experienced an interesting vision while returning home one night from the government land office at Lexington, Missouri, that exemplified the grandeur and high expectations of the area. He wrote:

> When I had traveled about two-thirds of the way across the prairie, riding on horseback, I heard the cooing of the prairie hens. I looked northward and saw, apparently with my natural vision, a beautiful city, the streets of which ran north and south. I also knew there were streets running east and west, but could not trace them with my eye for the buildings. The walks on each side of the streets were as white as marble, and the trees on the outer side of the marble walks had the appearance of locust trees in autumn. This city was in view for about one hour-and-a-half, as near as I could judge, as I traveled along. When I began to descend towards the Crooked River the timber through which I passed hid the city from my view. Every block in this mighty city had sixteen spires, four on each corner, each block being built in the form of a hollow square, within which I seemed to know that the gardens of the inhabitants were situated. The corner buildings on which the spires rested were larger and higher than the others, and the several blocks were uniformly alike. The beauty and grandeur of the scene I cannot describe. While viewing the city the buildings appeared to be transparent. I could not discern the inmates, but I appeared to understand that they could discern whatever passed outside. Whether this was a city that has been or is to be I cannot tell. It extended as far north as Adam-ondi-Ahman, a distance of about twenty-eight miles. Whatever is revealed to us by the Holy Ghost will never be forgotten.[11]

This vision may have been symbolic of the spiritual grandeur of the future New Jerusalem, or it may have been a vision of times past. Some scholars have suggested it might have been a vision of the biblical City of Enoch, which may have been located in this area but was taken into heaven due to the righteousness of those who lived there. Section 75 of the 1835 edition of the Doctrine and Covenants makes a connection between the land of Zion and the city of Enoch. The Lord instructed the Saints to establish a "storehouse for the poor of my people, both in this place [Kirtland] and in the land of Zion, or in other words, the city of Enoch." Likewise, Moses 7:62 states that the City of Enoch would return to Zion:

> Righteousness and truth will I cause to sweep the earth as with a flood, to gather out mine elect from the four quarters of the earth, unto a place which I shall prepare, an Holy City, that my people may gird up their loins, and be looking forth for the time of my coming; for there shall be my tabernacle, and it shall be called Zion, a New Jerusalem. And

the Lord said unto Enoch: Then shalt thou and all thy city meet them there, and we will receive them into our bosom, and they shall see us; and we will fall upon their necks, and they shall fall upon our necks, and we will kiss each other; and there shall be mine abode, and it shall be Zion, which shall come forth out of all the creations which I have made; and for the space of a thousand years the earth shall rest. (Moses 7:62–64)

William W. Phelps wrote a hymn, commonly called "Adam-ondi-Ahman," that portrays the early Saints' view of the lands in the Far West region. (The hymn is also known as "This Earth Was Once a Garden Place"):

This earth was once a garden place,
With all her glories common,
And men did live a holy race,
And worship Jesus face to face,
In Adam-ondi-Ahman.

We read that Enoch walked with God,
Above the power of mammon,
While Zion spread herself abroad,
And Saints and angels sang aloud,
In Adam-ondi-Ahman.

Her land was good and greatly blest,
Beyond all Israel's Canaan,
Her fame was known from east to west,
Her peace was great, and pure the rest
Of Adam-ondi-Ahman.

Hosanna to such days to come,
The Saviour's second coming,
When all the earth in glorious bloom
Affords the Saints a holy home,
Like Adam-ondi-Ahman.[12]

In view of this exciting new knowledge, many Church members began to move to Jackson County beginning in 1831 and continuing over the next two years, with Independence as the center place. The Saints understood that a city was to be built, beginning at the temple lot, and that at some point this city would be the New Jerusalem spoken of in biblical prophecies and in the newly published Book of Mormon (D&C 84:2–5, 31–33). These early Mormon settlers in the Far West region deemed it a privilege to live and make their homes in such a choice land.

Notes

1. The name *Mormon* is a nickname attributable to the Church's belief in the Book of Mormon as well as the Bible.
2. There are no remaining structures from the 1830s in Far West Proper. However, Charles C. and Sarah Rich's log cabin has been identified and can be visited about four miles south of Far West in Mirable. Charles Rich was ordained an apostle in the LDS Church in 1849.
3. Several early Mormon journal accounts indicate that Joseph taught that the Garden of Eden was in Jackson County, Missouri. See Samuel Miles, Autobiography, 5; Edward Stevenson biography, 59; Cowley, *Wilford Woodruff—His Life and Labors*, 481; and Lee, Autobiography.
4. In 1838, the name of the Church was changed to The Church of Jesus Christ of Latter-day Saints. This change was made while the Church was located in Far West.
5. The term *Lamanites* refers to a group of people in the Book of Mormon that are believed to have been ancestors of certain American Indians.
6. *History of the Church,* 2:254.
7. See note 3 herein.
8. *Journal of Discourses*, vol. 18, 342–43.
9. McConkie, *Mormon Doctrine*, 20.
10. *History of the Church*, vol. 2, 386–87.
11. Philo Dibble autobiography, in *Faith Promoting Classics*, 86–87. The date of this vision is not indicated in Dibble's account, but it appears to have been early in the Far West era (fall of 1836). He refers to it before other events that occurred in Far West and in the context of recording land sales as they commenced to settle Caldwell County.
12. *Hymn* no. 49. This hymn was written by William W. Phelps in 1835. It was sung at the dedication of the Kirtland Temple and at several high council meetings at Far West.

Chapter 2

BEFORE FAR WEST: THE CHURCH IN MISSOURI, 1831–36

T HE MORMONS SETTLED IN JACKSON County in five principal communities: Independence, Colesville,[1] the Whitmer Settlement, the Prairie Settlement, and the Big Blue River Settlement. By the fall of 1833 there were ten branches of the Church in the area,[2] and an estimated 1,000 to 1,200 Church members lived there.

The Mormon presence in Jackson County was short, however. In November 1833, they were forced by the local settlers (hereinafter called anti-Mormons)[3] to leave their homes. Much has been written about the history of the Mormons in Missouri and their expulsion from Jackson County, and only a summary will be given here.[4] A basic awareness of these events is necessary to understand the Far West era.

Causes for the Conflict

At the time, Missouri was the western frontier of the United States and was sparsely settled. To some degree, it attracted a rough and law-less element.[5] To the west of Missouri was Indian territory, now the state of Kansas. Jackson County, named for General Andrew Jackson (then president of the United States), was settled principally by people from Tennessee and farther south. Clay County, immediately north and sep-arated from Jackson County by the Missouri River, had been named for Henry Clay, Jackson's opponent in the presidential contest of 1828. Its settlers were mostly Kentuckians. The city of Independence was the seat of Jackson County and was situated about three miles south of the Mis-souri River and twelve miles east of the state boundary line. It contained a courthouse built of brick, two or three mercantiles stores, and twenty or more private dwellings. Poorer settlers lived in log cabins without glass windows or finished floors, and many of the settlers—women as well as men—dressed entirely in skins. Their food was also coarse, usually consisting of wild meat, wild honey, pork, and corn bread prepared in the most primitive manner. Those financially well-to-do lived a better lifestyle.[6]

There were many differences between the Mormons and their neighbors. The Mormons mostly came from the northeastern United States, and by comparison to the local settlers, were more educated and more refined in their speech and manner of dress.[7] Also, many of the Mormons descended from the Puritans and had many puritanical traditions and habits, while the local settlers did not have such a background. Sabbath-breaking, profanity, cockfighting, drunkenness, and gambling were common for many of the locals.[8]

Slavery was a major political issue at the time. The Mormons did not own slaves and for the most part were against slavery, while the settlers of Jackson County were mostly from the South and were either slaveholders or advocates of slavery.[9] Missouri was a slave state and had enacted laws prohibiting freed slaves from moving into that state. Since Mormon policy encouraged Church members, regardless of race or color, to gather to the center state of Zion, some Missourians feared a possible infiltration of former slaves—a development they could not tolerate. However, this possibility appears to have been more theoretical than actual.

The local settlers became increasingly uneasy with the large growth in the Mormon population, and they feared that the Mormons would be able to gain political control of the county, even though the Mormons did not run for public office. However, some Church members contributed to these fears by boasting that many more Mormons would soon be moving into the county, that it was the promised land of their inheritance, and that they would eventually possess it to the exclusion of others.[10] A few local ministers added fuel to the fire with their preaching against the Mormons. One local reverend taught that "the Mormons are the common enemies of mankind and ought to be destroyed."[11]

Local settlers tended to fear the neighboring Indians, but the Mormons were more friendly and attempted to preach religion to them. The old settlers became suspicious that the Mormons intended to somehow use the Indians against them.[12] The Black Hawk War of 1832 was still a fresh memory, and many Indians were located near the Missouri borders in present-day Kansas.

Ultimately, however, the Mormon religion was the source of most conflicts.[13] In July 1833, the local settlers adopted a document that the Mormons call the "Manifesto of the Mob."[14] We quote in part from it to show the spirit of the times:

> We, the undersigned, citizens of Jackson county, believing that an important crisis is at hand, as regards our civil society, in consequence of a pretended religious sect of people that have settled, and are still settling in our county, styling themselves "Mormons;" and intending, as we do, to rid our society, "peaceably if we can, forcibly if we must," and believing as we do, that the arm of the civil law does not afford us a guarantee, or at least a sufficient one, against the evils which are now inflicted upon us, and seem to be increasing, by the said religious sect, deem it expedient, and of the highest importance, to form ourselves into a company for the better and easier accomplishment of our purpose—a purpose which we deem it almost superfluous to say, is justified as well by the law of nature, as by the law of self-preservation.
>
> It is more than two years since the first of these fanatics, or knaves, (for one or the other they undoubtedly are) made their first appearance amongst us, and pretended as they did, and now do, to hold personal communication and converse face to face with the Most High God; to receive communications and revelations direct from heaven; to heal the sick by laying on hands; and, in short, to perform all the wonder-working miracles wrought by the inspired Apostles and Prophets of old.
>
> We believed them deluded fanatics, or weak and designing knaves and that they and their pretensions would soon pass away; but in this we were deceived. The arts of a few designing leaders amongst them have thus far succeeded in holding them together as a society; and since the arrival of the first of them, they have been daily increasing in numbers; and if they had been respectable citizens in society and thus deluded, they would have been entitled to our pity rather than to our contempt and hatred; but from their appearance, from their manners, and from their conduct since their coming among us, we have every reason to fear that, with but very few exceptions, they were of the very dregs of that society from which they came, lazy, idle, and vicious. This we conceive is not idle assertion, but a fact susceptible of proof, for with these few exceptions above named, they brought into our country little or no property with them and left less behind them, and we infer that those only yoke themselves to the "Mormon" car who had nothing earthly or

heavenly to lose by the change; and we fear that if some of the leaders amongst them, had paid the forfeit due to crime, instead of being chosen ambassadors of the Most High, they would have been inmates of solitary cells. But their conduct here stamps their characters in their true colors. More than a year since, it was ascertained that they had been tampering with our slaves, and endeavoring to sow dissensions and raise seditions amongst them. Of this their "Mormon" leaders were informed, and they said they would deal with any of their members who should again in like case offend. But how spacious are appearances. In a late number of the Star, published in Independence by the leaders of the sect, there is an article inviting free negroes and mulattoes from other states to become "Mormons," and remove and settle among us. This exhibits them in still more odious colors. It manifests a desire on the part of their society, to inflict on our society an injury that they know would be to us entirely insupportable, and one of the surest means of driving us from the country; for it would require none of the supernatural gifts that they pretend to, to see that the introduction of such a caste amongst us would corrupt our blacks, and instigate them to bloodshed.

They openly blaspheme the Most High God, and cast contempt on His holy religion, by pretending to receive revelations direct from heaven, by pretending to speak unknown tongues, by direct inspiration, and by divers pretenses derogatory to God and religion, and to the utter subversion of human reason.

They declare openly that their God hath given them this county of land, and that sooner or later they must and will have possession of our lands for an inheritance; and, in fine, they have conducted themselves on many other occasions, in such a manner, that we believe it a duty we owe to ourselves, our wives, and children, to the cause of public morals, to remove them from among us, as we are not prepared to give up our pleasant places and goodly possessions to them or to receive into the bosom of our families, as fit companions for our wives and daughters, the degraded and corrupted free negroes and mulattoes that are now invited to settle among us.

Under such a state of things, even our beautiful county would cease to be a desirable residence, and our situation intolerable. We, therefore, agree that after timely warning, and receiving an adequate compensation for what little property they cannot take with them, they refuse to leave us in peace, as they found us—we agree to use such means as may be sufficient to remove them, and to that end we each pledge to each other our bodily powers, our lives, fortunes and sacred honors.[15]

Hostilities Commence

The hostilities commenced in Jackson County in July 1833. The anti-Mormons demanded that the Mormons sign a written promise to leave the county and close their newspaper. They also demanded that all Mormon-owned stores cease business and that no additional Mormons settle in Jackson County. A dozen anti-Mormons delivered the ultimatum to six local Mormon leaders. The shocked Mormon leaders replied that they would have to consult with Church leaders in Kirtland and that it would take three months to receive an answer.

This response infuriated the already agitated anti-Mormons. They thoroughly vandalized the home of William W. Phelps and then went looking for the Mormon press, which they tore apart.[16] They then went to the homes of Bishop Edward Partridge and another member, Charles Allen, pulled them from their homes, and tarred and feathered them in the public square, surrounded by hundreds of the anti-Mormon group.

The next day, the Mormons sought redress from the state government, but Lieutenant Governor Lilburn Boggs, who resided in Independence, surveyed the scene, shook his head, and remarked that it would probably be best if the Mormons just left.

The Mormons refused to move, and the anti-Mormons issued another ultimatum. One-half of the Mormons had to leave by January 1, 1834, and the other half were to leave by April 1, 1834. The Mormons approached the governor for relief from these illegal actions but to no avail. Meanwhile, the anti-Mormons roamed the streets under a red flag, which was a token of blood.

The anti-Mormons were dissatisfied with the Mormons' response, and violence began on October 31, 1833. The Mormons were scattered in several different communities and settlements. The anti-Mormons first attacked the Whitmer Settlement and destroyed more than a dozen homes. Two Mormon men, George Beebe and Hiram Page, were tied to a tree and whipped. The anti-Mormons did not find David Whitmer at home, so they pulled his wife outside by her hair and then destroyed the home.

The next night, the anti-Mormons attacked the Mormon settlement at the Big Blue River, six miles west of Independence. They found one elderly man, David Bennett, ill and unable to move. They beat him up, shot him in the head, and left him for dead. Miraculously, Bennett lived.

Several Mormons decided to defend themselves and rode toward the sounds of conflict. When the anti-Mormons saw the Mormons coming, they opened fire at the Mormons. The Mormons fired back, and one anti-Mormon was hit in the leg. The anti-Mormons briefly retreated but regrouped and went on a rampage, pillaging and ransacking several homes.

Tensions were high for the next few days. Three Mormon men, John Corrill, Isaac Morley, and Sidney Gilbert, brought charges against one Missouri man for pillaging a store, but the man was promptly acquitted. The man then filed a counter suit against the three Mormons, who were arrested and taken to jail.

On November 4, 1833, the anti-Mormons seized the ferry that Porter Rockwell operated at the Big Blue River Settlement. A gun battle ensued that day—the Battle of the Big Blue River—in which nineteen Mormons approached a group of fifty anti-Mormons. The Mormons retreated into cornfields, and when the anti-Mormons followed them, another group of thirty or so Mormons came upon their rear. Although only seventeen of the Mormons had guns, they managed to frighten off the anti-Mormons. Two anti-Mormons and one Mormon (Andrew Barber) were killed by gunfire. Another Mormon, Philo Dibble, was shot three times in the stomach but miraculously recovered.

The anti-Mormons regrouped and determined to drive the Mormons from the county. They spread vicious rumors that the Mormons had aligned themselves with the Indians and were planning to massacre the entire state. This news reached the courtroom where Corrill, Morley, and Gilbert were about to stand trial, and the sheriff had to guard them away to protect their lives from angry spectators.

When the governor heard the fabricated story that the Mormons were planning a combined massacre with the Indians, he sent the Jackson County militia to protect Independence. However, the militia was led by Colonel Pitcher, an avowed anti-Mormon, and many members of the militia were in the groups that were attacking the Mormons. Meanwhile, the Mormons gathered a group of about two hundred, led by Lyman Wight, to ride to Independence and free the three Mormon men being held as prisoners.

Thus, the two groups headed for what appeared to be a major and potentially dangerous confrontation, but moments before they met, Lyman Wight learned that the three Mormons had been set free and that Mormon leaders had decided to evacuate the county. He therefore dispersed his group.[17] However, Colonel Pitcher decided to take advantage of the Mormons. He shrewdly confessed that he and his fellow anti-Mormons had been at fault and suggested that the Mormons should, as an act of good faith, surrender their weapons temporarily. Lyman Wight agreed on the condition that the anti-Mormons would surrender their guns as well. Colonel Pitcher agreed and took the Mormons' weapons. However, the anti-Mormons were not required to turn over their weapons, and the Mormons' weapons were never returned.

With the Mormons unarmed, the anti-Mormons had the license they needed. They immediately launched what one writer has called "an unabashed orgy of destruction."[18] Mormon homes were burned or looted, and the Mormons were forcibly driven out of the county.

In freezing November temperatures, the Mormons fled their homes for safety, with nowhere to go for shelter. Many were caught, tied, and flogged, and some were shot while attempting to run. Some who were ill or aged died from the cold and exposure. Others died later from conditions brought about by the exposure. Lyman Wight said he witnessed 190 women and children driven across thirty miles of prairie "thinly crusted with sleet, and [he] could easily follow their trail by the blood that flowed from the lacerated feet on the stubble of the burnt prairie."[19] John Greene described the serious state of affairs:

> Horrible to relate, several women thus driven from their homes gave birth to children in the woods and the prairies, destitute of beds or clothing, having escaped in fright. It is stated, on the authority of Solomon Hancock, an eye-witness, that he, with the assistance of two or three others, protected 120 women and children, for the space of 8 or 10 days, who were obliged to keep themselves hid from their pursuers, while they were hourly expecting to be massacred—and who finally escaped into Clay County, by finding a circuitous route to the ferry.[20]

While fleeing from their homes in this forced exodus, many Mormons witnessed a brilliant meteor shower on the night of November 13, 1833.[21] Parley P. Pratt recorded:

> All the firmament seemed enveloped in splendid fireworks, as if every star in the broad expanse had been hurled from its course, and sent lawless through the wilds of ether. Thousands of bright meteors were shooting through space in every direction, with long trains of light following in their course. This lasted for several hours, and was only closed by the dawn of the rising sun. Every heart was filled with joy at this majestic display of signs and wonders.[22]

Most of the Mormons left Jackson County to the north, crossing the Missouri River by the ferry at Wayne City, north of Independence. It was a laborious and time-consuming process for so many to cross the river. A smaller group left Jackson County to the south and went to Van Buren County (now Cass County) for the winter.

After leaving Jackson County, the majority of the Mormons settled in adjoining Clay County, Missouri, to the immediate north of Jackson County across the Missouri River. Those who did not settle in Clay County were in nearby counties, such as adjoining Ray County to the east of Clay.

The residents of Clay County welcomed the refugees at first, but times were generally difficult there for the now homeless Mormons. David Pettigrew described the conditions in Clay County: "While living in Clay County, many of our dear brothers and sisters died from the hardships and exposure they had gone through, and many were forced to live in sickly places for lack of a better; in places too, that no others would attempt to live in. The majority of the people looked upon us as poor deluded people, and thought many of us were Christians and honest."[23]

Arrival of Zion's Camp and Establishment of the Missouri High Council

In May 1834, about two hundred men, under the direction of Joseph Smith, organized themselves into a quasi-military organization called Zion's Camp. They left their homes in Ohio and elsewhere, and marched to Missouri for the purpose of assisting the Mormons who had been forced from their homes in Jackson County. Zion's Camp arrived in Clay County in the latter part of June 1834. The camp members had left Ohio with the intent to restore the Mormons to their homes in Jackson County, but as they approached Missouri, a quasi-military group of local settlers, mostly from Jackson County, came out to meet them. It appeared that there would be a battle between the two groups, but when the two opposing forces were camped on different sides of the Fishing River, ready to meet, an incredible thunderstorm suddenly arose. It damaged the ammunition of the local militia and filled the normally mild river to incredible heights between the two groups, effectively precluding the battle.

Shortly thereafter, the members of Zion's Camp were attacked with a scourge of cholera, a disease that affects the digestive system and often causes death. About seventy members of the camp contracted the disease, and thirteen members of the camp died as a result.[24]

© Janet Lisonbee

Zion's Camp memorial at Mound Grove Cemetery,
Independence, Missouri.

On June 22, Joseph Smith indicated he had received a revelation on the banks of the Fishing River, stating that Zion's Camp was not to fight, and chastising the Saints in general for their transgressions:

> Behold, I say unto you, were it not for the transgressions of my people, speaking concerning the church and not individuals, they might have been redeemed even now.
>
> But behold, they have not learned to be obedient to the things which I required at their hands, but are full of all manner of evil, and do not impart of their substance, as becometh Saints, to the poor and afflicted among them;
>
> And are not united according to the union required by the law of the celestial kingdom;
>
> And Zion cannot be built up unless it is by the principles of the law of the celestial kingdom; otherwise I cannot receive her unto myself.
>
> And my people must needs be chastened until they learn obedience, if it must needs be, by the things which they suffer. (D&C 105:2–6)

After these events, Zion's Camp was disbanded, and most members of the camp returned to Ohio and elsewhere. A few remained in Missouri to establish homes.

While he was in Missouri, Joseph Smith also organized a high council, or the "High Council of Zion, to provide leadership for the church in Missouri."

> On the third of July [1834, a Thursday], the High Priests of Zion assembled in the yard of Col. Arthur's, where Lyman Wight lived, in Clay County, and I [Joseph Smith] proceeded to organize a High Council, agreeable to the revelation and pattern given at Kirtland, for the purpose of settling important business that might come before them, which could not be settled by the Bishop and his council. David Whitmer was elected president, and William W. Phelps and John Whitmer assistant presidents. The following High Priests, viz., Christian Whitmer, Newel Knight, Lyman Wight, Calvin Bebee, Wm. E. McLellin, Solomon Hancock, Thomas B. Marsh, Simeon Carter, Parley P. Pratt, Orson Pratt, John Murdock and Levi Jackman, were appointed councilors.[25]

After this, Joseph Smith returned to his home in Ohio, and the Missouri Mormons settled into Clay County and did the best they could to establish homes and farms. They were not certain as to how long they might be there but were planning to return to Jackson County, where they believed they had a legal right to be.

NOTES

1. The Colesville settlement was named after the Saints from Colesville, New York, who emigrated as a group to the area after a short stay near Kirtland.
2. Canon, *Far West Record*, 65.
3. Many Mormons referred to these anti-Mormon forces as *mobbers*, and that term was frequently used in Mormons accounts of the Jackson County experience.
4. More detailed accounts can be found in *History of the Church*, vol. 1, pages 426–38, and Joseph Fielding Smith, *Essentials of Church History*, pages 156–67. The information in this section is taken from those sources unless specifically noted otherwise.
5. See discussion in *History of the Church*, vol. 3, introduction, page 20.
6. Whitney, *History of Utah*, vol. 1, 76.
7. See discussion in *History of the Church*, 3:20–21.
8. Ibid.
9. Whitney, *History of Utah*, 1:76.
10. See discussion in *History of the Church*, vol. 3, introduction, pages 32–42.
11. *History of the Church*, 1:372, footnotes.
12. *History of the Church*, 3:29–32

13. *History of the Church*, 3:47, et seq.

14. Among the hundreds of names attached to the document were Lewis Franklin, jailor; Samuel C. Owens, county clerk; Russel Hicks, deputy county clerk; R. W. Cummins, Indian agent; James H. Flournoy, postmaster; S. D. Lucas, colonel and judge of the court; Henry Chiles, attorney-at-law; N. K. Olmstead, M. D.; John Smith, justice of the peace; Samuel Weston, justice of the peace; William Brown, constable; Abner F. Staples, captain; Thomas Pitcher, deputy constable; Moses G. Wilson and Thomas Wilson, merchants (*History of the Church*, vol. 1, 376).

15. *History of the Church*, 1:374–76

16. Two young Mormon girls, Mary Elizabeth Rollins [Lightner] and her sister Caroline were able to save many of the pages of the Book of Commandments, as it was then called, which later became known as the Doctrine and Covenants.

17. *Times and Seasons*, 35; Wight, *Mormon Redress Petitions*, 653.

18. Dewey, *Porter Rockwell*, 19.

19. Lyman Wight testimony before Nauvoo Municipal Court, July 11, 1843 (*History of the Church*, 1:435n).

20. John Greene, *Expulsion of the Mormons*, 23; *Journal of Discourses*, 1:13, 107.

21. These magnificent "falling stars" were seen as far away as Ohio (*History of the Church*, 1:439).

22. *Autobiography of Parley P. Pratt*, 103.

23. David Pettigrew Journal, *An Enduring Legacy*, 3:202.

24. The names of the deceased are John S. Carter, Eber Wilcox, Seth Hitchcock, Erastus Rudd, Alfred Fisk, Edward Ives, Noah Johnson, Jesse B. Lawson, Robert McCord, Eliel Strong, Jesse J. Smith, Betsey Parrish (the wife of Warren Parrish and one of the eleven women traveling with the camp), and Warren Ingalls. Several local members also contracted the disease while assisting camp members, and Algernon Sidney Gilbert, as well as a young girl living with him, Phebe Murdock, died (*History of the Church*, 2:120).

25. *History of the Church*, 2:122–24. Note: there were only two stakes in the Church at that time, one in Kirtland and the other in Missouri.

Chapter 3

THE CREATION OF
CALDWELL COUNTY

O NE UNIQUE FEATURE OF CALDWELL County, Missouri, is that it is the only county in the United States that was created specifically as a home for Mormons. It was established as a place where the Mormons could live by themselves, unmolested by others and without the friction that arose between them and their Gentile neighbors in Jackson and Clay Counties. This peaceful coexistence proved to be an elusive objective, however, as the Church maintained a presence in Caldwell County for less than three years (1836–39).

Events Leading to the Creation of Caldwell County

After the forced exodus from Jackson County in November 1833, the people of Clay County were at first sympathetic to Church members. They welcomed them and treated them well. The prevailing thought, however, was that the Mormons' stay would only be temporary. When it became apparent to the old settlers that the Mormons would not be able to return to their homes in Jackson County soon, if at all, the old settlers expressed some misgivings about permitting the Mormons to remain. The local citizens were also concerned by the fact that some of the Mormons purchased land in Clay County and began to establish farms.[1] However, the Mormons were generally held in high regard by the residents of Clay County.

Many years after the Mormons left Missouri, Alexander Doniphan wrote: "While the Mormons resided in Clay County they were peaceable, sober, industrious, and law-abiding people, and during their stay with us, not one was ever accused of a crime of any kind."[2]

Nevertheless, by 1836, residents of Clay County began to grow weary of the increasing number of Church members gathering in their county. The old feelings of negative excitement eventually returned. Slavery flourished in Clay County, and the Mormons' anti-slavery stance was not welcomed. There were only five hundred registered voters in Clay County in 1830 (the latest census before 1836), and the Clay County locals feared that a large number of Mormon residents would be able to out-vote them.

The Mormons were reminded that they had originally been offered refuge in Clay County only until they could be restored to their homes in Jackson County. Since that was no longer likely to occur, the people of Clay County came to the conclusion that the Mormons should leave and extended a formal notice to this effect. On June 29, 1836, the non-Mormon portion of Clay County drew up a petition asking the Mormons to remove from the county. A committee presented the petition to the local Church leaders. Three reasons were cited for this action against the Mormons:

1. They are eastern men, whose manners, habits, customs, and even dialect are essentially different from our own.

2. They are non-slaveholders, and opposed to slavery, which, in this peculiar period when abolition has reared its deformed and haggard visage in our land, is well calculated to excite deep and abiding prejudices in any community where slavery is tolerated and practiced.

3. They are charged with maintaining a constant communication with the Indian tribes on our frontier, with declaring, even from the pulpit, that the Indians are a part of God's chosen people and are destined by heaven to inherit this land, in common with themselves.[3]

The Mormons were not formally charged with any crimes or misdemeanors and the document went on to say:

> We do not vouch for the correctness of these statements; but whether they are true or false, their effect has been the same in exciting our community. In times of greater tranquility, such ridiculous remarks might well be regarded as the offspring of frenzied fanaticism; but at this time our defenseless situation on the frontier, the bloody disasters of our fellow citizens in Florida and other parts of the south, all tend to make a portion of our citizens regard such sentiments with horror, if not alarm.[4]

The petition admitted "that they had not the least right under the laws of the country and the Constitution to expel them by force," but they did earnestly urge the Mormons to seek some other abiding place where the manners, habits, and customs of the people would be more consonant with their own. For this purpose "we would advise them to explore the Territory of Wisconsin. This country is peculiarly suited to their conditions and their wants."[5] The local citizens also offered to assist the Mormons in finding and relocating to a suitable place.

The Mormons met to consider a response. They held a public meeting in Clay County on July 1, 1836, which was well attended.[6] The Mormons decided to agree to move and to accept the offer for assistance from the citizens of Clay County. They responded with a written resolution and appointed Thomas B. Marsh, Lyman Wight, and Samuel Bent as a committee to deliver the response to the local citizens, with Thomas Marsh as spokesmen.[7] The response indicated the Mormons would agree to move, and they expressed gratitude for the kindness shown to them by the citizens of Clay County but denied all accusations of wrongdoing on their part, in particular that they advocated the overthrow of slavery, maintained a correspondence with the Indians, and claimed entitlement to the land without purchase. The resolution provided:

> Resolved first, for the sake of friendship, and to be in a covenant of peace with the citizens of Clay County, and they to be in a covenant of peace with us, notwithstanding the necessary loss of property, and expense we incur in moving, we comply with the requisitions of their resolutions in leaving Clay County, as explained by the preamble accompanying the same and that we will also exert ourselves to stop the tide of emigration of our people to this county.
>
> Resolved second: That we accept the friendly offer verbally tendered to us by the committee yesterday, to assist us in selecting a location, and removing to it.[8]

Thomas B. Marsh said that in presenting the Mormons' response to General Atchison and the citizens group of Clay County, he was "enabled to speak so feelingly in relation to our previous persecutions and expulsions that General Atchison could not refrain from shedding tears."[9]

The citizens group then held a second meeting at Liberty on July 2, 1836, and issued a reply accepting the Mormons' resolution and committed to assist in the relocation process.

Developing Tensions

Although the exodus from Clay County was generally peaceable, undercurrents of mob activity arose against the Church, fueled by several local ministers. Although these excitements did not lead to widespread physical persecution or mob activity at the time, they increased the tension between the Mormons and local settlers. Apparently, some of the men who had driven the Mormons from Jackson County came into Clay County to cause troubles

Joseph Smith taught that Church members should continue to gather to Missouri and "situate themselves to be in readiness to move into Jackson" [as of September 11, 1836], "which is the appointed time for the redemption of Zion."[10] As the date approached, however, it was obvious that the political and cultural problems that had prompted the Mormons' expulsion from Jackson County had not been solved. It appeared as though the persecutions of old would resume. David Pettigrew recorded the hostile feelings that existed:

> The old feelings and excitement of Jackson County now began to show itself in Clay. It was first started by the ministers of the gospel such as Edwards and Balden, Baptist ministers, and others soon followed. They soon had the people to arms and, I suppose, made the people believe they were doing God a service. I am satisfied that many of their leading men were from Jackson County, for the same spirit was manifested over again. We were now forced to take up arms in self-defense. The excitement had got to its highest pitch and their head men such as Judge Cameron, Judge Birch and others made several speeches to the people which seemed to allay somewhat their excitement. They came to the conclusion to give us Caldwell County and that we should live there by ourselves, and thither we moved. . . . On a visit to Clay County, while on my way I saw for the third time the mob spirit. I saw a large company of men, who appeared to be mustering, and I found out they were making arrangements and preparing to go against the Mormons.[11]

Similar feelings were beginning to arise against the Mormons in Ray County as well. John Murdock described the conditions he found when he arrived from Kirtland on July 14, 1836:

> When we landed on Crooked River, in Ray County, we found from one to two hundred families . . . encamped in this neighborhood. Some by the wayside, some in the woods, and some in buildings of different descriptions, all in suspense, waiting to know what to do; for the inhabitants of Clay County had rose [risen] up in defiance of law and

gospel, and forbid any further move of our brethren into that county and had passed a decree that those who were in the county should leave. Now these brethren were from the far east, strangers in a strange land, and to add to their affliction, some of them nearly moneyless and many of them sick, and others daily sickening and they might well use the words of the poet, "We have no home nor where to go."[12]

Brother Murdock and John Corrill met with the Ray County citizens group on July 30, 1836, to present the Mormons' case, but to no avail. Of this experience he recorded: "I, in company with Elder John Corrill met the Ray County Committee, and laid our complaint before them, and desired of them that if we could not have a home with them that they would grant us the privilege of settling on Shoal Creek in the Territorial part of the state; and after calling in a meeting of the county, they granted the latter but would not let us live with them."[13]

The Legislature Creates Two New Counties

The state legislature developed a solution to this so-called Mormon problem. With the assistance of Attorney Alexander Doniphan, an elected representative from Clay County, arrangements were made in the state legislature to create two new counties out of the northern portions of Ray County and to allot one of them, Caldwell County, exclusively to the Mormons. Daviess County was also created out of Ray County at the same time but could be settled by both Mormons and non-Mormons.

The bill passed on December 26, 1836, thus establishing the new county.[14] The county offices were to be in the hands of the Mormons, and they were to have a representative in the general assembly of the state.

Those involved in these processes believed the creation of the new county was a complete and satisfactory solution to the Mormon problem. The Missourians were satisfied because they had a poor opinion of the prairie soil of the new county and doubted whether it would ever be made really valuable. Moreover, they wished to rid themselves of the presence of the Mormons, who they regarded as clannish and exclusive, as well as unpleasantly peculiar. The Mormons were satisfied because they wished for peace and wanted to enjoy their religion undisturbed by others and now had a home of their own.[15]

As then established and as it exists today, Caldwell County is generally rectangular in shape and is approximately twenty-four miles from east to west and eighteen miles from north to south. The new county was named after Captain Matthew Caldwell, who had served in the Revolutionary War as the commanding officer of Alexander Doniphan's father.[16]

Daviess County was named after Colonel Joseph H. Daviess, who also served with Doniphan's father in the Revolutionary War. Daviess was killed in 1811 at the Battle of Tippecanoe, Indiana.[17]

Notes

1. Roberts, *A Comprehensive History of the Church*, 1:413.
2. *Kansas City Journal*, June 5, 1881; *Saints Herald*, 28:197.
3. *History of the Church*, 2:450.
4. Ibid. The principal "bloody disasters" referred to was the so-called Second Seminole War in Florida, which began in 1835 and lasted until 1842.
5. *History of the Church*, 2:450.
6. Ibid., 2:452–53.
7. Marsh, Autobiography in *Millennial Star* 26, 391.
8. Roberts, *A Comprehensive History of the Church*, 1:416.
9. Thomas Marsh Autobiography in *Millennial Star* 26, 391.
10. Jesse, *Personal Writings of Joseph Smith*, 349.
11. Pettigrew, *An Enduring Legacy*, 3:203.
12. *John Murdock Journal*, 16.
13. *John Murdock Journal*, 16.
14. Ward, *A Brief History of Caldwell and Livingston Counties, Missouri* [hereafter referenced as *History of Caldwell County*].
15. Ibid., 116–18.
16. Ibid., 105.
17. Ibid.

Chapter 4

THE MORMONS SETTLE CALDWELL COUNTY

T
HE FIRST MORMON SETTLERS IN Caldwell County came
from Clay County and began to settle Far West in large numbers
during the fall of 1836. Steady growth occurred after that, as comparatively
smaller groups of Mormons continued to move to Caldwell County from
the eastern states and Canada. These Church members typically traveled
to the Far West area in small companies consisting of a few wagons and
families. However, a significant influx occurred in 1838. Joseph Smith and
his family left Kirtland, Ohio, in January 1838, and arrived in Far West in
March. Soon thereafter, in April 1838, Joseph received a revelation indicating, in part, that the Mormons should gather to Far West and other nearby
environs (D&C 115:17–18). Thus, Far West became a significant gathering
place for the young Church. Most of the Mormons living in Kirtland soon
came to Far West, as did many from other states and Canada. Two large
groups arrived in 1838: one group of over two hundred wagons arrived from
Canada in June, and another large group of several hundred, known as Kirtland Camp, arrived in October. Joseph Smith sent the latter group to settle
Adam-ondi-Ahman because of crowded living conditions at Far West.

As Church members continued to settle in Far West, Caldwell County
became crowded, and the Mormon settlements spread into adjoining
Daviess, Livingston, Clinton, and Carroll Counties. The initial concept in
establishing Caldwell County for the use of the Church was that Mormon
settlements outside the county were supposed to be made after obtaining
permission from local inhabitants. The Mormons assumed they had permission when they paid for the purchase of property in another county.[1] Nevertheless, the expansion into other counties was a factor that contributed to the

later difficulties between the Church members and local Missourians.

Prior to the arrival of the Mormons, Caldwell County was largely unpopulated, with only seven families living there. They were bee hunters, and their business was not profitable because the land was mostly prairie. In fact, due to the scarcity of timber, Caldwell County was generally regarded by the locals as worthless.[2]

The Mormons took an interest in the Far West area as early as the spring of 1836, even before the citizens of Clay County formally asked them to leave. A few Mormon settlers exiled from Jackson County were already in the area.[3]

Shortly after the public meetings held in Clay County in July 1836, the Church appointed a committee of three men to explore the area for possible settlement: Morris Phelps, Joseph Clayton, and Wheeler Baldwin. These three men left their homes on July 31, 1836, and returned with a favorable report. Morris Phelps, one of the committee members, described Caldwell County as "a beautiful rich and fertile country though mostly prairies. [The] land was high, and was beautifully situated for farming, also with groves of timber beautifully shading the small streams and many springs of water that gently made their way into North Grand River, equally dividing the prairie, leaving them sufficiently large to permit farms on each side of the timber. We made our location on Log Creek and bought out three of the Missourians the only settlers in that grove of timber."[4]

The Church then appointed a committee of "wise men" to acquire lands for the Church membership in Caldwell County in accordance with a revelation given in December of 1833, which directed the Mormons to appoint a committee of honorable and wise men to purchase lands in Missouri (D&C 101:69–73). William W. Phelps wrote: "There were four men appointed in a private meeting in the Temple at Kirtland as 'wise men' to purchase all the land in Jackson County and in the regions round about for money. I was ordained president of this new quorum, with Edward Partridge, John Whitmer and John Corrill for my assistant wise men. We did the best we could, and I have the documents to claim some thousands of acres of this purchase from Uncle Sam."[5] Isaac Morley assisted these men in their endeavors.[6]

William W. Phelps and John Whitmer chose the site for Far West. The official entry of the town site was made on August 8, 1836. The north half was entered in the name of William W. Phelps and the south half in the name of John Whitmer, but both men merely held the land in trust for the Church.[7]

The money ($1,450) used for the purchase had been collected from Church members in Tennessee and Kentucky by Elisha H. Groves and

Thomas B. Marsh, President of the Quorum of Twelve Apostles, in the summer of 1836. These two men were sent on a mission to raise this money for "poor bleeding Zion" by William W. Phelps and John Whitmer, members of the Missouri Presidency (generally equivalent to a stake presidency in the Church today).[8] This money was turned over to Phelps and Whitmer for the purchase of land in Far West, with the general understanding that Phelps and Whitmer purchased the lands in trust for the Church. However, as discussed in a later chapter, the manner in which the funds were used to acquire lands became a source of controversy in the Church and led to the removal of these two men from the presidency.

Bishop Edward Partridge assisted in locating land for purchase and recorded the following:

> After my arrival at home [from a trip to Ohio for dedication of the Kirtland Temple] I spent a few days in attending to my own affairs; then in company with Bro. W. W. Phelps, I took a tour in looking at the country north. We found a mill site on Shoal Creek, about 35 miles N.E. of Liberty that suited us very well. We went out again in company with Brother Morley and Corrill, looked out some corners and Brother Corrill went and entered seven 80-acre tracts. Brothers Phelps and Corrill soon after looked out and entered thirteen more. In the meantime I visited the church, and brethren that were coming in, or had just arrived.[9]

In laying out Far West, the general plan was to follow the pattern for the cities of Zion outlined by Joseph Smith in connection with the establishment of Independence a few years earlier.[10] The original town site at Far West was made one mile square and was approved by the Missouri High Council in April 1837.[11] The city was divided by streets running at right angles into regular blocks, except that a large public square (ten acres) was laid off in the center of town, designed for a temple site and other public buildings. This square was approached from all four points of the compass by four principal avenues, eight rods wide (132 feet).[12] Other streets were five rods wide (82.5 feet).[13]

The original town site was expanded to two miles square under the direction of Joseph Smith when he visited Far West in November 1837. This expansion was due to the growth of the community, which was beginning to exceed expectations. As part of this plan, the city blocks were also expanded to include four acres instead of 396 square feet as originally designed.[14]

Shortly after the visit of the committee of three, the Mormons from Clay County began to settle the new area. As a result of the arrival of the Mormons and the legislature's creation of the new county for Mormons, most of the non-Mormon settlers in Caldwell sold their farms and moved out.

The Mormons settled along Shoal Creek and heavily along the southern townships of Caldwell County, closest to Ray County. The Mormon settlers were able to purchase land through the government land office in Lexington, Missouri (about forty miles away), initially for as little as $1.25 per acre. They could also acquire property directly from any Missouri settlers who owned land. By July 1837, due to increasing demand, land prices increased to as much as ten dollars per acre.[15]

The Mormons were excited as they arrived on the new land, and many recorded favorable impressions of it. Luman Shurtliff wrote, "On the 2nd of June [1838] we reached Far West, Missouri. I thought this the most beautiful county I ever saw and felt to rejoice that I and my family had been permitted to gather with the Saints in such a good land where I expected to live until the Saints went to Jackson County."[16]

Lyman Littlefield wrote that Far West "abounded in delightful locations. A high rolling prairie, with a black loam soil, interspersed with groves of timber and producing in many places heavy crops of delicious grasses for stock grazing or for the cutting of hay, and watered here and there by clear streams of running water—made it a desirable region for settlers on the public domain."[17] He also wrote, "Upon a delightful and sightly location the city of Far West was surveyed and soon a beautiful and thriving town sprang up as if by magic. The Latter-day Saints, with their habits of industry and thrift, in a little time were established in comfortable and happy homes and the voice of praise and thankfulness to the Almighty was heard in their abodes and in newly erected places of worship."[18]

Nearly all of the first houses in Far West were log cabins, and the majority of Mormon settlers in Far West were poor. Many were able to acquire and improve only forty acres of land.[19] This was due in large part to their banishment from Jackson County and the circumstances of their temporary stay in Clay County. In Far West, every head of family was guaranteed a home, and if he was unable to buy one, it was given him from the lands held by the trustees of the Church.[20] In a few months, however, some frame homes were built, a portion of the lumber being brought from lower Ray, and a portion being whip-sawed. Perhaps the first house was built by one Ormsby, in the summer of 1836.[21] It is believed that John Whitmer's house was built in January 1837.[22]

Local histories indicate that the Mormons in Far West built several hundred homes, four dry goods stores, three family grocery stores, several blacksmith shops, two hotels, a printing shop, and a large schoolhouse that doubled as a church and courthouse.[23] By the time the Mormons left Missouri, there were an estimated ten and fifteen thousand people living in Caldwell, Daviess, and other nearby counties. The Mormon community centered at Far West encompassed over two thousand farms and approximately 250 thousand acres.[24]

Far West served as the county seat, and court was held in the schoolhouse until the county seat was moved to Kingston in 1843. The schoolhouse was also used as a place for public meetings, worship services, and as a meeting place for the Far West High Council of the Church. There was also a cemetery west of town that was used during the Mormon era.[25]

Levi Jackman, a member of the high council, described the growth of the new community:

> It was finally settled that we should go north to a new county and live by ourselves, which we were willing to do. This was afterwards called Caldwell County. The most of us left Clay County and settled our new home that season. We laid out a town on a beautiful elevated place and called it Far West. We soon organized our city and county. I was elected one of the Justices of the Peace, and had considerable business to do. We were prosperous and happy for a season.
>
> The winter following the Legislature set off this territory into different counties, viz., Livingston, Daviess, and Caldwell . . . emigration rapidly increased . . all the land fit for cultivation was purchased. Large farms were in cultivation the first summer. Some had grain to share. A city was laid off on a high commanding eminence on the prairies which could be seen for several miles distant. They commenced building in the fall of 1836. And in August 1837 there was seven stores in the city and about one hundred and twenty dwelling houses, and thickly settled around and the prairies were beautiful with elegant farms everything appeared to flourish. Peace, plenty, and tranquility appeared to flow from the houses of every citizen of the county.[26]

Emily Young, the daughter of Bishop Edward Partridge, gave a good description of the early efforts in settling the County. She wrote:

> Father moved his family into a piece of timber, about three miles from the place where Far West was afterwards located. Father and the brethren that were with him built log huts and prepared us as well

as they could for the coming winter. The timber in which we were camped was mostly hickory, with some black walnut, and hazel bushes were plentiful, and all were loaded with nuts, and when the frost came they dropped from the trees and lay so thick on the ground all around us that the children were kept pretty busy gathering them up. We gathered several bushels, and feasted on nuts through the winter, if with little else. As father's eldest children were all girls, my sister Harriet and I had to act the part of boys and help him with his work, such as milking the cows and going to the prairie and assist him in loading hay, and sometimes we would carry the chain when he surveyed the land.

After Far West was laid out father built another house and we moved into the city. The Saints from all parts of the world, where the Gospel had been preached, began to gather in, and the place was rapidly built up.[27]

Another early settler, Nancy Tracy, arrived with her husband and children in Caldwell County from Kirtland in October 1836, after a difficult journey. They found the members beginning to establish homes, although their circumstances were challenging:[28]

> Building had begun, but not a house was finished. The Saints were in destitute conditions and circumstances in consequence of persecution and being driven from their homes. It was the same with us. Our clothes and shoes were giving out. When we camped, my husband went to work with a will. He cut prairie grass for the cattle in the winter, and cut logs and built us a cabin, covered it with what they called shocks, split out of the timber, a floor of the same kind. The chimney was of sod. Never did anybody enjoy a mansion or appreciate more than I did the humble abode. When I went into it, the cold and storms were getting severe. It was the last part of November, and some provisions were the next things to look after. There was no alternative but to take team and go 30 miles over the bleak prairie to a settlement to get flour and earn some money on which to live. So my husband started out and left me with the children just coming down with whooping cough. He found work and earned 100 pounds of flour and a barrel of shelled corn. When he started for home, it was so freezing cold in crossing the prairie that he nearly froze to death. When he felt himself going to sleep, he was just able to rally himself and jump out of the wagon and then he didn't dare get in again, but ran and jumped until he got his blood to circulate. He was alone and in the night the wolves howled around him, but he got home safely at last with our winter's supply of bread stuffs.
>
> We could get no vegetables, but game was plentiful, such as deer, turkeys, and prairie chickens. My husband had a good gun and was a

good marksman and often brought down deer, which supplied us with meat, as they were fat. I made candles of their tallow. Wood was plentiful, and with an open fireplace and our tallow candles the evenings were pleasant, and we were indeed happy and thankful to the Lord for his blessings, feeling that he was ever mindful of those that trusted in him. I never felt to complain or murmur in our trials and afflictions.[29]

Joseph Smith's Arrival at Far West

In January 1838, Joseph Smith hastily left Kirtland out of fear for his safety. Sidney Rigdon accompanied him. Of his departure, Joseph wrote, "On the evening of the 12th of January [1838] about ten o'clock, we left Kirtland on horseback, to escape mob violence, which was about to burst upon us under the color of legal process to cover the hellish designs of our enemies, and to save themselves from the just judgment of the law."[30] Joseph and Sidney waited in Norton, Ohio, for a few days until their families joined them. Then they continued their journey in covered wagons to Far West. Wintry conditions created a long and tedious journey, and Joseph and Sidney were in danger from the pursuit of their enemies. Joseph was soon separated from Sidney Rigdon, who took a different route.

During the early part of the journey, Brigham Young, who had left Kirtland on December 22, 1837, joined the Prophet. In Dublin, Indiana, the Prophet took work cutting wood to obtain the necessities of life. Through the influence of Elder Young, a Brother Tomlinson sold some property and gave the Prophet three hundred dollars to help him on his way.[31]

On March 14, 1838, Joseph Smith arrived at Far West with his family. He recorded this account by letter to the Mormons in Kirtland:

> Dear and well-beloved brethren—Through the grace and mercy of our God, after a long and tedious journey of two months and one day, I and my family arrived safe in the city of Far West, having been met at Huntsville, one hundred and twenty miles from the place, by my brethren with teams and money, to forward us on our journey. When within eight miles of the city of Far West, we were met by an escort of brethren from the city, vis: Thomas B. Marsh, John Corrill, Elias Higbee, and several others of the faithful of the west, who received us with open arms and warm hearts, and welcomed us to the bosom of their society. On our arrival in the city we were greeted on every hand by the Saints, who bid us welcome to the land of their inheritance.[32]

Joseph was welcomed enthusiastically by the Missouri Mormons, who, for the first time, would have their beloved Prophet living among them. Many of the members in Missouri had known Joseph for several years. A substantial number of the Missouri Mormons joined the Church in Ohio and were among the earliest converts to the Church. Also, a good portion of the Missouri Mormons were from the Colesville, New York, branch and had been baptized in 1830. The Prophet had visited Missouri several times, and many of the Missouri Mormons had associated with him on visits to Kirtland. For example, the Missouri Church leaders had spent several months in Kirtland in connection with the dedication of the Kirtland Temple in March 1836.

Ebenezer Robinson wrote of his feelings when the Prophet Joseph Smith arrived at Far West:

> The arrival of Joseph Smith and his first counselor, Sidney Rigdon, at Far West was a cause of great rejoicing among the Saints. They had fled from the intrigues of a dangerous conspiracy in Kirtland, originating in the bosoms of those very men who had been blessed with the enlightening influences of the spirit of God, which flowed to them through the channel of the gospel which the angel from the courts of glory had revealed to the very man whom they persecuted; . . . . Truly, 'a Prophet is not without honor save in his own country and with those of his own household.'
>
> Joseph Smith, Jr., was held in very high esteem by the masses of the people, members of the Church, and looked upon as being invested with powers and qualifications far above all other men, being, as they thought, a great Prophet of God, like unto Moses, and that like Elisha, he could tell their actions, and almost their thoughts, when absent from them. They rejoiced to think they were permitted to live to see the day when prophets and apostles were restored to the earth again, therefore there was great rejoicing when he arrived among them.[33]

Sidney Rigdon's Arrival

When the Rigdon family arrived three weeks later on April 4, 1838, Joseph heard they were coming and was on the lookout for them. He met them just as they were coming into the village. According to the account of John Rigdon (Sidney's son), the following took place:

> [Joseph] shook hands with my father [Sidney] and my mother with tears in his eyes and thanked God that we had got to the journey's end. Joseph Smith led us to Thomas Marsh who was then the President of the Quorum of the Twelve. This was on Saturday. On Sunday they

were going to have a meeting and Sidney Rigdon was to preach.

All the Mormons in Far West came to hear him. There was a large schoolhouse outside the village where the meeting was to be held. There was no standing room. They took out the windows, the weather being warm, and got up into the window spaces. Some had to remain outside. He preached for two hours. It was one of his great efforts.[34]

Other Mormons Leave Kirtland for Far West

With Joseph gone to Far West, the majority of Mormons in Kirtland and other areas began to make plans to follow him west to Missouri in the next few months. Most of them made great sacrifices in order to gather at Far West. In addition to the difficulty required to uproot themselves and leave their homes behind, many had to sell their homes for a loss or abandon property all together. The journey from Ohio to Missouri was long and difficult, and the Mormons were often met with accident, disease, or occasionally the death of a family member. Some had to stop to repair their wagons, and others had to work odd jobs along the way to raise funds needed to be able to continue their journey. Others met with persecution along the way, particularly as they crossed the state of Missouri in the fall of 1838.

William Draper was one who left his Kirtland home behind without receiving fair compensation for it. Of his experience he said:

> I expected the avails of my little farm and home to supply me with means to get me another home if I should ever be so happy as to reach Far West where we were all aiming to go and make a permanent home as we thought then. But let me here say that I was sadly mistaken and seriously disappointed, for instead of having means to buy me another home in Far West, lo and behold a Christian gentile had me in his clutches and swindled me out of my little home so I never got one dime for the whole.[35]

William Cahoon made a similar sacrifice in leaving Kirtland in the spring of 1838. He wrote:

> I left behind me a good lot all paid for, for which I labored very hard to get, also a good seven-room house well furnished and owned by myself. . . I could not dispose of it, so I turned the key and locked the door and left it, and from that day to this, I have not received anything for my property, which is in the hands of strangers. However, we left it and went on our journey, pitching tents for a house. After a long and tiresome journey we arrived at Far West, 5 May 1838, and we rejoiced to find the Saints prospering and in good spirits.[36]

Warren Foote left Kirtland on May 6, 1838. He described the hazards of travel and harassments received along the way:

> All being in readiness we started for far off Missouri about noon. Father's family now consists of my sister Almira, myself and Sister Clarissa, and her husband George Gates [married in March or April]. There are three other families in company with us, namely, Stephen Markham, Abel Lamb, and Jefferson Dimick. We have one team apiece, and we are all dependent on S. Markham for expenses, and teams. We met with some accidents this afternoon. In going up a little hill, Elder Lamb's horses stopped, and let the wagon run backward off a dugway and upset the wagon, with his wife, and four children. She struck on a fence, and hurt her back, but not seriously. I was walking a short distance behind the wagon when the accident occurred. We soon got it righted up again, and had not gone far before the kingbolt of another wagon broke. They fixed it so as to get as far as Russell Center, where they got it mended. We drove a mile south of the village, and pitched our tents, and put on our wagon covers. Mr. Markham had some trouble with some fellows, who said that he owed them, but the truth is, they are persecuting him because he is a "Mormon." Many who left Kirtland had to steal away privately because of persecution. Their persecutors would swear out writs of attachments, and follow them, and attach their teams or goods, they would then have to stop and have a trial or pay an unjust demand; and sometimes both. Samuel Smith, a brother of the Prophet Joseph, had to secrete himself at Father's house a short time, to evade his pursuers. Mr. Markham put $116.00 into my hands for safe keeping, until he could get rid of his persecutors.[37]

Anson Call had an interesting encounter during his journey with some of the men who had been involved in driving the Mormons out of Jackson County in 1833. He left Kirtland in March 1838 and after traveling to Wellsville, Ohio, on the Ohio River, left his family to travel ahead and prepare a place for them. He went in company with Almon Babbitt and fell in company with Asael Smith and his wife (Joseph Smith's uncle and aunt) and George Gee and his wife. The party traveled to Missouri on a steamboat. He wrote:

> While passing up the Missouri River there was a gentleman who came to our room and said that he had learned there were Mormons on the boat. . . . The gentleman said, "Where are you going?" "To Far West, sir," was the reply. The man then remarked, "I am sorry to see so respectable a looking company journeying to that place." Brother

Smith said, "Why so?" He replied, "Because you will be driven from there before six months." "By whom?" "By the Missourians, gentlemen," said he. My father spoke and said, "Are there not human beings in that country as well as others?" He said, "Gentlemen, I presume you are not aware of the gentleman you are talking to." The reply was, "A Missourian, I presume." The gentleman again spoke, "Yes, gentlemen, I am Colonel Wilson of Jackson County. I was one of the principal actors in driving the Mormons from that county and expect to be soon engaged in driving them from Caldwell County."

He advised us to stop in some other place, for if we went to Far West we were surely to be butchered. We told him we were no better than our brethren and if they died, we were willing to die with them. "Gentlemen," he said, "you appear to be very determined in your minds. Mormonism must and shall be put down." He read to us a letter which he had just received from [Grandison] Newell, which consisted of a bundle of falsehoods concerning our people in Kirtland. "Thrice as false, Joe's career must and shall be stopped." He then started for the door. I then remarked, "If you will stop a moment or two, I will tell you the way it can be done, for there is but one way of accomplishing it." "What is that, Sir?" he said. I answered, "Dethrone the Almighty and Joe's career is ended and never until then." He left us very abruptly.

We soon landed at Jefferson City. I went off the boat in connection with other passengers. Wilson then gave me an introduction to about a dozen of the Jackson County boys, Governor Boggs included. He told them I was a Mormon going to Caldwell County. They then said, "Ha, ha," with a sneer.[38]

Kirtland Camp

A group of more than five hundred Mormons left Kirtland together in early July 1838 to travel to Far West, a journey that would take them 870 miles.[39] This group was known as Kirtland Camp, sometimes called the Kirtland Poor Camp. Most of the members who had the means to travel on their own got an earlier start, but a large number of members were still left in Kirtland, and many of them were among the poor. The concept of Kirtland Camp was that by journeying together, these remaining members could share the burdens and expenses of the journey. An extensive account of the organization and journey of the Kirtland Camp is found in the *History of the Church*.[40]

Kirtland Camp was established and organized under the direction of the Presidency of the Seventy. Many Church members were concerned about the condition of the poor Mormons remaining in Kirtland but were overwhelmed about the seeming impossibility of moving them to

Missouri. At a meeting held in the Kirtland Temple on March 10, 1838, to discuss the subject, the following took place:

> The Spirit of the Lord came down in mighty power, and some of the Elders began to prophesy that if the quorum would go up in a body together, and go according to the commandments and revelations of God, pitching their tents by the way, that they should not want for anything on the journey that would be necessary for them to have; and further that there should be nothing wanting towards removing the whole quorum of Seventies that would go in a body, but that there should be a sufficiency of all things for carrying such an expedition into effect.
>
> President James Foster arose in turn to make some remarks on the subject, and in the course of his address he declared that he saw a vision in which was shown unto him a company (he should think about 500) starting from Kirtland and going up to Zion. That he saw them moving in order, encamping in order by the way, and that he knew thereby that it was the will of God that the quorum should go up in that manner.
>
> The Spirit bore record of the truth of his assertions for it rested down on the assembly in power, insomuch that all present were satisfied that it was the will of God that the quorum should go up in a company together to the land of Zion.[41]

The camp adopted a constitution to govern its conduct.[42] The company was organized with James Foster, Zerah Pulsipher, Joseph Young, Henry Harriman, Josiah Butterfield, Benjamin Willer, and Elias Smith at the head as counselors to lead the camp.

The Kirtland Camp left at noon on July 6, 1838, and traveled south seven miles the first day. There are various accounts of the actual number of members, but the *History of the Church* lists the company as consisting of 529 souls—256 males, 273 females, and 105 families.[43] Other accounts suggest generally similar numbers, with over 500 members. One account indicates there were 27 tents, 59 wagons, 97 horses, 22 oxen, 69 cows, and one bull.[44] During the long journey to Missouri, however, many members of the Kirtland Camp split off, stopped to visit relatives, or had to delay their journey due to breakdowns or illness, and only approximately one-half of the original group arrived together at Far West in early October.

Jonathan Dunham was the engineer, and Jonathan H. Hale was the commissary of Kirtland Camp. The business of the engineer was to go through the settlements and towns and buy provisions cheaply and bring a wagon load to the camp each night. The rations were given out once a day to the several families according to their number; he that gave in money and he that had none to give all fared alike. There was a regular order in starting; the bugle was sounded for all to rise in the morning at the same time; also to say prayers and eat breakfast at a certain time, and all started together and every wagon kept in its place.[45]

John Pulsipher recorded some of the experiences the Kirtland Camp encountered on its journey:

> Our enemies had threatened never to let us go out of Kirtland two wagons together, but when we got ready to start, the largest company of Saints that had ever traveled together in this generation started out in good order without an enemy to oppose us. We traveled along in fine order and after a few hundred miles we got out of money and stopped and worked about a month at Dayton, Ohio, and got means to pay our way thru to Missouri. While at Dayton the devil entered our camp and got possession of one of the sisters. She was in awful pain and talked all the time and some of the time in rhyme. The Elders administered to her. The evil spirits left her and entered another person and on being rebuked again would enter another and so continued a good part of the night. But when the devil was commanded in the name of Jesus Christ to leave the camp, he went and was very mad. He went thru the whole camp, made a roaring noise, knocked over chairs, broke table legs and made awful work.
>
> We again pursued our journey, sometimes the weather was good and sometimes bad. Sometimes our tents would blow over in the rain storms in the night when all within—beds, people and all—would get as wet as drowned mice, but we could sleep in wet beds and not get sick by it. The people in the towns, cities and country thru which we passed looked and gazed at us as we passed along. Sometimes they tried to stop us. Once they threw eggs at us just because we were Mormons. At one certain city in Missouri the people tried to stop us. They already had the artillery placed in the street. As we came up they were determined to fire the cannon right at our company, but father talked to them till finally they gave up the notion and let us pass unmolested, except a few of our head men whom they took and cast in prison but the Lord delivered them and they came on and overtook the company the next night.
>
> We traveled in fine order, for we would have order. If people would not obey the rules and keep good order they were labored with and if they would not repent and reform they were turned out of the company.[46]

Daniel McArthur wrote of the opposition the group encountered while traveling to Missouri:

We were told by men and women that we would not be permitted to reside long in that state, and when we had gotten into the state we were met by an armed mob who told us that we would catch Hell in a short time, which caused the hearts of some of the Saints who were along to feel quite faint. We were traveling in a large camp, 550 of us, when we started from Kirtland; men, women, and children, being the first camp of the kind that the Saints had undertaken. But the Saints continued to pray unto God to cause the hearts of the people of Missouri to be softened toward them and to open up the way that they might get through in safety, which He did for all those who continued to persevere their travels."[47]

When Kirtland Camp arrived within five miles of Far West, they were met by Joseph Smith, Hyrum Smith, and Sidney Rigdon, who conducted the group to Far West. The large group camped for the night around the temple cellar, which had been dug a year earlier. By this time, Far West and Caldwell County were becoming crowded, so the Prophet directed the group to settle at Adam-ondi-Ahman to the north. He accompanied them there the next day, where camp member John Pulsipher said, "We found the handsomest country I ever saw. We bought land and went to work building houses and mills."[48]

Upon the arrival of Kirtland Camp in Adam-ondi-Ahman on October 4, 1838, Joseph recorded:

Thursday, October 4. This is a day long to be remembered by that part of the Church of Jesus Christ of Latter-day Saints, called the Camp, or Kirtland Camp No. 1 for they arrived at their destination and began to pitch their tents about sunset, when one of the brethren living in the place proclaimed with a loud voice:

"Brethren, your long and tedious journey is now ended; you are now on the public square of Adam-ondi-Ahman. This is the place where Adam blessed his posterity, when they rose up and called him Michael, the Prince, the Arch-angel, and he being full of the Holy Ghost predicted what should befall his posterity to the latest generation."[49]

Later Arrivals—Fall 1838

The opposition encountered by incoming Mormons generally grew worse as the fall of 1838 approached. Those who arrived in the fall were met with increased opposition, and some were actually turned back by vigilante groups.

Bathsheba Bigler Smith (who later became the wife of Apostle George A. Smith) traveled to Far West from Virginia with her mother, brother, and sisters Sarah and Melissa, in company with two brothers-in-law and one uncle and their families. Her father stayed in Virginia to settle his business but intended to join them at Far West in the spring, bringing with him, by water, farming implements and house furniture. She wrote:

> On arriving in Missouri, we found the state preparing to wage war against the Latter-day Saints, the nearer we got to our destination the more hostile the people were. As we were traveling along, numbers of men would sometimes gather around our wagons and stop us. They would inquire who we were, where we were from, and where we were going to. On receiving answers to their questions, they would debate among themselves whether to let us go or not; their consultation would result generally in a statement to the effect of, "As you are Virginians we will let you go on, but we believe you soon will return for you will quickly become convinced of your folly."[50]

Just before crossing the Grand River, Bathsheba Smith's group met another company of eastern Saints traveling to Far West, which had originally been part of Kirtland Camp. They were led by Joseph Young, one of the seven presidents of the Seventy. After spending the evening together, the two companies separated and crossed the river at two different ferries to continue the journey. Bathsheba Smith's company arrived at Far West in safety, but the other company stopped at Haun's Mill on October 28, 1838, and were there on the day of the attack. Joseph Young described some of the opposition encountered on their trip:

> On the thirteenth day of October I crossed the Mississippi at Louisiana, at which place I heard vague reports of the disturbances in the upper country, but nothing that could be relied upon. I continued my course westward till I crossed Grand river, at a place called Compton's Ferry, at which place I heard, for the first time, that if I proceeded any farther on my journey, I would be in danger of being stopped by a body of armed men. I was not willing, however, while treading my native soil, and breathing republican air, to abandon my object, which was to locate myself and family in a fine, healthy country, where we could enjoy the society of our friends and connections. Consequently, I prosecuted my journey till I came to Whitney's Mills, situated on Shoal creek, in the eastern part of Caldwell county.
>
> After crossing the creek and going about three miles, we met a party of the mob, about forty in number, armed with rifles, and mounted on horses, who informed us that we could go no farther west, threatening us with instant death if we proceeded any farther. I asked them the reason of this prohibition; to which they replied, that we were

"Mormons;" that everyone who adhered to our religious faith, would have to leave the state in ten days, or renounce their religion. Accordingly they drove us back to the mills above mentioned.

Here we tarried three days; and, on Friday, the twenty-sixth, we re-crossed the creek, and following up its banks, we succeeded in eluding the mob for the time being, and gained the residence of a friend in Myer's settlement. On Sunday 28th of October, we arrived about noon at Haun's mills; where we found a number of our friends collected together, who were holding a council, and deliberating on the best course for them to pursue, to defend themselves against the mob, who were collecting in the neighborhood, under the command of Col. Jennings of Livingston; and threatening them with house burning and killing.[51]

Notes

1. Ward, *History of Caldwell County,* 118.
2. *Journal of Discourses*, 13:108.
3. Ward, *History of Caldwell County,* 116.
4. *Journal of Morris Phelps*, LDS Family and Church Historical Department Archives.
5. Phelps, *A Short History of W. W. Phelps' Stay in Missouri.*
6. *Far West Record*, 103.
7. Ward, *History of Caldwell County,* 120.
8. *Elder's Journal*, vol. 1, No. 3, 37–38.
9. Edward Partridge Journal, 196.
10. Ward, *History of Caldwell County,* 121; *History of the Church*, 1:423.
11. Ibid. and *Far West Record*, 110.
12. Roberts, *Comprehensive History of the Church*, 1:423.
13. Ibid.
14. *Far West Record*, 119–21, 125.
15. *Messenger & Advocate,* July 1837, 529.
16. Luman Shurtliff Autobiography, 7
17. Littlefield, *Reminiscences of Latter-day Saints*, 33.
18. Ibid.
19. Ward, *History of Caldwell County,* 121.
20. Ibid., 119.
21. Ibid.
22. Ibid.
23. *History of the Church*, 3:43, citing *History of Caldwell County,* 121.
24. Ward, *History of Caldwell County.*
25. Ibid., 121.
26. Levi Jackman Autobiography, 20.
27. Young, "Autobiography," *Woman's Exponent*, vol. 14, no. 2 (1885), 10.
28. Nancy Tracy Autobiography, 14–15.
29. Ibid. 15–16.
30. *History of the Church*, 3:1.
31. Ibid., 3:2; Smith, *Essentials of Church History*, 205.

32. Ibid., 3:10.
33. Robinson, *The Return 1*, 131–32.
34. Rigdon, *Life of Sidney Rigdon*, Dialogue 1:30-31.
35. William Draper Autobiography, 4–5.
36. William Cahoon Autobiography, in *Reynolds Cahoon and Sons*, 85.
37. Warren Foote Autobiography, typescript, 14–15.
38. *Journal of Anson Call*, 4–5.
39. *History of the Church*, 3:101.
40. Ibid., 3:87–148. An excellent account of the Kirtland Camp is also found in Backman, *Heavens Resound*, 352–67.
41. *History of the Church*, 3:88–89.
42. Ibid., 3:90–91. A list of the members of this camp who signed the Camp Constitution is also included on pages 91–93.
43. *History of the Church*, 3:100
44. John Pulsipher Autobiography, 2.
45. Ibid.
46. Ibid., 3.
47. Daniel McArthur Autobiography, 5.
48. John Pulsipher Autobiography, 3.
49. *History of the Church*, 3:147–48.
50. Bathsheba Bigler Smith, Autobiography, 3–4.
51. *History of the Church*, 3:183.

Chapter 5

Daily Life in Far West

AS THE MORMONS BEGAN TO settle Far West, daily life consisted mostly of building homes, establishing and putting in crops, spinning and making cloth into clothes, and preparing meals.

During the Far West era, the majority of the Mormons made their living by farming, and they owned farmland in areas outlying Far West. However, a number of families also had property in the city and lived there. One example is Levi Hancock, who arrived in Far West in 1836. He wrote:

> In November I bought me a farm in Caldwell County. I built a house sixteen feet square of logs and a small one for a shop. I hired rails made and fenced four acres and planted it to corn. I built a brush fence around my pasture. I bought and paid for ten acres in the city of Far West and partly paid for a city lot near the Temple block, where I desired living. I had in all sixty acres of good land besides my city lot paid for. I had cows, hogs, and one good mare, sheep and hens a plenty and was in a good way to live with plenty to eat.[1]

Joseph Smith generally encouraged the Mormons to live in the city itself, even if they made their living by farming. For example, at a meeting on August 6, 1838, Joseph Smith said, "I addressed the meeting . . . on the duty of the brethren to come into cities to build and live, and carry on their farms out of the cities, according to the order of God."[2]

Living conditions were difficult for the Mormons as they settled the new frontier. Nancy Tracy described the conditions at Far West:

> When spring came, my husband procured 40 acres of land three miles from Far West . . . . He planted corn and other things. We raised

quite a crop. We still lived in the city, and all things moved along nicely. We believed we had found a permanent resting place. Brother Joseph, his brother Hyrum, and their father and their families had come up to Far West; so we were blessed again with their presence and council and could hear the words of life and salvation that flowed from their lips. Before we realized any benefit from our crops, we had to live very close, sometimes having to gather greens and dig roots to make a meal. Shoes and clothing were out of the question just at this time, but after a while a man by the name of Adam Lightner came in and brought a stock of goods and set up a store. I got sewing to do and got store pay for my work. However, we had peace. The spirit of mobocracy had lulled. We could go to meeting and enjoy our religion, and at present, no one interfered, but how long was it going to last? We shall see.

We built a cabin on our farm and moved into it the next season in order to be near my husband's work. We had an ox team, so we could go over to Far West for meetings. There was a nice grove of timber on the place and a stream of water. Wild turkeys roosted in the trees around the house, and we surely had to look out for rattle snakes, especially in the fall. When the hickory nuts were ripe, they would fall on the roof, and everything was so nice.[3]

When the Mormons were able to cultivate the land, the rich Missouri soil produced abundantly. Samuel Miles remembered, "My father's farm, two miles south of Far West, on the rich prairie and bottoms of a branch of Log Creek, produced phenomenal growths of vegetables, etc. Among other things a mammoth muskmelon was being developed. Father said, 'We will give this to the Prophet'. I watched over it with great care, and we had much satisfaction when it was ripe in presenting it to Joseph and receiving his thanks."[4]

The Mormons frequently took extra steps to improve their farms as well. When Elder Jenson visited the area in 1888, a local resident pointed out the difference between Mormon farms and other farms: "Nearly every one of the Mormons planted locust trees around their buildings which was something the Missourians never thought of doing, and these have now grown and spread, until there are locust groves nearly on every farm where the Mormons resided."[5]

Stores in Far West

Several members opened dry goods stores in Far West to accommodate the growing demands of the incoming Mormons. George M. Hinkle, Samuel Musick, Waldo Littlefield in partnership with Calvin Graves, and Adam Lightner were known store owners. Horace Martin Alexander also established a small general store. A record book of sales from the store states: "Saleratus 2 lbs. 30 cents, Candles 25 cents, Calico 50 cents."[6] Lyman Littlefield wrote of the store operated by his father:

> In August, 1836, the Saints commenced settling in Caldwell County. My father moved there and selected a place about two miles south of Far West, on the road leading to Liberty, Clay County. In addition to opening a farm, he formed a partnership with Mr. Calvin Graves, and purchased a stock of dry goods and family groceries and commenced business in Far West. Also, they took a stock of goods to Grand River, in Daviess County. In both of these places they were selling many goods and prospering. About this time. . . . [I] clerked in the store at Far West. Father purchased a farm on Dog Creek, about half way between Far West and Adam-ondi-Ahman, which was generally called the "half way house," where he moved his family, but still continuing to sell goods.[7]

Another store owner, who was not a member of the Church, was Adam Lightner. His wife, Mary Elizabeth Rollins Lightner,[8] who was a member, wrote the following about Adam's store:

> Shortly after [we were married] our people moved to Far West, Caldwell County, and soon had a flourishing town, and a settlement all around of farms, etc. The brethren persuaded Mr. Lightner to go there and keep a store for their accommodation, as the Church was not able; for the most of them had been stripped of all they had. He concluded to go and build a log house for his store, and leave me in Liberty until it was completed. We soon left for Far West, my husband furnishing the supplies for the brethren until they could harvest their crops. It was customary among the Missourians to credit the farmers a year. Mr. Lightner followed the rule, for he knew they could not pay until they could earn the money.[9]

Lyman Wight, Simeon Carter, and Elias Higbee ran a leather store.[10] The Whitmers owned and operated a hotel.[11]

The Mormons were called upon to assist the poor who arrived in Far West. Martha Thomas wrote, "Brother James Allred called on him [her husband] and his brother, Henry, to join the big field company. They wanted to fence a large field for the benefit of the poor. They wanted all the tools for farming that could be spared, oxen, horses, cows, and work when called on."[12]

The Church established the equivalent of a bishop's storehouse in Far West. Chapman Duncan wrote about his experience with consecrating his property to the Church:

> In the month of May I found myself at Far West. The second season
> it was settled. . . . I was doing business in the church store for Bishop
> Vinson Knight. Here I will remark at the time or about this time of
> going into the store I and my brother took an inventory of our property
> and it amounted to $1,500, nearly all of which we consecrated or deliv-
> ered to the bishop for the Church. A portion of the property that we
> handed over was 1 wagon, 2 horses, and harness, 30 acres fenced, and
> heavy crop of corn, house and stable, outhouses, bees, gang of hogs.[13]

Anson Call wrote:

> While at Far West I happened in . . . the church store, and my atten-
> tion was called by Vincent Knight who was opening some boxes of goods.
> Says he, 'Joseph will be much pleased with these.' He had been very uneasy
> about the translation of the Bible and the Egyptian Records. 'Here they
> are,' placing them on the table. Said he to me, 'If you will take one of
> these, I will the other and we will carry them over to Joseph's office.' There
> we found Joseph and six or seven other brethren. Joseph was much pleased
> with the arrival of the books, and said to us, 'Sit down and we will read
> to you from the translations of the Book of Abraham.' Oliver Cowdery
> then read until he was tired, when Thomas Marsh read making altogether
> about two hours. I was much interested in the work.[14]

Schools in Far West

School districts were soon formed, and a schoolhouse was planned for
each district. David Pettigrew wrote, "We soon had schools started in school
districts and our children were benefited by the learning they received."[15]
"There were also many persons of education and accomplishment. School
teachers were plentiful and schools were numerous. . . . The Mormons
very early gave attention to educational matters. There were many teachers
among them and school houses were among their first buildings."[16]

Caldwell County history indicates the first schools were taught by
Mormons. Then referring to the local educational work at Kingston, the
present county seat, the historian says, "In the vicinity of Kingston, the
first school was taught by a young lady Mormon, Miss Mary Ann Duty, in
an abandoned Log Cabin on Log Creek. This was the summer of 1836."[17]

Joseph Holbrook helped to build one of the schools, among other
buildings, in Far West. He wrote:

> My wife Nancy had a son born January 31, 1837, at about 4 o'clock
> in the afternoon and I named him Joseph Lamont Holbrook at my house
> on Plum Creek. I have built a house and assisted others in building so that
> I had plenty to do and the brethren paid me well for it. I built an office for

Bishop Edward Partridge in Far West and finished it. I also built a dwelling house for him. I built two other dwelling houses, for Morgan Gardner and George Slade; I also built a school house in the district where I lived, 22 feet square, besides farming considerable each year.[18]

According to William W. Phelps, "Our school section was sold at auction, and although entirely a prairie, it brought, on a year's credit, from $3.50 to $10.21 per acre, making our first school fund five thousand and seventy dollars. Land cannot be had around town now much less than ten dollars per acre."[19]

Erastus Snow, a teacher in Far West, wrote, "On the 13th of December [1838], I was married to Artimesia Beman and during the winter I taught school in Far West.[20]

One of his students, Samuel Miles wrote, "I attended school in Far West that winter which was taught by Erastus Snow and thus had the privilege of associating with the [youth] of many of our prominent leaders."[21]

John Murdock also taught one of the schools. During an evening spelling school a young man hugged a girl, causing a stir in Far West. According to the *Far West Record*, this issue wound up before the Far West High Council for consideration: "Jacob Gates testifies that Br. Murdock was at his house, the subject of spelling schools, in the evening was introduced, which he disapproved of also, mentioned about a young man's undertaking to hug a girl in an evening meeting but mentioned no names, he disapproved of evening schools and meetings on account of the young people being light minded & tended to draw away their minds from the studies."[22]

One seventeen-year-old Mormon girl, Eliza Lyman (and perhaps others), hired out as a schoolteacher away from Far West. She wrote:

> While here, I went about thirty miles from home and taught school for three months, not hearing a word from home while I was away and I did not see a person while there that I had ever seen before, but the Lord watched over me and returned me in safety to my parents again. I would never advise anyone to let a girl go away as I did then with entire strangers, to dwell with strangers. It was no uncommon thing in those times for our Mormon girls to go out among the Missourians and teach their children for a small remuneration. I received but 13 dollars and my board for the three months that I was gone. . . . I was at this time about 17 years old.[23]

Civic Duties at Far West

Far West was the county seat, and court was held in the schoolhouse. Justices of the peace were appointed in the different townships, and all the political machinery of the county was controlled by the Mormons. The county militia, which was almost exclusively composed of Mormon men, was organized and formed under the laws of the state, with George W. Hinkle as the leader.[24]

Elias Higbee was appointed to be the first judge of the newly formed county,[25] and Dimick Huntington was appointed to be the Far West city constable.[26] Levi Jackman, Amasa Lyman, and Albert Petty served as justices of the peace at Far West.[27]

On May 27, 1837, William W. Phelps was appointed postmaster at Far West. On July 4, he executed the necessary bonds for the faithful discharge of his duties as postmaster, and he was duly commissioned as postmaster on August 26, 1837, his commission being signed by Amos Kendall, at Washington, DC.[28] In August of 1838, William W. Phelps resigned from this position, and Sidney Rigdon took his place. "This day the citizens of Caldwell county assembled at Far West, and organized by calling Elias Higbee to the chair, and appointing George W. Robinson secretary. William W. Phelps having resigned the office of postmaster, it was voted unanimously that Sidney Rigdon be recommended to the Postmaster General, as the person of our choice to fill the place of William W. Phelps, as postmaster in this city."[29]

The versatile Phelps, who was a publisher and songwriter, was also appointed and commissioned as a justice of the county court for Caldwell County. His commission was signed by Missouri's new governor, Lilburn W. Boggs.[30]

The Elders' Journal

The Mormons began to publish what was known as the *Elders' Journal* at Far West in the summer of 1838. The *Messenger and Advocate*, the monthly paper printed in Kirtland, was discontinued, and the *Elders' Journal* took its place. The first issue of the *Journal* was published in Kirtland in October of 1837. In January of 1838, the print shop in Kirtland was destroyed by fire, and printing of the *Journal* did not resume until July 1838 in Far West.

In the first issue of July 1838, the *Elders' Journal* introduced itself:

> It is, we presume, generally known, that this paper was commenced in Kirtland, Ohio, in October last; but by reason of the great persecution against the Saints in that place, the paper had to be stopped; and through the craft of wicked men, they got possession of the printing office, and knowing they could not hold it, it was burned.[31] The paper is

now about to be resuscitated in this place, to be conducted as set forth in the former prospectus. It will be issued in a few weeks, and sent to the former subscribers, as previously stated. We send this prospectus to arouse the Saints to energy in obtaining subscribers. We hope the elders abroad will not fail to use their influence to give as general a circulation as possible. The *Journal* will be edited by Joseph Smith, Jr., and published by Thomas B. Marsh at Far West, Caldwell County, Missouri. Terms One dollar per annum, paid in advance. All letters must be postpaid, and directed to the publisher."[32]

Elisha Groves was sent to Kirtland to obtain donations for the Far West Temple that was to be built. He arrived in Kirtland in February 1838, and while there, he obtained a printing press and in the spring returned to Far West.[33] This press was used to print the Church publications.

On May 8, 1838, the Prophet recorded, "In the afternoon, I answered the questions which were frequently asked me, while on my last journey but one from Kirtland to Missouri, as printed in the *Elders' Journal,* vol. 1, Number II, pages 28, and 29."[34] He also recorded, "Some time in July [1838] we succeeded in publishing the third number of the *Elders' Journal*; Joseph Smith, Jun., editor; Thomas B. Marsh, printer and publisher. In this number of the *Journal* was published the following Epistle of David W. Patten, one of the Twelve Apostles of the last days."[35]

Also, a copy of Sidney Rigdon's famous Fourth of July address was furnished to the editor and printed in Far West. It was printed in pamphlet form, in the printing office of the *Elders' Journal,*[36] and its availability was announced in the *Elders' Journal.*[37]

The *Elders' Journal* was the same size as its predecessor, *Messenger and Advocate,* and the printed matter on each page contained two columns measuring 8.25 by 4.25 inches. It was edited by Joseph Smith and published by Thomas B. Marsh, but Don Carlos Smith, the youngest brother of the Prophet, took immediate charge of the printing establishment. Only two editions were published at Far West because the paper was suspended in consequence of the persecutions. On the night that Far West was surrounded by General Lucas's mob militia, the type was buried in Brother Dawson's yard in Far West, and it remained there until the spring of 1839, when it was dug up by Elias Smith, Hyrum Clark, and others,[38] and taken to Quincy, Illinois, and eventually to Nauvoo, where it was afterward used for the publication of the *Times and Seasons.* Thus, only four numbers of the *Journal* (two in Kirtland, Ohio, and two in Far West) were published.[39]

The citizens of Far West also made attempts to publish a newspaper. On August 6, 1838 (election day), a group gathered together to decide on developing a local newspaper. "In the afternoon, the citizens of Far West assembled in the school house and organized the meeting by calling Judge Elias Higbee to the chair, and appointing George W. Robinson, secretary. I stated to the meeting, that the time had come when it was necessary that we should have a weekly newspaper, to unite the people, and give the news of the day. It was unanimously agreed that such a paper be established, and that President Sidney Rigdon should be the editor."[40] Ebenezer Robinson, who also helped in the printing office in Kirtland, worked in the printing office.[41]

Mormon Births

More than one hundred Mormon children were born in Caldwell counties during the few years the Church maintained a presence there.[42] There were other births in other Mormon communities in Livingston and Ray counties.

Perhaps the most generally well-known of such children among Mormons is Joseph Fielding Smith, who grew up to be the sixth president of The Church of Jesus Christ of Latter-day Saints. He was the son of Hyrum Smith and Mary Fielding Smith and was born in Far West on November 13, 1838, just twelve days after his father, Hyrum, was arrested and taken to prison with the Prophet Joseph and several other men. The young baby nearly lost his life in the persecutions in Far West that occurred at the time of his birth. The birth of her son and the arrest of her husband resulted in shock and physical suffering for Mary Fielding Smith, and for months she was confined to her bed in a very serious condition. While in this condition of poor health, a mob entered her house, searched it and broke open her treasure chest, scattered things about, and stole valuable documents and other things of worth. In the confusion, a mattress, laying on the floor for an extra bed, was thrown onto the bed where the baby was sleeping, smothering him. When he was discovered after the mob left, he appeared dead, but he was revived by Mary's sister, Mercy, who was her constant companion and nurse.[43]

Another famous birth at Far West is Alexander Hale Smith, the eighth child (and fourth surviving) of Joseph and Emma Smith.[44] Emma gave birth to Alexander on June 2, 1838. He later became patriarch of the Reorganized Church of Jesus Christ of Latter Day Saints (now the Community of Christ).

Marriages

There were a number of Mormon marriages during the Far West era. Sarah Pea Rich recorded the unusual events that led to her marriage to Charles C. Rich:

After a while the two elders returned to our house that first preached there, and the one that baptized me said to me, Sister Sarah, while I was at Kirtland I recommended you to a very worthy young man who is an elder in the Church, and when I told him of you said he, "that same girl has been recommended to me twice before, and now I must hunt her up," so when I inquired his name, it was the same as the two others had recommended to me. We all wondered, thinking how strange this all should be!

So about a month from that time I heard there was a letter in the post office for my father, and he not being at home I rode to the post office, about a mile away and got the letter, and on opening the letter I found one enclosed directed to me, and on opening mine found it was this same young man that had been recommended to me so many times before writing. I truly was struck with wonder and surprise. As a matter of course, it set me to thinking of the matter, and could not help but think the hand of the Lord had something to do in this matter; as I had always prayed to the Lord that I might be led by His Spirit in selecting a companion for life, and to guide me in this matter. I still have that letter and will copy the same in this book, although it was written fifty years ago.

Although we wrote several letters to each other after the one mentioned before we saw each other, the first one has been preserved with the greatest of care as a momento of our "first acquaintance by letter." It was almost six months after I received this letter before my father sold his property in Illinois and moved to Missouri and after father got to Far West, it was about two weeks before I met with the young man referred to; his name was Charles C. Rich. It was in a public meeting that our eyes first rested on each other, and without anyone pointing us out to each other, we knew each other at sight; and in four months from the time we first met, we were married on the 11th day of February, in Far West, Caldwell County, Missouri. So my many friends can see the hand of the Lord had something to do in our acquaintance and marriage. . . .

As Far West was a place every body lived in log houses, so my husband had built a nice little hewed log house and got it ready to live in by the time we were married. It was seven miles from Far West, near my husband's fathers. So I left my father's house in Far West and we moved to our cozy and happy home, and we thought we were the happiest couple in all the land. My husband had a beautiful prospect for a nice farm with plenty of timber and water, and our plans were laid for a comfortable and happy home in the near future. Our religion being first with us in all things.[45]

Charles C. and Sarah Rich's cabin, Mirable, Missouri.

Margaret T. McMeans Atkinson married Abraham O. Smoot under unusual circumstances in Far West on November 11, 1838. Brother Smoot had counseled with the Prophet Joseph about the marriage, and the Prophet advised him to take her, saying "She is a woman of God and you will be blessed."[46] They were married while he was under arrest as a prisoner. Orson F. Whitney wrote about this event:

> When Caldwell and Daviess counties were invaded by the Missourian mobs, and peace was changed to war and desolation, A. O. Smoot girded on his arms and went forth to the field of strife in defense of his people. He was in several skirmishes with the enemy, and at the surrender of Far West became a prisoner in the hands of the State forces. While yet a captive, confined to the limits of the fallen city, he married Margaret Thompson McMeans Atkinson, a widow with one child; a woman of noble presence and noble character, who will be remembered and revered as "Ma" Smoot.[47]

There were many other, perhaps more ordinary, marriages at Far West. For example, Ethan Barrows wrote, "The spring of '36, I started to Zion, arrived in Clay County, Missouri in July. Started from Kirtland with Gad Yale and family. We left from Clay County to what was afterwards called Caldwell County in the following October where I married Lorena Covey, January 1, 1837. Bought some land and settled one and 1/2 miles from the city of Far West."[48]

Chapman Duncan recorded, "In the month of May, the first Monday, 18, I married a lady by the name of Rebecca Rose, daughter of Andrew Rose, who lived on Log Creek. I moved my wife on a farm that my brother Homer and myself had bought in April."[49]

Deaths

Unfortunately, many Mormons died during the Far West era. Many died of illness, in childbirth, accidents, or old age; others died due to violence or exposure to the elements caused by the persecutions by the Missouri mobs. It is believed that many of these people were buried in the Far West Burial Grounds, located on present-day Kerr Road about one mile west of the temple site, currently owned by the Community of Christ. The graves at this location are not marked, however. Others were buried on their family farms, which was a common practice at that time.

Celia Steepleford Woodland, wife of John Woodland Jr., lost her mother at Adam-ondi-Ahman. "While at this place Sister Woodland's mother died on October 27, 1838. The mobs were so bad that they could not go after lumber to make the coffin, so they buried her in a Clother box which was not long enough and her feet stuck out about six inches, a scene which was a trial that they never forgot. It was in the dead of winter and they had no shelter except a wagon and some quilts held up by brush."[50]

Hiram Dayton was having difficulty in securing a home for his family and was living in a rented home in which the owner wanted possession. During their move, his daughter took sick and died within a few days. He recorded:

> We stayed there for two weeks and then had to give possession to the owner. Some days after this, a merchant heard my conversation with several friends and the owner of the house had just left. I was talking about what I should do. He, the merchant, proposed giving myself and team and labor to freight merchandise for him and some of his friends. He said the Missourians would get drunk and steal his goods. He had a log cabin and a stable one and a half miles from the city which he said we could occupy. I loaded up what things I could take and moved out there. One of my daughters [Nancy], the one who had been well all through my sickness, rode horseback without saddle or blanket. She caught a violent cold while going out there, and took sick in a few days and lived about two weeks and died. I took her body down to the city [Far West] to bury her. The ground was frozen very deep. I was very feeble and not being able to dig her grave, I asked several bystanders to assist me, but I could not get them to help me at all. I then borrowed some tools and went to the graveyard where a Negro came to me and said, "Massah, I will dig the grave and bury your daughter."[51]

Henry and Rachel Thomas, an elderly couple who joined the Church and made the journey from Kentucky, died shortly after their arrival at Far West. Their daughter Rachel wrote:

> We now bade farewell to all kindred, which was a sad affair, especially to father and mother Thomas. They belonged to the Church but were too old to stand the journey. Brother Woodruff had blessed them and said they would yet stand in Zion. So they did for we sent for them and in the fall they came by water. They soon died and were buried side by side on Log Creek, Missouri. Father was a revolutionary soldier under Washington. He was 84 years old and Mother, 78. This ends 1837.[52]

Three-year-old Annica MacArthur suffered death through accident. Her brother, Daniel, recorded:

> After the fuss was settled in Daviess County, the Saints all moved up to Far West, Caldwell County to the time they were permitted to stay in the state. So my father, after moving into the above county, went to work and put himself up a log house to stay in through the winter by the side of a small stream called Log Creek. Here my father stayed until March 1839, and while here my little sister, Annica, got burned to death by her clothes catching a fire which broke out from a little playhouse that she and her little playmates had built under a large white oak tree.[53]

John E. Page, one of the Quorum of the Twelve, buried his wife, Lorain Stevens Page, and two children as a result of the persecutions. He wrote:

> On the 14th day of May 1838, I started with a company of Saints, made up of men, women and their children, for the state of Missouri, where we landed, in the first week of October, with a company occupying thirty wagons, at a place there called DeWitt, some six miles above the outlet of Grand River, on the north side of the Missouri River, where we were attacked by an armed mob, and by them barbarously treated for near two weeks.
>
> We then went to Far West, Caldwell County, where we united with the general body of the Church, and with them participated in all the grievous persecutions practiced on the Church by means of a furious mob, by which means I buried my wife and two children as martyrs to our holy religion, who died through extreme suffering for the want of the common comforts of life, which I was not allowed to provide even with my money.[54]

Asahel Lathrop's wife and three children also died due to exposure after being driven from their homes. Asahel was notified by a non-

Mormon that the residents of Livingston County intended to drive every Mormon from the state and that he must leave immediately or would be in danger of losing his life. He wrote:

> At this time my family some of them were sick but after listening to the entreaties of my Companion to flee for safety I committed them into the hands of God and left them it being on Monday morning and in a short time after I left there came some time on fifteen men to my house and took possession of the same and Compelled my wife to Cook for the same and also made free to take such things as they saw fit and whilst in this situation my child died, which I have no reason to doubt was for the want of care which owing to the abuse she received and being deprived of rendering that care that she would had she been otherwise situated my boy was buried by the Mob my wife not being allowed to pay the last respects to her child. I went from my home into Davis county and applied to Austin A King and General Atchison for advise as they were acting officers in the State of Missouri and there was men called out to go and liberate my family which I had been absent from some ten or fifteen days and on my return I found the remainder of my family confined to their beds not being able the one to assist the other and my house guarded by an armed force. I was compelled to remove my family in this situation on a head to a place of safety this together with all the trouble and for the want of care was the cause of the Death of the residue of my family as I have no doubt which consisted of a wife and two more children as they Died in a few days after the arrival to my friends such was my situation that I was obliged to assist in making my own coffins.[55]

Joseph Smith's Residence

When Joseph Smith arrived in Far West, he and his immediate family temporarily resided with the George W. Harris family near the public square of Far West. Joseph wrote, "On the 14th of March, as we were about entering Far West, many of the brethren came out to meet us, who also with open arms welcomed us to their bosoms. We were immediately received under the hospitable roof of Brother George W. Harris, who treated us with all possible kindness, and we refreshed ourselves with much satisfaction."[56]

In July of 1838, the high council voted that the bishop purchase George M. Hinkle's house and cook stove for Joseph.[57] Several sources and local oral tradition locate this structure approximately two hundred yards southwest of the temple site.[58] In an 1889 publication, LDS historian Andrew Jenson wrote, "The house in which Joseph Smith once lived, which stood 200 yards southwest of the temple foundation, was recently torn down and the logs used in building a stable."[59]

Jacob D. Whitmer (a son of John Whitmer) described Joseph's home: "It was a one story, frame building, with two rooms."[60] Joseph Smith III recalled, "The house had two rooms, one the living or 'keeping' room and the other a bedroom. Into this latter, the door leading from the keeping room opened inwardly, opposite a window in the end of the building."[61]

The Smiths had a white dog named Major. Joseph Smith, III, recalled:

> I remember this dog particularly from the fact that upon one occa-
> sion, the baby (Alexander H. Smith) was set down by him as he lay
> upon the floor. The baby pulled his ears, which hurt him so [Major had
> been in a fight and had his ears chewed until they were sore], that he
> growled fiercely. Father punished him severely for this, boxing his ears
> soundly. This treatment resulted in his never afterwards lying quietly
> when a child was placed near him. He would spring to his feet imme-
> diately and go away, evidently never forgetting the punishment he had
> received from growling at the baby.[62]

Hyrum Smith's Residence

In the spring of 1838 Hyrum Smith and his family moved to Far West and, according to family tradition, lived in a home a mile west of the temple site near present-day Kerr Road. Some sources place the location as "the northeast corner of the southwest quarter of Section 9, Mirabile Township (Twp 56-N, Range 29).[63] President George Albert Smith visited Far West in 1946 and indicated that the Hyrum Smith home was across the street from the site of the old cemetery at Far West, which is about one mile west of the public square.[64] It is believed that Hyrum lived west of town, even though the high council granted him two lots in the city on March 3, 1838.[65] These were lots number 2 and 3 in block 8 and were directly north of the public square, about eight to nine hundred feet north of the southwest cornerstone of the Far West Temple.

Church Meetings

During the Far West era, the Church continued the pattern for meetings that had been set in Kirtland. Every Thursday evening, prayer and testimony meeting was held, and every Sunday there were alternately preaching and communion services. The Mormons attended these meetings regularly, but according to one early Mormon's account, few of them had teams, and those who had them were forced to keep them working their crops all week, so they rested their horses on the sabbath day and walked to church. "Sunday after Sunday," he wrote, "quite a crowd of men, women, and children could be seen wending their way to the Central City."[66]

William W. Phelps wrote: "Our meetings, held in the open prairie, were larger than they were in Kirtland, when I was there. We have more . . . to bless, confirm, and baptize every Sabbath."[67] Samuel Miles recorded, "I recollect the Prophet in 1838, in Far West, Missouri, calling the people together from the city and country round about for conference and general instruction, at the frame schoolhouse. The building would not accommodate the people, and it being in the warm season, the congregation assembled on the outside in the open air."[68]

The Mormons met together on April 6, 1838, to hold a conference and to celebrate the anniversary of the organization of the Church. Ebenezer Robinson, the clerk for the meeting, recorded this account:

> Agreeable to a resolution passed by the High Council of Zion . . . the Saints in Missouri assembled in this place, to celebrate the anniversary of the Church of Jesus Christ of Latter-day Saints, and to transact church business, Joseph Smith, Junior, and Sidney Rigdon presiding. The meeting was opened by singing, and prayer by David W. Patten, after which President Smith, Junior, read the order of the day. . .
>
> The meeting then proceeded to business. George Morey was appointed Sexton, and Dimick Huntington, assistant; John Corrill and Elias Higbee, Historians; George W. Robinson, General Church Recorder, and Clerk to the First Presidency; Ebenezer Robinson, Church Clerk and Recorder for Far West, and Clerk of the High Council; Thomas B. Marsh, President pro tempore of the Church in Zion, and David W. Patten and Brigham Young, his assistant Presidents.
>
> After one hour's adjournment, meeting again opened by David W. Patten. The bread and wine were administered, and ninety-five infants were blessed.[69]

On Sunday, July 29, 1838, the Prophet was on his way to Adam-ondi-Ahman with Hyrum Smith and Sidney Rigdon when he met Heber C. Kimball on the public square and asked him to preach to the congregation and give them a history of his recent mission to England, "saying it would revive their spirits and do them good." Elder Kimball complied and said, "Although I was hardly able to stand. I related many things respecting my mission and travels, which were gladly received by them, whose hearts were cheered by the recital, while many of the elders were stirred up to diligence and expressed a great desire to accompany me when I should return to England."[70]

Church members at Far West heard Joseph Smith preach on many occasions. Lyman Littlefield wrote of the Prophet Joseph Smith:

> And here, in Far West, his admiration and respect for him person-
> ally, as well as for his calling, was heightened day by day. We watched
> his intercourse with the people, and listened to his preaching from the
> stand, with sentiments of profound respect and pleasure. There was
> something in his manner, his countenance and spirit that was not asso-
> ciated with mortal man that we had ever looked upon before. Sidney
> Rigdon was a fine-looking man, polished in address and powerful in
> oratory; but he was far behind Joseph in the possession of those mag-
> netic powers of the mind which attracted the multitude, and chained
> the attention of his auditors. In comparison, Rigdon's eloquence was
> delightful, like the ripple of the merry brooklet that glides over its peb-
> bled bed or dashes down a narrow declivity; but the testimony of Joseph
> struck through the heart, and, like the thunder of the cataract, declared
> at once the dignity and matchless supremacy of the Creator.[71]

David Osborn described an outdoor meeting in which the Prophet Joseph Smith spoke while standing on a wagon box while visiting Far West in November 1837:

> I settled 10 miles north of Far West in the year 1837. There was
> then but a few houses in that place. The same fall father Smith and
> family, Joseph and Sidney and others arrived. Notice was given and
> nearly everyone gathered to see and hear the Prophet. There was no
> meeting house and a wagon was provided for a stand. Therefore the first
> sight I had of Joseph Smith was then on that wagon box.
>
> He had quite a green or boyish appearance at first, but he had not
> spoken long till he assumed a more manly appearance, even that of a
> man of God. He spoke of Adam, Enoch, Noah, Moses, the patriarchs
> and some of the prophets, telling what keys each one held, and the
> work he accomplished in his day down to Jesus and the apostles.
>
> Now says he, having told you so much about these ancient men of
> God, I will proceed to tell you something of myself. Some of you have
> known me and heard my testimony, but many of you have not. You
> have heard many things about me and what I have been doing, some
> things were true and some were not; the world had called me a fool.
> Well I don't wonder at it. I suppose I have acted to them like a fool, the
> Lord has shown me many things concerning the ancients of this conti-
> nent, with their record and my mind was so much absorbed in regard to
> these things and the great responsibilities resting upon me as a servant of
> God, and having had but little experience in regard to worldly matters, I
> do not blame people for thinking me a fool; indeed, we are all fools. We

know but little, hence the necessity of the Lord teaching us something.

Says he, I bear testimony to you in the name of the Lord, that the Book of Mormon is true and the testimony I expect to meet in the day of judgment. For this testimony I have suffered persecution, but I expect to suffer much more. If I obtain the glory which is set before me I expect to wade through much tribulation.

He told us that Peter, James and John, having held the keys of the kingdom in their day had come and conferred the same upon him and his brethren. He quoted the saying of the Savior that the time would come when "every secret thing should be proclaimed on the house-tops." Thus I have proclaimed these secret things, if not on the house top, it is upon the wagon top.[72]

Concerns of the Prophet

There are indications, however, that all was not well in Far West among the members of the Church. On one occasion, Joseph is reputed to have said:

Brethren, we are gathering to this beautiful land to build up Zion; Zion which is the pure in heart. But since I have been here I perceive the spirit of selfishness. Covetousness exists in the hearts of the Saints which is not becoming those who receive the spirit of the gospel. Here are those who begin to spread out buying up all the land they are able to get to the exclusion of the poorer ones who are not so much blessed with this world's goods, thinking to lay foundations for themselves, only looking to their own individual families and those who are to follow them. Now I want to tell you that Zion cannot be built up in any such way. We are called out from this world to learn God's ways, to become one, looking each to his brother's interest and welfare, the widow, the fatherless, and poor without distinction. I see signs put out, beer signs, speculative schemes are being introduced. This is the way of the world, Babylon indeed, and I tell you in the name of the God of Israel, if there is not repentance with this people and a turning from such ungodliness, covetousness, and self-will, you will be broken up and scattered from this choice land to the four winds of heaven. For the Lord will have a people who will serve him and keep his commandments humbly, each one seeking his neighbor's welfare, to preach the gospel, gather the poor, and aid them and build up a holy city.[73]

David Osborn similarly wrote about a discourse given by the Prophet:

[At] the conclusion of his discourse he reproved the brethren who had purchased government land and dividing it and selling it out at a high price to their poor brethren, and other matters of speculation and iniquity which was going on in the Church. Now says he, you call me a prophet. If I am it is my privilege to prophesy which I will do, and when you go home, write it down and remember it. You think you have suffered much already by the hand of your enemies, but if you don't cease this thing and take a different course and be more faithful, your enemies will again come upon you in greater numbers and you will not find a resting place in the state of Missouri.[74]

Notes

1. Levi Hancock Autobiography, 57–58.
2. *History of the Church*, 3:56.
3. Nancy Tracy Autobiography, 16.
4. Samuel Miles, "Recollections," *Juvenile Instructor* 27, 174.
5. Jenson, *Historical Record*, 684.
6. Black and Porter, *Life Sketch of Horace Alexander*, 1.
7. Littlefield, *Reminiscences of Latter-day Saints*, 33.
8. Mary Elizabeth Rollins Lightner is remembered by many as one of the two young girls who, along with her sister Caroline, saved a number of the printed pages of the Book of Commandments (which is now part of the Doctrine and Covenants) when the vigilante group attacked the Church's printing office in Independence in 1833.
9. "Mary Elizabeth Rollins Lightner," *The Utah Genealogical and Historical Magazine* 17, 198.
10. The Far West High Council voted to uphold these brethren in this endeavor. *Far West Record*, 114.
11. *Historical Record*, January 1889, Jenson—Caldwell County, 723.
12. Martha Thomas autobiography, in Daniel Thomas Family History, 15.
13. Chapman Duncan Autobiography, 7.
14. Call, Anson Call Biography, 33
15. Pettigrew, *An Enduring Legacy*, 3:203.
16. Oliver Cowdery, Biography, 79.
17. Ward, *History of Caldwell County*, 80, 99.
18. Joseph Holbrook Autobiography, 38–39.
19. William W. Phelps Biography, 82–83.
20. Erastus Snow Autobiography, 47.
21. Samuel Miles Autobiography, 6.
23. Eliza Lyman Autobiography, 5.
24. Ward, *History of Caldwell County*, 117.
25. Johnson, *Mormon Redress Petitions, Greene's Expulsion of the Mormons*, 27–28.
26. Dimick B. Huntington Autobiography, 14.
27. *Far West Record*, 270, 282; *LDS Biographical Encyclopedia*, 1:96.
28. William W. Phelps Biography, 83.
29. *History of the Church*, 3:56.
30. William W. Phelps Biography, 83.
31. The question of who actually burned the printing house in Kirtland has been both controversial and difficult to prove. Many early members suspected it was burned by enemies of the Church, but there are indications that it may have been burned by a member who did not want to see it used by the enemies of the Church.

32. *Elders' Journal* (July 1838), 34.
33. Elisha H. Groves Autobiography, 4.
34. *History of the Church*, 3:28–30
35. Ibid., 3:48–49
36. Ebenezer Robinson, *The Return 1* (November 1889), 171.
37. *Elders' Journal* (Aug 1838), 54.
38. *History of the Church*, 4:398.
39. Jenson, *Historical Record* (March 1889), 844.
40. Jesse, *The Papers of Joseph Smith*, 2:265–66.
41. Ebenezer Robinson, *The Return* 1, 172.
42. The authors have compiled a list of such births by a review of Susan Easton Blacks' multi-volume *Early Membership* works, but this list is not all-inclusive.
43. Smith, *Life of Joseph F. Smith*, 123–24; Black, *Who's Who in the Doctrine and Covenants*, 292.
44. The earlier children were Alvin, who died June 15, 1828; twins, Thaddeus and Louisa, who died April 1, 1831; adopted twins, Joseph (who died six months later) and Julia Murdock Smith; Joseph III born November 6, 1832 and later became president of the Reorganized Church of Jesus Christ of Latter-day Saints; and Frederick Granger Williams, who was born in July of 1836.
45. Sarah Rich Autobiography, 20–24.
46. Carter, *Heart Throbs of the West*, 3:126.
47. Whitney, *History of Utah*, 4:99–100.
48. Ethan Barrows Autobiography.
49. Chapman Duncan Autobiography, 7.
50. Woodland, in "Early Membership."
51. Hiram Dayton Autobiography, 1–2 (grammar standardized).
52. Lisonbee, "Missouri Mormon Burials," 55.
53. Ibid., 46.
54. John Page Autobiography, 103.
55. Lathrop, *Mormon Redress Petitions*, 265–66 (grammar and spelling standardized).
56. *History of the Church*, 3:8.
57. *Far West Record*, 197.
58. Ward, *History of Caldwell County*, 122.
59. Jenson, *The Historical Record*, 722.
60. Ibid.
61. Howard, *The Memoirs of President Joseph Smith III*, 3.
62. Ibid.
63. Dyer, *Refiner's Fire*, 225.
64. *Journal History*, July 20 1946, 6.
65. *Far West Record*, 144.
66. Brush, *Autumn Leaves*, 4:66.
67. William W. Phelps Biography, 82.
68. Samuel Miles "Recollections," *Juvenile Instructor* (1892) 27:174.
69. Robinson, *The Return*, 132.
70. Heber C. Kimball Journal in Helen Whitney, 9.
71. Littlefield, *Reminiscences of Latter-day Saints*, 35–36.
72. David Osborn Autobiography 63–64.
73. *Autobiography of Edward Stevenson*, 2.
74. David Osborn Autobiography, 64

Chapter 6

CHURCH GOVERNANCE
AND REVELATIONS

WHEN THE MORMONS SETTLED AT Far West, the governing body of the Church in the area was the high council, then called the High Council of Zion. Due to the evolving organization of the early Church, the Far West High Council served a more significant role in terms of church administration than is the case today with a typical stake high council. The Church leadership as it exists today under the First Presidency and Quorum of Twelve Apostles had not fully developed during the Far West era.

When Church members moved to Far West, there were only two stakes in the Church, one in Missouri and the other at Kirtland, eight hundred miles away.[1] In addition, the Quorum of the Twelve, which was organized in 1835, was heavily involved in missionary work and was not as involved in the administration of the Church as it is today. The Twelve would eventually assume greater authority than the two high councils, but this did not occur until 1841 in Nauvoo, when the Twelve began to take their place next to the First Presidency.[2]

In March 1835, the revelation contained in Doctrine and Covenants 107 was given, outlining priesthood responsibilities and placing the two "standing high councils" in the Church (Kirtland and Clay County, Missouri; the latter subsequently became the Far West High Council) in a unique position. The revelation indicated that "the Standing High Councils, at the stakes of Zion, form a quorum equal in authority in the affairs of the Church, in all their decisions, to the quorum of the presidency or to the traveling High council (Quorum of the Twelve)" (D&C 107:36–37). This differs from the Church today when stake high councils do not enjoy a position equal in authority to the First Presidency or the Twelve. Thus, the powers and position of the two standing high councils of Kirtland and Zion have never since been duplicated.[3]

When Joseph Smith came to Missouri with Zion's Camp, he organized the first high council in Missouri on July 3, 1834.[4] During the next few years, one of these men passed away (Christian Whitmer), and four were called to be apostles (William McLellin, Thomas Marsh, Parley P. Pratt, and Orson Pratt). Thus, when Joseph Smith visited Far West in November 1837, he reorganized the Far West High Council by replacing these five men. The members of the new high council were John Murdock, Solomon Hancock, Elias Higbee, Calvin Bebee, John M. Hinkle, Thomas Grover, Simeon Carter, Lyman Wight, Newel Knight, George M. Hinkle, Levi Jackman, and Elisha H. Groves.[5]

At a conference held at Far West on November 7, 1837, the First Presidency of the Church was reorganized under the direction of Joseph Smith. Frederick G. Williams was released as a counselor and Hyrum Smith appointed in his stead. Further, David Whitmer, John Whitmer, and William W. Phelps were sustained as the Presidency at Far West.[6]

The Far West High Council and presidency were supposed to meet together as a group of fifteen men[7] and were involved in a number of significant cases and decisions. For example, at a meeting on April 7, 1837, the council discussed and approved the original city plat for Far West and resolved to commence building a house of the Lord in Far West. This was decided even though Joseph Smith had not approved the building of a temple.[8] Subsequently, at a meeting on August 5, 1837, the high council voted to "go on moderately" and build a temple in Far West "as we have means."[9]

Another unusual issue was that the Far West High Council, at its meeting held on May 13, 1838, approved the use of Church funds to obtain land and salaries for Joseph Smith and Sidney Rigdon.[10] A few months earlier, on December 23, 1837, they had approved making payments to members of the committee (Elisha Groves, Jacob Whitmer, and G. M. Hinkle) for the building of the temple for expenses incurred and services performed.[11] At a meeting on December 7, 1837, the council determined that it was "antiscriptural" to pay themselves for their time and services.[12]

The *Far West Record* includes the minutes of several meetings of the Far West High Council, from which it is possible to glimpse the workings of the early Church.[13] A sample of these meetings is as follows.

1. April 24, 1837, at Far West.[14] The main topic of this meeting was charges against Lyman Wight for erroneously teaching that the Book of Covenants printed in Kirtland was a telestial law, while the Book of Commandments printed at Independence was a celestial law. Lyman Wight made the necessary acknowledgements of error.

2. March 24, 1838, at Far West Schoolhouse.[15] Joseph Smith was present at this meeting. The council considered a dispute between individuals over the hugging of a girl in public, and also adopted a procedure that high councilors who were frequently absent would be replaced.

3. April 14, 1838, at Far West Schoolhouse.[1] Concluded that an elder with independent views of the Word of Wisdom and authority of the high council regarding revelations was found to err in spirit, but did not deserve punishment.

4. June 28–29, 1838, at Far West.[17] Considered various disciplinary matters, including a dispute about the division of timber among partners. The council overturned the bishop's decision to disfellowship a father who was accused of speaking unduly harshly to his children.

A review of the minutes indicates that the high council meetings were conducted with prayer and hymns. One of the hymns they sang frequently was "This Earth Was Once a Garden Place" by William W. Phelps. This hymn is commonly known today as "Adam-ondi-Ahman" and reflects the significance of the Far West area to the Church.

Quorum of the Twelve

The Quorum of the Twelve Apostles underwent a significant reorganization during the Far West era, due primarily to the fact that several of the original apostles called in 1835 left the Church and David Patten was killed in the Battle of Crooked River in October 1838. In total, six new apostles were called during the Far West era:

- John E. Page
- Wilford Woodruff
- Willard Richards
- John Taylor
- George A. Smith
- Lyman Sherman

The first four men were called in July 1838 (D&C 118:6). George A. Smith and Lyman Sherman were nominated by the First Presidency in a letter sent from Liberty Jail in January 1839. Elders Page and Taylor were ordained apostles at a high council meeting in Far West on December 19, 1838.[18] George A. Smith and Wilford Woodruff were ordained at the Far West temple site on April 26, 1839,[19] and Willard Richards was ordained while serving a mission in England in 1840. Lyman Sherman died at age thirty-four before he could be ordained.[20]

The Work of Joseph Smith in Far West

Joseph Smith spent the first few weeks after arriving in Far West teaching the Mormons and getting settled. Then he and Sidney Rigdon began the task of writing the history of the Church. While living in Far West, Joseph wrote the personal account of the Restoration that is now included in the Pearl of Great Price as Joseph Smith—History.[21]

Joseph also spent time looking for other nearby lands where the Mormons could settle. As discussed in a later chapter, in May 1838, he led a group of surveyors northward for the purpose of laying off stakes of Zion in Daviess County and establishing the city of Adam-ondi-Ahman. He organized a stake there in June 1838.

Revelations in Far West

Far West was a place of revelation for the Prophet and the Church. Eight sections of the Doctrine and Covenants (113–20) were written or received at Far West and Adam-ondi-Ahman during the year 1838, and three additional sections (121–23) were written or received while Joseph Smith was a prisoner in Liberty Jail in Liberty, Clay County, Missouri, as a result of his arrest at Far West in November 1838.

Section 113

Shortly after he arrived in Far West, the Prophet provided answers to certain questions interpreting the writings of the Old Testament prophet Isaiah. Joseph recorded that shortly after the arrival of his brother Samuel at Far West, "while walking with him and certain other brethren, the following sentiments occurred to [his] mind,"[22] including those recorded in section 113.

Section 114

On April 18, 1838, Joseph Smith received a revelation directing Apostle David Patten to prepare to serve a mission with the other members of the Twelve the following spring.

Section 115

On April 26, 1838, Joseph Smith received a revelation that is now Doctrine and Covenants section 115. This revelation did four main things.

First, it gave the Church the name used today: "For thus shall my church be called in the last days, even The Church of Jesus Christ of Latter-day Saints" (D&C 115:4). Prior to this revelation the Church had generally been called the Church of Christ or the Church of the Latter-day Saints.

Second, the revelation designated Far West as a holy ground: "Let the city, Far West, be a holy and consecrated land unto me; and it shall be called most holy, for the ground upon which thou standest is holy." This language is similar to that used in Exodus 3:5, when Moses stood on the mount and spoke with the Lord face-to-face.

Third, the revelation directed the Church to build the temple in Far West.

Finally, this revelation designated Far West as a gathering place for the Mormons, the new center place in Missouri: "And again, verily I say unto you, it is my will that the city of Far West should be built up speedily by the gathering of my Saints; And also that other places should be appointed for stakes in the regions round about, as they shall be manifested unto my servant Joseph, from time to time" (D&C 115:17–18).

The Revelations of July 8, 1838: Sections 117–20

July 8, 1838, was also an important day of revelation for the Prophet. He received several revelations that day, including sections 117–20 of the Doctrine and Covenants.[23] Joseph Smith recorded the following in his history about this day: "The three revelations which I received January 12, 1838, the day I left Kirtland, were read in the public congregation at Far West; and the same day I inquired to the Lord, 'O lord! Show unto thy servant how much thou requirest of the properties of thy people for a tithing,'[24] and received the following answer, which was also read in public.

The answer to this question is in Doctrine and Covenants sections 119 and 120, conveying the law of tithing as practiced in the Church today: "And after that, those who have thus been tithed shall pay one-tenth of all their interest annually; and this shall be a standing law unto them forever, for my holy priesthood, saith the Lord" (D&C 120:4).

Section 120 also states that tithing funds shall be disposed of by a council composed of the First Presidency, Presiding Bishop and his council, and the Quorum of Twelve.

Another revelation received on July 8, 1838—Doctrine and Covenants section 117—was directed to three brethren still living in Kirtland: Newel K. Whitney, William Marks, and Oliver Granger. The first two brethren were directed to "settle up their business speedily and journey from the land of Kirtland, before I, the Lord, send again the snows upon the earth" (D&C 117:1). Included in that revelation is a reference to the Far West area being the land where Adam dwelt: "Is there not room enough on the mountains of Adam-ondi-Ahman, and on the plains of Olaha Shinehah, or the land where Adam dwelt, that you should covet that which is but the drop, and neglect the more weighty matters? Therefore, come up hither unto the land of my people, even Zion" (D&C 117:8–9).

Doctrine and Covenants section 118 was also received on this date. This revelation was directed to the Twelve in response to the Prophet's inquiry, "Show us thy will, O Lord, concerning the Twelve." It provides that the Twelve should be reorganized to replace the fallen apostles, calling John Page, Wilford Woodruff, and Willard Richards as the new apostles. It also states that the Twelve should serve a mission starting the next spring "over the great waters" and that this mission was to begin in "the city of Far West, on the twenty-sixth day of April next [1839], on the building-spot of my house, saith the Lord" (D&C 118:5).

Joseph Smith received one last revelation on July 8, 1838, relating to the standing of William W. Phelps and Frederick G. Williams. However, it is not included in the Doctrine and Covenants. "Verily, thus saith the Lord, in consequence of their transgressions their former standing has been taken away from them, and now, if they will be saved, let them be ordained as Elders in my church to preach my Gospel and travel abroad from land to land and from place to place, to gather mine elect unto me, saith the Lord, and let this be their labors from henceforth. Amen."[25]

Sections 121–23

While incarcerated in Liberty Jail, the Prophet wrote a letter directed "to the Church of Latter-day Saints at Quincy, Illinois, and Scattered Abroad, and to Bishop Partridge in Particular." This letter was started on March 20, 1839, and completed on March 25. Portions of that letter were regarded of such special value that they were placed in Doctrine and Covenants 121–23.[26]

After hearing the reports of the destruction of property; the violence against the Mormons in Far West and their forced exodus into Quincy, Illinois; and, after spending several months in the dark, cold prison, the Prophet exclaimed, "O God! Where art Thou! . . . How long shall Thy hand be stayed, and Thine eye, yea Thy pure eye, behold from the eternal heavens, the wrongs of Thy people, and of Thy servants, and Thy ear be penetrated with their cries?" Joseph continued to write, "And when the heart is sufficiently contrite, then the voice of inspiration steals along and whispers, 'My son, peace be unto thy soul; thine adversity and thine afflictions shall be but a small moment" (see D&C 121:1–7 for the full account).

Joseph continued:

> Ignorance, superstition and bigotry . . . is oftimes in the way of the prosperity of the Church; like the torrent of rain from the mountains, that floods the most pure and crystal stream with mire, and dirt, and filthiness, and obscures everything that was clear before, and all rushes along in one general deluge; but time weathers tide; and notwithstanding we are rolled in the more of the flood for the time being, the next surge peradventure, as time rolls on, may bring to us the fountain as clear as crystal, and as pure as snow; while the filthiness, flood-wood and rubbish is left and purged out by the way.
>
> How long can rolling water remain impure? What power shall stay the heavens? As well might man stretch forth his puny arm to stop the Missouri river in its decreed course, or turn it up stream, as to hinder the Almighty from pouring down knowledge from heaven, upon the heads of the Latter-day Saints. (D&C 121:33)

In this letter, Joseph warned:

> And if there are any among you who aspire after their own aggrandizement, and seek their own opulence, while their brethren are groaning in poverty, and are under sore trials and temptations, they cannot be benefited by the intercession of the Holy Spirit. . . .
>
> Behold, there are many called, but few are chosen. And why are they not chosen? Because their hearts are set so much upon the things of this world, and aspire to the honors of men, that they do not learn this one lesson—that the rights of the Priesthood are inseparably connected with the powers of heaven, and that the powers of heaven cannot be controlled nor handled only upon the principles of righteousness.[27]

Further in the letter is what is now known as section 122 of the Doctrine and Covenants, instructing Joseph that "if the very jaws of hell shall gape open the mouth wide after thee, know thou, my son, that all these things shall give thee experience, and shall be for thy good. The Son of Man hath descended below them all; art thou greater than he?"[28]

The latter part of the letter that is now contained in Doctrine and Covenants 123 instructed the Mormons to document the sufferings and abuses and damages to their properties that were inflicted upon them in Missouri and present them to the heads of the government. In accord with the Prophet's letter, Church members prepared various claims over the next few years and presented many of these to government authorities. These various claims are commonly referred to as the Mormon Redress Petitions.

Notes

1. A third stake was organized in June 1838 at Adam-ondi-Ahman in Daviess County.
2. See *History of the Church,* 4:402–404.
3. Dyer, *The Refiner's Fire*, 139–42.
4. *History of the Church*, 2:122–24.
5. Ibid., 2:522–23, and *Far West Record*, 121–22.
6. Ibid., 2:522–23 and *Far West Record*, 121–22.
7. *Far West Record*, 71, note 2.
8. Ibid., 103.
9. Ibid., 118.
10. Ibid., 186, and *History of the Church*, 3:31–32.
11. Ibid., 133–34.
12. *History of the Church*, 2:527–28.
13. However, there are no minutes for the entire year 1835, and most of the year 1836. During this period of time, many of the Missouri Church leaders were on missions or in Kirtland, Ohio, preparing for the dedication of the temple. There are also no minutes of meetings between October 6, 1838, and December 13, 1838, due to the persecutions at Far West (*Far West Record*, 223, note 1).
14. *Far West Record*, 111.
15. Ibid., 153–57.
16. Ibid., 179.
17. Ibid., 190–92.
18. Ibid., 223–24.
19. *History of the Church*, vol. 3, 337.
20. Black, *Who's Who in the Doctrine and Covenants*, 262. Brother Sherman went to visit the Prophet in prison after his arrest in November 1838 but took cold while on that trip and died soon after returning home. Brother Sherman is described as having been a man of great integrity and a powerful preacher (Benjamin Johnson, *My Life's Review*, 52–53).
21. See Joseph Smith—History, Pearl of Great Price, JS—H 1:2 and 1:60, and *History of the Church*, 3:268.
22. *History of the Church*, 3:9–10.
23. Ibid., 3:44.
24. The location and content of the three revelations Joseph referred to that were received in Kirtland is not known. These revelations are not printed in the Doctrine and Covenants or in any other LDS publication. Diligent efforts

have been made to find them in the LDS Church Historian's Office, but they have never been located. See *History of the Church*, vol. 3, 44.

25. *History of the Church*, 3:46 footnotes.
26. See *History of the Church*, 3:289–305 for the complete letter.
27. Ibid., 121:34–35.
28. Ibid., 122:7–8.

Chapter 7

ADAM-ONDI-AHMAN

THE MORMONS ESTABLISHED ANOTHER COMMU-
NITY at Adam-ondi-Ahman (commonly called Diahman by the
Mormons) in Daviess County, about twenty-five miles north of Far West.
Adam-ondi-Ahman was the focal point of the Mormon settlements in
Daviess County and also figured prominently in the Mormon War of
1838.

Most of the growth at Adam-ondi-Ahman occurred in 1838. Not long
after Joseph Smith arrived in Far West, he began looking for other nearby
lands where the Mormons could settle. The Church was growing, with
members continually moving into Missouri, and the habitable portions of
Caldwell County soon became crowded. Further, in the revelation received
on April 26, 1838, the Mormons were directed to look for other places to "be
appointed for stakes in the regions round about, as they shall be manifested
unto my servant Joseph from time to time" (D&C 115:17–18).

On May 18, 1838, Joseph led a group of surveyors northward for
the purpose of laying off stakes of Zion in Daviess County. Among this
group were Elder David W. Patten, an apostle, and Bishop Edward Partridge.[1] When Joseph Smith arrived in the area with the survey team, he
found three or four Mormon families already living there, and he made
his headquarters in Lyman Wight's log cabin. Lyman Wight operated a
ferry on the Grand River at the bottom of Tower Hill.

Joseph was inspired by what he saw and proclaimed a new community. He
indicated the area had a connection to the Nephites of the Book of Mormon,
for he spotted "an old Nephitish Altar and Tower," and then received a revelation that said Spring Hill was named by the Lord Adam-ondi-Ahman

because, he said, "it is the place where Adam shall come to visit his people, or the Ancient of Days shall sit, as spoken of by Daniel the Prophet."[2]

Other revelations indicate that the concept of Adam-ondi-Ahman was known within the Church as early as 1832,[3] before the location was known, just as the concept of the city of the New Jerusalem was revealed before Jackson County was settled. Joseph Smith taught that in the valley of Adam-ondi-Ahman, Adam assembled his posterity three years before his death and bestowed upon them his blessing. On that occasion the Lord appeared to them, and Adam's posterity arose and blessed Adam, calling him Michael, the Prince, and Arch-angel. Also there, the Lord administered comfort to Adam and said unto him, "I have set thee to be at the head; a multitude of nations shall come of thee, and thou art a prince over them forever" (D&C 107:53–55).

The land was beautiful. The city was laid out on a high, elevated piece of ground rising from two to four hundred feet above the Grand River. From the high elevations visitors can see long distances in several directions. In the *Elders' Journal* of August 1838, Adam-ondi-Ahman was described as follows:

> Adam-ondi-Ahman is located immediately on the north side of Grand River, in Daviess County, Missouri, about twenty-five miles north of Far West. It is situated on an elevated spot of ground, which renders the place as beautiful as any part of the United States, and overlooking the river and country round about, it is certainly a beautiful location. And when we look upon this beautiful situation, with the transcendent landscape which surrounds it, attended with all the above-named advantages, we are ready to say truly this is like unto the land which the Lord our God promised to his Saints in the last days.[4]

The town site was two miles square and was laid out in lots of an acre each, in the center of which was the temple lot of four acres.[5] The city of Adam-ondi-Ahman was laid out in a similar pattern to that designed for Independence, Far West, and later Nauvoo, with large streets running to the square of one another. The center square of each city included plans for a temple, storehouses, places of worship, and schools.

Growth of Adam-ondi-Ahman

Joseph and his party remained in Daviess County for several weeks surveying the lands. The Mormons intended to eventually purchase all of the lands between Adam-ondi-Ahman and Far West when the lands went up for sale and they had the resources to do so.

The Mormons settled in Daviess County as Caldwell County filled up. There was a steady stream of wagons coming to the area, and a large group of two hundred wagons arrived from Canada in June of 1838; many of these newcomers began to settle in Daviess County.[6] In addition, on October 2, 1838, the Kirtland Camp of several hundred members arrived at Far West, and Joseph Smith took them to Adam-ondi-Ahman to settle as a group because Caldwell County was becoming crowded.

David Osborn was one of the first Mormon settlers in Daviess County, arriving in the spring of 1837. He described the conditions he experienced:

> I bought land and commenced a farm in Daviess County, 12 miles north of Far West, cleared, fenced and put into corn eight acres. Also built a good white-oak log cabin the first season. Also dug a well some 35 feet deep, but got no water in the fall. I took a tour in company with Elisha H. Groves and Francis Case on Grand River some 60 miles north, bee hunting. We were from home six weeks and got about five barrels of beautiful honey. Though it rained about one week while we were out, the richest tree we found contained 11 1/4 gallons, though I heard of 20 gallons being taken from one tree. Next spring, I commenced making rails, and fencing another field in the prairie. I enclosed, broke and planted in corn, potatoes, pumpkins, etc., 10 acres more. This proved to be a good season for crops. I raised 400 or 500 bushels of corn and vegetables in abundance. On the 19th of April this year, which was 1838. We had another son added to our family and as I was afraid this would be my last son, I called him after my own name. The health of my family was good except little William who was still afflicted, being entirely helpless. He was a great burden to his mother.[7]

It is estimated that from June to October 1838 the population of the two-mile square city of Adam-ondi-Ahman increased to four to five hundred people. By October there were two hundred houses there.[8] Another six hundred Mormons were scattered throughout Daviess County.

Approximately 90 percent of the Mormons in Daviess County settled on the land under "preemption rights," meaning that the government had not yet made the land available for purchase.[9] However, the Mormons believed that they would eventually own the land and thus worked hard to build their farms. The U.S. government planned to offer this land for sale in November 1838. This land ownership issue would ultimately prove to be one of the causes of the Mormon War.

The arrival of Kirtland Camp in early October added greatly to the size of the community. Many camp members were impressed by the beauty of the area. One member of the camp, John Pulsipher, wrote, "Joseph directed us to camp at night around the Temple cellar in Far West and then go thirty miles north to strengthen a small settlement at Adam-ondi-Ahman. We found the handsomest country I ever saw. We bought land and went to work building houses and mills."[10]

Benjamin Johnson, also a member of Kirtland Camp, described his arrival:

> On approaching Far West we were met by the Prophet, who came out to meet us, and I felt joy in seeing him again. As my sisters, Delcena and Julia, wives of L. R. Sherman and A. W. Babbitt, were both living in Far West, I had expected to remain there also, but I was counseled by the Prophet to proceed to [Adam-ondi-Ahman] Diahman to assist with others in strengthening that place against mobs gathering there from the adjoining counties.
>
> On our arrival at Diahman, our camp was pitched upon the town plat which had just been surveyed by direction of the Prophet, and of course each one was anxious to obtain the most eligible, or first choice of lots. As I was young and unmarried my choice would come near the last under the rule of "oldest served first." So when it was my choice I found I must take the top lot on the promontory overlooking the Grand River valley, or go farther away and lower down than I wished to. So I chose the upper, which at first appeared rocky, but which made the other lots appear almost enviable. When, after a few days, the Prophet accompanied us to this spot, and pointed out those rocks as the ones of which Adam built an altar and offered sacrifice upon this spot, where he stood and blessed the multitude of his children, when they called him Michael, and where he will again sit as the Ancient of Days, then I was not envious of anyone's choice for a city lot in Adam-ondi-Ahman.[11]

Another member of Kirtland Camp, Daniel McArthur, wrote: "[We] were sent by the Prophet Joseph to Daviess County more than a day or two before we commenced to build a city to be called Adam-ondi-Ahman. Some of us cut house logs, others hauled them to the spot and others put them up, and so by doing, a city sprang up in a very short time, and while we were busy building and providing for the winter."[12]

George A. Smith, who was later called as an apostle, recorded, "I assisted my father in building a two-story log house on a lot in Adam-ondi-Ahman. I helped to raise 25 log houses in 25 days."[13]

Orange Wight, the son of Lyman Wight, recalled fond memories of sociality at Adam-ondi-Ahman:

> Adam-ondi-Ahman was visited a number of times by the Prophet Joseph Smith and I became still better acquainted with him being now 14 years old, I could comprehend and appreciate all or nearly all he would say. He was very kind and sociable with both young and old. We often bathed in the limped waters of Grand River, although but a boy I was invited to bathe with them. At one time we had a jolly time—yes and at other times. There was Joseph the Prophet, my father [Lyman Wight], Sidney Rigdon, and several others, our amusement consisted in part seeing Brother Rigdon swim. He was so corpulent that he was forced to lay on his back to swim, he would swim in that way until his shoulders would strike the sand bar then he could turn but would flop back in deep water.[14]

The Stake at Adam-ondi-Ahman

On June 28, 1838, Joseph Smith organized a stake at Adam-ondi-Ahman, making it the third stake in the Church, after Kirtland and Far West. The meeting to establish the stake was held at a grove near Lyman Wight's home.[15]

John Smith, the prophet's uncle who had arrived in the area a few weeks earlier, was called as stake president. The counselors in the stake presidency were Reynolds Cahoon and Lyman Wight. Vincent Knight was chosen as acting bishop. The high council consisted of John Lemon, Daniel Stanton, Mayhew Hillman, Daniel Carter, Isaac Perry, Harrison Sagers, Alanson Brown, Thomas Gordon, Lorenzo D. Barnes, George A. Smith, Harvey Olmstead, and Ezra Thayer. Those who were not already high priests were ordained to the office that day.[16]

Adam's Altar

Joseph Smith taught that Adam offered sacrifices during his life. On one occasion an angel appeared to Adam while he was offering sacrifices and taught him the meaning of the law of sacrifice as a type of the forthcoming sacrifice of Jesus Christ (Moses 5:6–8).

The Prophet stated that certain rock formations found at Adam-ondi-Ahman were sacrificial altars used by Adam. These may or may not have been the altar involved in the angelic appearance, but they were probably typical of what would have been used by Adam so long ago.

The accounts describing Adam's altar at Adam-ondi-Ahman were typically made several years after the fact and thus vary in their particulars.

There was probably more than one ancient structure in the area.

Oliver Huntington described the valley of Adam-ondi-Ahman as follows: "It was a most glorious and joyfully handsome prairie of two or three [miles] in length and in full view of the ground where both Adam's altar and tower once stood, only a few trees were between us and the altar, yet all three places were just on the edge of the prairie."[17]

Heber C. Kimball gave an account of the altars on the occasion of the dedication of the temple site at Adam-ondi-Ahman in 1838:

> While there, we laid out a city on a high elevated piece of land, and set the stakes for the four corners of a temple block, which was dedicated, Brother Brigham Young being mouth; there were from three to five hundred men present on the occasion, under arms. This elevated spot was probably from 250 to 500 feet above the Grand River so that one could look east, west, north or south, as far as the eye could reach; it was one of the most beautiful places I ever beheld...The Prophet Joseph called upon Brigham, myself and others, saying, "Brethren, come, go along with me and I will show you something." He led us a short distance to a place where were ruins of three altars built of stone, one above the other, and one standing a little back of the other, like unto the pulpits in the Kirtland Temple, representing the order of the three grades of priesthood. "There," said Joseph, "is the place where Adam offered up sacrifice after he was cast out of the garden." The altar stood at the highest point of the bluff. I went and examined the place several times while I remained there."[18]

Abraham Smoot and Alanson Ripley also aided in surveying the site at Adam-ondi-Ahman. Years later when Wilford Woodruff and others were visiting at the home of Brother Smoot in Provo to administer to his sick wife, Smoot related an experience which had occurred in June 1838:

> Abraham Smoot said that "he and Alanson Ripley, while surveying at that town [Adam-ondi-Ahman]. . . came across a stone wall in the midst of a dense forest of underbrush. The wall was 30 feet long, 3 feet thick, and 4 feet high. It was laid in mortar or cement. When Joseph Smith visited the place and examined the wall he said it was the remains of an altar built by Father Adam and upon which he offered sacrifices after he was driven from the Garden of Eden. He said that the Garden of Eden was located in Jackson County, Missouri. The whole town of Adam-ondi-Ahman was in the midst of a thick and heavy forest of timber and the place was named in honor of Adam's altar. The prophet explained that it was upon this altar where Adam blessed his sons and his posterity, prior to his death.[19]

An account by Chapman Duncan is also insightful:

[Joseph] said to those present, "get me a spade and I will show you the altar that Adam offered sacrifice on." . . . We went forty rods north of my house. He placed the spade with care, placed his foot on it. When he took out the shovel full of dirt, it bared the stone. The dirt was two inches deep on the stone I reckon. About four feet or more was disclosed. He did not dig to the bottom of the three layers of good masonry well put wall. The stone looked more like dressed stone, nice joints, ten inches thick, eighteen inches long or more. We came back down the slope, perhaps fifteen rods on the level. The Prophet stopped and remarked that this place where we stood was the place where Adam gathered his posterity and blessed them, and predicted what should come to pass to later generations.[20]

Luman Shurtliff described the altar as "a pile of rock about two feet high and ten or twelve feet broad. This is said to be the altar where Adam offered up his sacrifice at the time he called all his sons together and blessed them and prophesied what should befall them in the latter days."[21]

In *History of the Church* by B. H. Roberts, we learn:

On the brow of the bluff stood the old stone altar, and near the foot of it was built the house of Lyman Wight. When the altar was first discovered, according to those who visited it frequently, it was about sixteen feet long, by nine or ten feet wide, having its greatest extent north and south. The height of the altar at each end was some two and a half feet, gradually rising higher to the center, which was between four and five feet high—the whole surface being crowning. Such was the altar at "Diahman" when the Prophet's party visited it. Now, however, it is thrown down, and nothing but a mound of crumbling stones mixed with soil, and a few reddish boulders mark the spot which is doubtless rich in historic events. It was at this altar, according to the testimony of Joseph Smith, that the patriarchs associated with Adam and his company, assembled to worship their God. Here their evening and morning prayer ascended to heaven with the smoke of the burning sacrifice, prophetic and symbolic of the greater sacrifice then yet to be, and here angels instructed them in heavenly truth.[22]

Adam-ondi-Ahman Today

The LDS Church owns many acres at Adam-ondi-Ahman and has established facilities to tour the area. However, there is little or no tangible evidence remaining of the city or the stones used in Adam's altar. The

© David O. Lloyd

1964 photo of altar stones. Author is the skinny girl on the right.

smaller stones were likely removed by visitors over the years. In 1966, LDS Church Mission President Alvin R. Dyer interviewed Clayt Barlow (then eighty-three years old), a long-time resident of Jameson (three or four miles north of Adam-ondi-Ahman), who had information regarding the larger stones. Mr. Barlow told how the larger stones at the altar site were removed in the early 1920s by a man named Joe Miller (with the permission of the land owner). Barlow had little information, however, regarding Mr. Miller, where he took the stones, or how he intended to use them.[23]

Notes

1. *History of the Church*, 3:34–35.
2. *History of the Church*, 3:35; D&C 116; and Daniel 7.
3. D&C 78:15, dated March 1832, provides, "That you may come up unto the crown prepared for you, and be made rulers over many kingdoms, saith the Lord God, the Holy One of Zion, who hath established the foundations of Adam-ondi-Ahman."
4. A. Ripley, *Elders' Journal*, Aug. 1838, 52.
5. Dyer, *Refiner's Fire*, 175.
6. *History of the Church*, 3:48.
7. Osborn, Autobiography, 15.
8. Bushman, *Joseph Smith, Rough Stone Rolling*, 346.
9. See *History of the Church*, 4:29; Jenson, *Historical Record*, 727.
10. Pulsipher Autobiography, 3.
11. Benjamin Johnson, *My Life's Review*, 36.
12. Daniel McArthur Autobiography, 5.
13. George Smith, "My Journal," *The Instructor* 82:14

14. Orange Wight Autobiography, 4.
15. *History of the Church*, 3:38.
16. *History of the Church*, 3:38–39.
17. Oliver Huntington Autobiography, 36–37.
18. Dyer, *Refiner's Fire*, 172–73, quoting Whitney, *Life of Heber C. Kimball*, 22.
19. Abraham Smoot Biography, 23. C. E. Berlin, the author, notes, "This stone structure should not be confused with the stone tower standing on the same hill but which Joseph Smith identified as a Nephite tower at least a month earlier than Smoot and Ripley could have discovered Adam's altar."
20. Chapman Duncan Autobiography, 37–38.
21. Luman Shurtliff Autobiography, 34.
22. *History of the Church*, 3:39.
23. Dyer, *Refiner's Fire*, 205–08.

Chapter 8

INTERNAL STRIFE
AND DISSENSION

T HE FAR WEST ERA WAS a period of significant internal strife for the Church. In the spring of 1838, the three members of the Missouri presidency of the Church—David Whitmer, William W. Phelps, and John Whitmer—were removed from office by the local members. Shortly thereafter, these three men were excommunicated, along with two other important leaders in the early Church: Oliver Cowdery and Apostle Lyman E. Johnson. These excommunications thus included two of the three witnesses to the Book of Mormon plates (David Whitmer and Oliver Cowdery) and one of the eight witnesses to the same (John Whitmer). Indeed, this was a time of great difficulty for the Church.

Removal of Missouri Presidency

The internal troubles in the Missouri church first came to a head in April 1837. The Far West High Council formally challenged two of the presidency, John Whitmer and William W. Phelps, on how they had used the $1,450 raised by contributions from Mormons in several southern states for the purchase of land in Far West—the fund for "poor bleeding Zion." However, Whitmer and Phelps had used the funds to buy land in their own names, then resold the land to incoming Mormons at a profit, which they retained, although each of the two men promised to donate $1,000 to the fund to build the Far West Temple. Some members complained about this.

The members also complained that the presidency made decisions without consulting with the high council, such as deciding to build a temple in Far West.[1] As originally constituted, the Missouri High Council consisted of fifteen members, three presidents and twelve councilors.[2]

In early 1837, however, complaints were made that the presidency in Far West not only met separately on occasion but did not seek high council approval for their decisions or discuss matters with them.

These issues were addressed in April 1837 with the high council and Elders David Patten and Thomas B. Marsh, who were apostles. With respect to the land purchases, John Whitmer and William W. Phelps made a reconciliation by agreeing to return the profits and convey the land to Bishop Partridge as agent of the Church. Their commitment to donate $1,000 each to the temple was cancelled. The group also collectively decided to proceed with the building of a temple at Far West.[3]

Problems continued, however, when William W. Phelps and John Whitmer made further attempts to profit from land deals. When Joseph Smith sought guidance from the Lord, he received a revelation in Kirtland on September 4, 1837, announcing that John Whitmer and William W. Phelps were in transgression and should be removed from their positions if they did not repent.[4]

Joseph Smith went to Far West in November 1837 to set the Church in order and to look for other suitable habitats for the Mormons to settle in northern Missouri. At a meeting held with the Far West High Council during his visit, a decision was reached to wait for the building of the temple until the Lord revealed it to be His will to have it commenced.[5]

After Joseph left Far West to return to Kirtland, problems resurfaced during the winter of 1837–38 between the stake presidency and high council in Missouri. By then, Oliver Cowdery had moved to Far West from Kirtland. He and the three men in the local presidency (David Whitmer, William W. Phelps, and John Whitmer) decided to sell some Church lands in Jackson County that were held in their names. The selling of these lands violated the Lord's directions that the Mormons should continue to hold claim on their lands in Jackson County, even if they could not presently dwell there (D&C 101:99). In fact, the members had been commanded in revelations given in 1833 and 1834 to continue to acquire lands in Jackson County whenever possible (D&C 101:70–74; 105:28–29; 103:23).[6]

The high council and Elders Thomas Marsh and David Patten of the Twelve appointed a committee to visit the presidency and Oliver Cowdery to inquire about their feelings.[7] The committee met with the four men, but generally adversarial relations existed. The presidents declared they had not broken revelations or the law of God in so doing, and if they were deprived of that privilege they would sell their possessions in Far

West and move. They further declared they would not be controlled by an ecclesiastical power or revelation whatsoever in their temporal concerns. Regarding the accusations concerning the Word of Wisdom, William W. Phelps said he had not broken it. Oliver Cowdery said he had drunk tea three times a day during the winter on account of his ill health. David and John Whitmer said they used tea and coffee, but they did not consider them to come under the head of hot drinks.[8]

The high council resolved that the men should be removed from office and that the case be laid before the Church at different meetings held in the homes of members at various settlements near Far West for that purpose.[9] On February 5, 1838, at a meeting attended by Church members, the high council tried John Whitmer and William W. Phelps for misusing Church funds and David Whitmer for willfully breaking the Word of Wisdom.[10] The *Far West Record* contains a detailed record of the proceedings and is included in the Appendix of this book.[11]

The situation was quite contentious. A significant issue in the meeting was whether the high council had jurisdiction to consider the case against the presidency. A number of brethren believed that they did not and that the matter should properly be brought before the bishop and his counselor, if at all, or before Joseph Smith personally.

Some of the members of the council spoke strongly against the presidency, while others spoke in their favor. According to the meeting minutes, George Morey contended "in a very energetic manner" that the actions of the presidency were iniquitous, and Apostle David Patten "spake with much zeal against this Presidency, and in favor of Br. Joseph Smith and that the wolf alluded to in his letter, was the dissenters in Kirtland."[12] Lyman Wight said that "all other accusations were of minor importance compared to their selling their lands in Jackson County, that they (Phelps and Whitmer) had set an example which all the members were liable to follow: he said that it was a hellish principle, and that they had flatly denied the faith in so doing."[13]

On the other hand, several men spoke in favor of the presidency or believed that the proceedings were hasty. Solomon Hancock "pled in favor of the Presidency, stating that he could not raise his hand against them."[14] John Corrill argued that the high council proceedings were illegal and the presidency should be tried before a proper tribunal, which he considered to be a bishop and twelve high priests. He also spoke in favor of the presidency and said that he could not raise his hands against them at present, although he did not uphold them in their iniquity."[15]

At the conclusion of the meeting, a vote was taken and "was unanimous, excepting eight or ten and this minority only wished them to continue in office a little longer, or until Joseph Smith came up."[16] Thus, the Far West High Council, with the approval of the local members, voted to remove the three men from the office of the presidency.

That decision was then presented to the Church membership and voted upon and approved at a series of four meetings held over a period of four days in February 1838 at several locations.[17] A new temporary presidency was chosen consisting of David Patten and Thomas B. Marsh. A short while later, this presidency was formalized under the direction of Joseph Smith, and Brigham Young was added as the third member.[18]

These actions and decisions led to bitterness and hard feelings among the brethren. Oliver Cowdery expressed his feelings in the following letter to his brother, Warren Cowdery, dated February 4, 1838:

> Messrs William W. Phelps, J. Whitmer and myself had a partial claim to a few lots in Independence, Mo. [which] we sold some time since on some of the Jackson suits costs. We quit claimed our interest in and to the same for a small sum (and glad to get that) which has caused considerable stir. Not long since, Messrs D and J Whitmer, William W. Phelps and myself were waited upon by (as they said) a committee of the High Council who said the church were dissatisfied with our conduct, &c. in selling those lots and not keeping the word of wisdom, and also in not teaching the church to fulfil the consecration law. I told them that if I had property, while I lived and was sane, I would not be dictated, influenced or controlled by any man or set of men by no tribunal of ecclesiastical pretenses what ever . . . .
>
> The . . . council met again and resolved not to have those men [David Whitmer,William W. Phelps and John Whitmer] to be their Presidents, and to call on the church to know if they would consent in the same. They [the High Council] say they have no legal accusation against them, but don't want them to preside over the church any longer. Tomorrow [February 5, 1838] is appointed for the first meeting of the church: the brethren [Whitmers and Phelps] won't go. They will note to the principle enough to go and answer to a tribunal which is no tribunal. . . . The council have concluded they have nothing to do with me.[19]

Excommunications

After this action was taken, it was just a matter of time until these three brethren in the presidency and Oliver Cowdery were formally removed from the Church. This occurred within the next few months. The charges against the men were generally similar to those raised previously by the high council. Apostle Lyman Johnson was also excommunicated but for different reasons all together.

First, two members of the Missouri stake presidency, William W. Phelps and John Whitmer, were excommunicated by the high council on March 10, 1838.[20] The principal charges against both men related to the misuse of funds donated by Church members to acquire lands at Far West, specifically the fund for "poor bleeding Zion." There were also charges against John Whitmer for violations of the Word of Wisdom.[21] This excommunication occurred just four days before Joseph Smith arrived from Kirtland to make Far West his residence.

Next, charges were brought against Oliver Cowdery, and he was excommunicated at a high council meeting on April 12, 1838, at the Far West Schoolhouse.[22] Joseph Smith and Brigham Young were in attendance, as well as the high council. The principal charges against Oliver Cowdery were that he sold land in Missouri contrary to revelation and that he had falsely accused Joseph Smith of adultery.[23] Oliver had raised objections about the Church's authority to be involved in temporal matters such as the right to sell private property.

Oliver refused to appear before the high council. However, he answered by letter and denied the Church's right to dictate how he should conduct his life. He asked that his fellowship with the Church be ended, and he was excommunicated.

The next day, David Whitmer and Lyman E. Johnson, an apostle, were each excommunicated. These meetings took place on April 13, 1838, also at the Far West Schoolhouse.[24] Joseph Smith and Brigham Young were in attendance as well. David Whitmer's charges were usurping too much authority, writing letters of dissension to apostates, and breaking the Word of Wisdom. The more significant charges against Lyman Johnson included attempting to vindicate the cause of apostates, filing vexatious lawsuits against some brethren, falsely claiming that Joseph Smith owed him $1,000, and physically assaulting Brother Phineas Young.

David Whitmer and Lyman Johnson refused to attend their respective cases but sent letters to the high council. David Whitmer's letter stated that the council did not have the authority to try him. The council considered his letter to be an affront, and it only served to hasten the decision that he be excommunicated without further investigation of the case.[25]

Two other notable members left the Church at approximately this time. At a trial held before the high council on May 11, 1838, William E. McLellin of the Quorum of the Twelve stated that he had no confidence in the leaders of the Church. He voluntarily left Far West to settle in Clay County.[26] Jacob Whitmer, one of the eight witnesses to the Book of Mormon plates and a brother to David and John, also left the Church. There are no records about whether formal Church disciplinary action was taken against him, but he became disaffected following the departure of his brothers from the faith.

The Salt Sermon—Danite Dissenters Leave Under Duress

This already tense situation between the members and the excommunicated men was made worse when Sidney Rigdon gave a public address at Far West on June 19, 1838, known as the Salt Sermon. It was so named because the text was based on Matthew 5:13 (or possibly 3 Nephi 12:13): "Ye are the salt of the earth: but if the salt have lost his savor, wherewith shall it be salted? It is thenceforth good for nothing but to be cast out, and trodden under feet of men."[27]

The premise of the speech was that this scripture should be applied to apostates and dissenters who had made profit off prejudicing the minds of the non-Mormons in the surrounding counties. This was taken by many to be a reference to the several Church leaders who had been excommunicated in the few months previous to this address. Therefore, a written communication was issued several days later to the principle dissenters advising them to leave the county under penalty of a "more fatal calamity." This document was signed by eighty-three men but was not authorized by the Church.

The majority of the signers were members of the Danite organization (also called Gideonites). There has been considerable debate among historians of the Mormon Far West era about the size of this paramilitary organization and the role that it played in Far West, as well as the extent to which it was sanctioned by Church leadership. However, it seems clear that a number of Mormon men belonged to it, that it held a number of secret meetings, and that it was led by Sampson Avard, Jared Carter and George W. Robinson. It began meeting in Far West to discuss how to deal with dissenters. Ebenezer Robinson stated that the eighty-three men who signed the petition calling for the removal of the Far West dissenters were the organizers of the Danite society.[28] The Danites were also involved, to an extent, in raising money for the Church and in attempting to influence political elections. There are indications that it was more prevalent among Mormon men in Daviess County than at Far West, that the First Presidency was at least tacitly aware of it, and that Sidney Rigdon possibly attended some Danite meetings.[29]

As a result of this letter, Oliver Cowdery, Lyman E. Johnson, William W. Phelps, John Whitmer, and David Whitmer immediately left Far West, fearing their safety. They were joined by Frederick G. Williams, who had been released as a member of the First Presidency of the Church in Kirtland in the fall of 1837, subsequently moved to Far West, and continued to associate with the Mormons.

John Corrill described the tensions that existed with respect to the dissenters in the *History of the Mormons*, presented to the Missouri legislature in January 1839, which discussed the history of the Church and many key events of the Mormon War.[30] He wrote:

> Notwithstanding, the dissenters had left the Church, yet the old strife kept up, and Church leaders complained about the ill treatment they had received from the dissenters and others; they had been harassed for seven or eight years, and were determined to bear it no longer. . . This kind of preaching was the chief topic of conversation for several months. Many Church members became disgusted with these things, and looked upon them as great inconsistencies, that would bring destruction upon the Church. But on the other hand, the dissenters kept up a kind of secret opposition to the Presidency and Church. They would occasionally speak against them, influence the minds of the members against them, and occasionally correspond with their enemies abroad, and the Church, it was said, would never become pure unless these dissenters were routed from among them. Moreover, if they were suffered to remain, they would destroy the Church. Secret meetings were held, and plans contrived, how to get rid of them. Some had one plan, and some another, but there was a backwardness in bringing it about, until President [Rigdon] delivered from the pulpit what I call the salt sermon; "If the salt have lost its savor, it is thenceforth good for nothing, but to be cast out and trodden under the feet of men," was his text, and although he did not call names in his sermon, yet it was plainly understood that he meant that dissenters, or those who had denied the faith, ought to be cast out and literally trodden under foot. He indirectly, accused some of them with crime.
>
> This sermon had the desired effect. Excitement was produced, in the Church, and, suffice it to say that in three or four days, several of the dissenters became much alarmed and fled from the place

in great fright, and their families soon followed, but their property was attached for debt. Necessity compelled others of the dissenters to confess and give satisfaction to the Church. This scene I looked upon with horror, and considered it as proceeding from a mob spirit. Thus the work of purifying was commenced, and now it must be carried out. Another thing was in the way; there was a good deal of murmuring, finding fault, and complaining against the First Presidency and others of the leaders for various causes, but more especially, on account of money which the Presidency had borrowed from time to time during the building of the Lord's house in Kirtland, and the carrying on their mercantile and banking operations. Some of the debts had been paid, but several remained unpaid, and many who had lost their farms in paying the New York debts felt bad, and they murmured and complained to that degree that the Presidency and Church got tired of hearing it, until they became determined to have it stopped.[31]

Aftermath

The internal strife in Far West resulted in hard feelings that led to the permanent separation of several of the men and their families from the Church. Of the five men who were excommunicated, only Oliver Cowdery and William W. Phelps came back to the Church. William W. Phelps went west with the Mormons, but Oliver Cowdery's health did not permit him to do so. David Whitmer, John Whitmer, and Lyman Johnson never rejoined the Church.

A brief mention is made below of the lives of the men who did not go west.

Oliver Cowdery

After his excommunication in Far West, Oliver moved to Tiffin, Ohio, where he practiced law for several years. In the spring of 1847, he moved to Elkhorn, Wisconsin. News reached the Mormons in Iowa, where they were gathering to prepare for the migration to Utah, that Oliver was interested in rejoining the Church. Brigham Young wrote him a letter inviting him to return.

Oliver traveled from Wisconsin to Kanesville, Iowa.[32] He first addressed the assembled congregation on October 21, 1849: "Friends and Brethren,—My name is Cowdery—Oliver Cowdery. In the early history of this Church I stood identified with her, and one of her councils, . . . not because I was better than the rest of mankind . . . I wrote, with my own pen, the entire Book of Mormon (save a few pages) as it fell from the lips of the Prophet Joseph Smith . . . that book is true."[33] The next month Oliver formally appeared before the high council and requested permission to rejoin the Church, and he was granted it. He is reported to have said, "Brethren, for a number of years, I have been separated from you. I now desire to come back. . . . I seek no station. I only wish to be identified with you."[34]

He remained in Iowa for a while to help Orson Hyde edit a newspaper, and in April 1849, he and his wife traveled to Richmond, Missouri, to

© Janet Lisonbee

Oliver Cowdery's grave site and memorial, Pioneer Cemetery, Richmond, Missouri.

visit her extended Whitmer family. He had a chronic lung condition, which advanced to consumption, and on March 3, 1850, he died at the home of David Whitmer in Richmond. Before doing so, he spoke to those present. He admonished his loved ones to live the teachings of the Book of Mormon and promised that if they did, they would meet him in heaven.[35]

David Whitmer

After leaving the Church, David Whitmer settled in Richmond, Missouri, where he lived until his death in 1888. He was recognized as an outstanding citizen and operated a livery and feed stable. The *Richmond Conservator* reported that "the forty six years of private citizenship on the part of David Whitmer, in Richmond, was without stain or blemish . . . If a life of probity, of unobtrusive benevolence and well doing for well nigh a half century, marks a man as a good citizen, then David Whitmer should enjoy the confidence and esteem of his fellow men." He affiliated briefly with a church organized by William McLellin, and in 1879, at the insistence of family members he organized a Church of Christ, which had a small congregation consisting mostly of his family and friends.[36]

He remained faithful to his testimony as a witness to the Book of Mormon plates. As the last surviving witness, he was interviewed far more extensively than the others. Just before his death, he called his

David Whitmer's grave site, Richmond City Cemetery, Missouri.

family and a few friends to his bedside. Turning to the attending physician, he said, "Dr. Buchanan, I want you to say whether or not I am in my right mind, before I give my dying testimony." The doctor answered, "Yes, you are in your right mind." David then bore testimony: "I want to say to you all, the Bible and the record of the Nephites is true, so you can say that you have heard me bear my testimony on my death-bed."[37]

A local paper, the *Richmond Democrat*, eulogized his life: "No man ever lived here, who had among our people more friends and fewer enemies. Honest, conscientious and upright in all his dealings, just in his estimate of men, and open, manly and frank in his treatment of all, he made lasting friends who loved him to the end."[38]

John Whitmer

John Whitmer lived the rest of his life in the Far West area after being excommunicated from the Church. After the Mormons left Far West in 1839, he took advantage of the low prices at which lands could be bought and succeeded in purchasing the principal part of the Far West town site. When he died at his residence at Far West, July 11, 1878, he was known as an extensive farmer (625 acres) and stock-raiser.[39]

As one of the eight witnesses, he was always true to his testimony of the Book of Mormon. Even in his darkest days and at the time he turned his back upon the Church, he declared in the presence of a number of local Missourians who were hostile to the Mormons that he knew the Book of Mormon was true. In 1878, Myron Bond wrote, "Old Father John Whitmer told me last winter, with tears in his eyes, that he knew as well as he knew he had an existence that Joseph translated the ancient writing which was upon the plates which he

John Whitmer grave site, Kingston City Cemetery, Missouri.

'saw and handled.' "[40] His nephew, John C. Whitmer, of Richmond, who was with him a few days before his death, told Elder Andrew Jenson in 1888 that John Whitmer bore testimony to the truth of the Book of Mormon until the last.[41] John Whitmer is buried in the Kingston cemetery just north of that community, about six miles east of Far West.

Lyman Johnson

Lyman Johnson was only twenty-three when he was ordained an apostle. He was the son of John and Elsa Johnson of Hiram, Ohio. Joseph and Emma lived in the family home for a while. Lyman's apostasy reportedly began in 1837 over a merchandising venture in Kirtland. He claimed that his loss of $6,000 was Joseph Smith's fault. He was disfellowshipped in September 1837 but was soon reinstated.

After his excommunication in Far West in 1838, Lyman remained friendly to the Mormons but did not rejoin the Church. He practiced law in Davenport and Keokuk, Iowa, in the 1840s and 1850s. He died in 1856 at the age of forty-five when a sleigh he was riding in fell through ice on the Mississippi River in Wisconsin.[42]

Notes

1. See *Far West Record* pages 107–08 for a detailed list of complaints against the Presidency.
2. Ibid., 71, note 2.
3. Ibid., 107–110 and 103.
4. *History of the Church*, 2:511.
5. Ibid., 2:521; and *Far West Record*, 119–20.
6. D&C 101:70-74; 105:28-29; and 103:23.
7. The committee consisted of brothers Hinkle, Grover, and Morey (*Far West Record*, 135).
8. *Far West Record*, 136. The Word of Wisdom was still new in the Church in 1838 and was not a commandment. The term "hot drinks" was not defined to mean "tea and coffee" until after the Far West era.
9. *Far West Record*, 136.
10. Ibid., 137–41; *History of the Church*, 3:3–4.
11. Ibid., 137–140. The minutes of the proceedings are included in the Appendix of this book.
12. Ibid., 138.
13. Ibid.
14. Ibid.
15. Ibid., 139.
16. Ibid.
17. These meetings were held at S. Carter's settlement (possibly Simeon Carter), Edmund Durfee's settlement, Nahum Curtis's dwelling house, and Haun's Mill (*Far West Record*, 139–40).

18. *Far West Record*, 141.
19. Ibid., 140.
20. Ibid., 145–50.
21. Ibid., 147–51.
22. Ibid., 162–71; *History of the Church*, 3:18–20.
23. This accusation related to Joseph's alleged polygamist marriage to Fanny Alger in Kirtland.
24. *Far West Record*, 171–79.
25. Ibid., 178.
26. *History of the Church*, 3:31.
27. See Baugh, *A Call to Arms*, 35. There is no known record of the exact words of the speech.
28. Robinson, *The Return 1* (Oct. 1889), 147.
29. Many resources discuss the Danite movement in more detail. Two examples of this are the *History of the Church*, 3:178–82 and Baugh, *A Call to Arms*, 36–43.
30. John Corrill was one of the missionaries called to Missouri in June 1831 (D&C 52:7). For many years he was an important Church leader in Missouri and was integrally involved in the early history of the Church in that state. Although he left the Church in 1838, he used his influence as the elected representative to the state legislature from Caldwell County to help the Church leave the state peacefully.
31. Corrill, *A Brief History of the Church of Christ of Latter Day Saints*, 29–30 (hereafter cited as *History of the Mormons*).
32. Kanesville is generally known as Council Bluffs, Iowa.
33. Jenson, *LDS Biographical Encyclopedia*, 1:249.
34. Ibid., 249–50.
35. Black, *Who's Who in the Doctrine and Covenants*, 75–76.
36. Ibid, 330.
37. Ibid.
38. Ibid.
39. Ibid., 333.
40. Myron Bond letter, *Saints Herald*, 15 August 1878, 254.
41. Jenson, *LDS Biographical Encyclopedia*, 1:252.
42. Ibid., 91; *Far West Record*, 272; and Black, *Who's Who in the Doctrine and Covenants*, 158–59.

Chapter 9

FAR WEST TEMPLE AND
JULY 4, 1838

B Y THE TIME THE CHURCH settled in Far West, the principles of building a temple were familiar to its members. In Jackson County, Missouri, in 1831, Joseph Smith had identified the temple site and placed it in a geographic position of preeminence at the center of Independence. That temple was never built because the Mormons were driven from Jackson County in November 1833. In Kirtland, Ohio, Church members began construction of a temple in June 1833. It was completed at great cost and sacrifice and dedicated on March 27, 1836. The Missouri church leaders (the high council including the local presidency) were in attendance at the dedication in Kirtland.

Accordingly, not long after the Mormons began settling in Far West, the local church presidency (David Whitmer, William W. Phelps, and John Whitmer) made a decision in early 1837 to build a temple there. It was to be in the center of the city near the public square. Their decision was unilateral, however, and therefore caused some concern among the local members. The local presidency had not consulted with the local high council, or with Joseph Smith, the president of the Church, who was far away in Kirtland.

The presidency's decision to build a temple was one of the issues that the Missouri High Council and Elders David Patten and Thomas Marsh of the Twelve addressed with the Missouri presidency in early 1837 (together with the use of funds to purchase land that led to their removal from office). At a meeting on April 7, 1837, the Missouri High Council and presidency met together with the two apostles resolved to commence building a House of the Lord in Far West. This was decided even though the building of a temple had not been approved by Joseph Smith.[1]

In the summer of 1837, preparations began for the building of the temple in the center of the town. The excavation was dug for the cellar under the prospective structure, 110 by 80 feet in area, and five feet in depth. The excavation was accomplished in about a half a day with more than five hundred men involved in the work.[2] LDS historian Andrew Jenson made this account of the occasion:

> On Monday, July 3, 1837, the weather being clear and beautiful, more than fifteen hundred Saints assembled in Far West, on the site previously chosen for the erection of a Temple, and at half past 8 o'clock in the morning, after prayer, singing and an address, they proceeded to break the ground for such a building. An excavation, 110 feet long and 80 feet wide, was nearly finished on that day. The spirit of God was poured out in a great measure upon the assembled Saints, who rejoiced exceedingly. On the following day a large meeting was held in the open prairie (no meeting house having as yet been erected at Far West), and several Missourians were baptized.[3]

Subsequently, at a meeting on August 5, 1837, the Far West High Council recommitted to "go on moderately" and build a temple in Far West "as we have means."[4]

Joseph Smith went to Far West in November 1837 to conduct Church business. In a meeting on November 7, 1837, Joseph met with the high council and some other elders and reconsidered the high council's earlier decision to build a temple at Far West. It was decided to wait for the building of the temple until the Lord revealed it to be His will to have it commenced.[5]

That direction was soon forthcoming, however, approximately six weeks after Joseph Smith arrived to make Far West his home. On April 26, 1838, Joseph received a revelation, which, among other things, directed the Church to build the temple in Far West and commence laying the foundation on July 4, 1838. This revelation provides:

> Let the city, Far West, be a holy and consecrated land unto me; and it shall be called most holy, for the ground upon which thou standest is holy.
>
> Therefore, I command you to build a house unto me, for the gathering together of my Saints, that they may worship me.
>
> And let there be a beginning of this work, and a foundation, and a preparatory work, this following summer;
>
> And let the beginning be made on the fourth day of July next; and from that time forth let my people labor diligently to build a house unto my name;

And in one year from this day let them re-commence laying the foundation of my house. (D&C 115:7–11)

The Far West Temple was to be 110 feet long by 80 feet wide. By comparison, the exterior walls of the Kirtland Temple, the first built in the Church, were 79 feet long and 59 feet wide.[6] Similar to the Kirtland Temple, the temple at Far West was to have three floors, the first to be devoted to the purpose of public worship and the other two to educational purposes. It was meant, therefore, to be both a house of worship and an institution of learning.[7]

Dedication of Far West Temple Site—July 4, 1838

July 4, 1838, was an important day for the Mormons in Far West. They laid the cornerstones for the Far West Temple pursuant to the commandment given on April 26. They also celebrated the nation's birthday and independence.

Joseph Holbrook wrote of this day, "[The] cornerstones of the temple were laid, they having been hauled to the spot before hand. My team helped to haul them. They were quarried from the ledge down west and

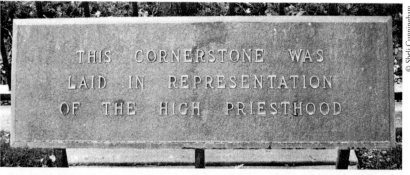

Far West Temple original cornerstone.

were about seven feet long, four feet wide and two feet thick by the First Presidency, Joseph Smith, Jr., and counselors and others."[8]

Joseph Smith's recorded account of this event suggests he was favorably moved by the occasion:

> July 4—the day was spent in celebrating the Declaration of Independence of the United States of America, and also by the Saints making a "Declaration of Independence" from all mobs and persecutions which have been inflicted upon them, time after time, until they could bear it no longer; . . . The corner stones of the House of the Lord, agreeable to the commandments of the Lord unto us, given April 26, 1838, were laid.
>
> Joseph Smith, Jun., was president of the day; Hyrum Smith, vice-president; Sidney Rigdon, orator; Reynolds Cahoon, chief marshal; George M. Hinkle and J. Hunt, assistant marshals; and George W. Robinson, clerk.
>
> The order of the day was splendid. The procession commenced forming at 10 o'clock a.m., in the following order. First, the infantry (militia); second, the Patriarchs of the Church; the president, vice-president, and orator; the Twelve Apostles, presidents of the stakes, and High Council; Bishop and counselors; architects, ladies and gentlemen. The cavalry brought up the rear of the large procession, which marched to music, and formed a circle, with the ladies in front, round the excavation. The southeast corner stone of the Lord's House in Far West, Missouri, was then laid by the presidents of the stake, assisted by twelve men. The southwest corner, by the presidents of the Elders, assisted by twelve men. The northwest corner by the Bishop, assisted by twelve men. The northeast corner by the president of the Teachers, assisted by twelve men. This house is to be one hundred and ten feet long, and eighty feet broad.
>
> The oration was delivered by President Rigdon, at the close of which was a shout of Hosanna, and a song, composed for the occasion by Levi W. Hancock, was sung by Solomon Hancock. The most perfect order prevailed throughout the day.[9]

Additional details are given by John Rigdon, the son of Sidney Rigdon:

> Colonel Hinkle had one company of uniformed militia. The Saints had a martial band with a bass drum and two small drums, and so a procession was formed to march, the uniform company of militia coming first and then the procession followed. We made quite a showing for a small town. After marching around the square, the militia came to the cellar [i.e., the temple excavation] and halted. There was

erected a stand to speak from. Joseph Smith, Hyrum Smith, Sidney Rigdon and several others took their places.[10]

Part of the celebration included a flag raising ceremony and the Hosanna Shout. Elder Parley P. Pratt wrote:

> On the Fourth of July, 1838, many thousands of our people assembled at the city of Far West, the county seat of Caldwell, erected a liberty pole, and hoisted the bald eagle, with its stars and stripes, upon the top of the same. Under the colors of our country we laid the corner stone of a house of worship, and had an address delivered by Elder Rigdon, in which was painted, in lively colors, the oppression which we had long suffered from the hand of our enemies; and in this discourse we claimed and declared our constitutional rights, as American citizens, and manifested a determination to do our utmost endeavors, from that time forth, to resist all oppression, and to maintain our rights and freedom according to the holy principles of liberty, as guaranteed to every person by the constitution and laws of our government. This declaration was received with shouts of hosannah to God and the Lamb, and with many and long cheers by the assembled thousands, who were determined to yield their rights no more, except compelled by a superior power.[11]

Near the close of the events, Solomon Hancock sang a song that his brother Levi Hancock wrote for the occasion at the request of Joseph Smith. The words of the "Freedom Song" are included in the Appendix of this book.[12]

Sidney Rigdon's Speech

Sidney Rigdon's oration at the ceremonies at the Far West temple site on Independence Day 1838 was powerful but proved to be controversial. His oratory stirred high emotions as he declared the Mormons' own declaration of independence from any further mob violence or illegal activity. Unfortunately, copies of the address fell into the hands of some Missouri officials, and the inflammatory portions increased the determination of the Missourians, and the violence believed necessary, to drive out the Mormons, in the fall of 1838.[13]

According to LDS historian B. H. Roberts, the speech expresses admiration for the free institutions of our government and urges their maintenance. It extols religious freedom and declares that all "attempts on the part of religious aspirants, to unite church and state, ought to be repelled with indignation." It reviews the establishment of the Church of Christ in the New Dispensation, its development, and the nature of the religion that was unfolded therein, with intelligence as a motive force. It also relates particulars about the Far West temple and the cornerstones that were being laid. Note is taken of the suffering that had been endured for the sake of this cause—from foes without and from foes within, for the Mormons had taken the spoiling of their goods; their cheeks had been given to the smiters and their heads to those who plucked off the hair. When smitten on the cheek, they turned the other, and this repeatedly, until they were wearied of being smitten and tired of being trampled upon. They had proved the world with kindness; they had suffered their abuse—abuse without cause—with patience, without resentment, until this day. And still persecution and violence did not cease.[14]

The controversial part of the speech was as follows:

> But from this day and this hour we will suffer it no more. We take God and all the holy angels to witness, this day, that we warn all men, in the name of Jesus Christ to come on us no more for ever, for from this hour we will bear it no more; our rights shall no more be trampled on with impunity; the man, or the set of men who attempt it do it at the expense of their lives. And that mob that comes on us to disturb us, it shall be between us and them a war of extermination; for we will follow them until the last drop of their blood is spilled; or else they will have to exterminate us, for we will carry the seat of war to their own houses and their own families, and one party or the other shall be utterly destroyed. Remember it then, all men. We will never be the aggressors, we will infringe on the rights of no people, but shall stand for our own until death. We claim our own right and are willing that all others shall enjoy theirs. No man shall be at liberty to come into our Streets, to threaten us with mobs, for if he does he shall atone for it before he leaves the place; neither shall he be at liberty to vilify and slander any of us, for suffer it we will not, in this place. We therefore take all men to record this day, that we proclaim our liberty this day, as did our fathers, and we pledge this day to one another our fortunes, our lives, and our sacred honors, to be delivered from the persecutions, which we have had to endure for the last nine years or nearly that time. Neither will we indulge any man, or set of men, in instituting vexatious law suits against us, to cheat us out of our rights; if they attempt it we say woe be unto them. We this day, then, proclaim ourselves free with a purpose and determination that never can be broken, No, never! No, never! No, never!"[15]

John Rigdon, Sidney's son, wrote the following about this event:

> The first half of this oration was a Fourth of July oration pure and simple. Not a word was said that could offend the ear of anyone. The next half was devoted to the building that was to be erected. The lower floor was to be devoted for worship. The upper story was to be

for school. They were to be so arranged so that they could give any student who might come a college education if he wished it. But in his closing remarks he made use of this language: "We have provided the world with kindness and have grown weary with well-doing, and if the Missourians shall attack us again, we shall carry the war to these very doors." It was reprinted that he had threatened to commence a war of extermination against the Missourians, but the little breeze that this remark occasioned soon wore off and all seemed to be well.[16]

A record of the speech was printed, and its availability was announced in the August 1838 edition of the *Elders' Journal*:

> In this paper, we give the proceedings which were had on the fourth of July, at this place, in laying the corner stones of the Temple about to be built in this city. The oration delivered on the occasion is now published in pamphlet form. Those of our friends wishing to have one can get it by calling on Ebenezer Robinson, by whom they were printed. We would recommend to all the Saints to get one, to be had in their families, as it contains an outline of the suffering and persecutions of the Church from its rise. As also the fixed determination of the Saints, in relation to the persecutors who are and have been continually, not only threatening us with mobs, but actually have been putting their threats into execution, with which we are absolutely determined no longer to bear, come life or come death, for to be mobbed any more without taking vengeance we will not.[17]

The Liberty Pole

The Mormons also erected a liberty pole at the public square as part of the ceremonies on July 4, 1838. It was made of white oak and was sixty feet in length. An American flag was raised and flown at the top of the liberty pole.

A short time later, however, lightning struck the liberty pole and seriously damaged it.[18] Some of the Mormons viewed this as a sign or indication of forthcoming events that would eventually deprive them of their liberties in the state of Missouri. "The thunder rolled in awful majesty over the city of Far West, and the arrows of lightning fell from the clouds and shivered the liberty pole from top to bottom; thus manifesting to many that there was an end to liberty and law in that state, and that our little city strove in vain to maintain the liberties of a country which was ruled by wickedness and rebellion. It seemed to portend the awful fate which awaited that devoted city, and the county and people around."[19]

Luman Shurtliff helped make the liberty pole but wrote that he was somewhat negatively impacted by Sidney's oration:

> I, with several others of my company, went into the timber of Goose Creek, got the largest tree we could and made a liberty pole, and on the 4th of July, 1838, the brethren and their families assembled in Far West to celebrate the day and to lay the cornerstone of our temple in the city of Far West. Early in the morning we raised the pole, raised the Stars and Stripes and then laid the cornerstone of our temple. We then assembled under the flag of our nation and had an oration delivered by Sidney Rigdon. This orator became quite excited and proclaimed loudly our freedom and liberty in Missouri. Although Sidney was a great orator and one of the leading brethren, his oration brought sorrow and gloom over my mind, and spoiled my further enjoyment of the day.
>
> After the services, the multitude dispersed. This was on Saturday. On Sunday a cloud came over Far West, charged with electricity, and lightning fell upon our liberty pole and shivered it to the ground. When the news reached me, I involuntarily proclaimed, "Farewell to our liberty in Missouri."[20]

Notes

1. *Far West Record*, 103.
2. Ward, *History of Caldwell County*, 121.
3. Jenson, *The Historical Record*, January 1889, 691.
4. *Far West Record*, 118.
5. *History of the Church*, 2:521; *Far West Record*, 119–20.
6. Robison, *The First Mormon Temple*, 36. By revelation, the interior court of the Kirtland Temple was to be 65 by 55 feet (D&C 94:4).
7. Roberts, *Comprehensive History of the Church*, 1:440.
8. Holbrook Autobiography, 39.
9. *History of the Church*, 3:41–42.
10. Rigdon, *Life of Sidney Rigdon*, 1:30–31.
11. Mormon Redress Petitions, *Parley Pratt History of Persecution*, 74.
12. Mosiah Hancock Autobiography 5–6. The Hancock brothers were related to John Hancock, the signer of the Declaration of Independence.
13. Roberts, *Comprehensive History of the Church*, 1:442–43.
14. Ibid., 1:440–41.
14. Ibid., *History of the Church*, 1:440–41.
15. Rigdon, *Life of Sidney Rigdon*, Dialogue 1:30–31.
16. *Elders' Journal* (Aug. 1838), 54.
17. It is difficult to determine the exact date the lightning struck the liberty pole from existing accounts. Some accounts place the lighting strike as the next day, others a few days, and some a few weeks. The exact date is not important, however; the important fact is that the event occurred.
18. Mormon Redress Petitions, *Parley Pratt History of Persecution*, 74–75.
19. Luman Shurtliff Autobiography, 33.

Chapter 10

CONFLICTS BEGIN— DAVIESS COUNTY AND DEWITT

THE RELATIONSHIP BETWEEN THE MORMONS and their neighbors began to deteriorate in Daviess County in the summer of 1838. One of the issues was that the large influx of Mormons moving into the county was changing political control, and another issue related to land ownership. Most of the land in Daviess County had not been officially sold by the government to settlers. Thus, most settlers in the county, including the Mormons, had settled on land under preemptive claims and hoped they would be able to purchase the land outright when it was offered for sale, which the government announced would be November 12, 1838. Thus, the Missourians who were responsible for expelling Church members from Daviess County knew that the members' land would shortly be offered for sale by the U.S. government. With the Mormons gone, the residents could purchase the improved land and reap the benefits of the Mormons' labor.[1]

Election Day in Gallatin

The situation escalated on August 6, 1838, when several members of the Church were not allowed to vote at an election for the state legislature in Gallatin, Daviess County. The Whig and Democratic parties were almost equally divided, and many local settlers believed the Mormons held the deciding vote or might even elect one of their own, even though there were no Mormon candidates on the ballot. The Mormons had been warned in advance that an effort would be made to prevent them from voting.

The conflict was instigated by William Penniston, the Whig candidate. Penniston had asked for Mormon support in his candidacy and became angry when the Mormons supported the Democrat candidate instead. He gave an inflammatory speech at the polls urging the old settlers to stop the Mormons from voting. Whiskey was passed around prior to the election.

A group of local men attacked a smaller group of Mormon men attempting to vote. One of the locals punched a Mormon and knocked him down. A vicious fight ensued.[2] Although several persons were seriously hurt in this fight, no one was killed. After the encounter, the presiding officer told the Mormon men they could vote, but they suspected it was a trap to lure them into a situation where they would not be able to defend themselves, and they left the area to go home.[3]

Result of Election Day Brawl: Rumors and Tensions

News of the incident spread quickly but was generally exaggerated, and consequently many locals became angry at the Mormons. Joseph Smith also got word by an express rider, but the news was also exaggerated—that two or three Mormons were lying dead in the streets of Gallatin and the mob was preparing to attack Adam-ondi-Ahman.

Joseph organized a group and went to Adam-ondi-Ahman to investigate, but when he found things quiet he went to see Adam Black, an early settler and the local justice of the peace who was known to be anti-Mormon. Adam Black was asked to sign an agreement of peace and did so, but after Joseph returned to Far West, Black claimed he'd been forced by 120 Mormons to sign the pledge of peace under threat of death. A warrant was soon issued for the arrest of Joseph Smith, Lyman Wight, and several others for harassment. They surrendered after a few days and appeared at a preliminary hearing before Judge Austin King on September 7, 1838.[4] Although the evidence against them was weak, Judge King ordered them to stand trial before the Daviess County Circuit Court on November 29 "to pacify the mob"[5] and then released them.

Local vigilante groups from Daviess and other counties, who were in some respects "mobs," began a siege of outlying Mormon settlers in Daviess County and other nearby counties in mid-August and September 1838. Under the command of Dr. William Austin, from Carroll County, who the people appointed as their leader,[6] the forces numbered two to three hundred men.[7] Some of the non-Mormons in Daviess County became agitated over the fact that Joseph Smith was not punished more severely, adding to the hostile environment in the county. Several Mormon families were intimidated and harassed in their homes. On one occasion, anti-Mormons fired on two Mormons, a man and a boy; the man escaped, but they took the boy prisoner. Some of Austin's forces also went to Richmond to get additional arms, but the Mormons intercepted the wagon on its way back to Daviess County and turned the weapons over to state militia forces.[8]

General Alexander Doniphan led a group of 500 state militia to quell the disturbance. A number of Mormon men from Caldwell County came north to join forces with Lyman Wight, who was a captain in the state militia in Daviess County.[9] When General Doniphan arrived, he placed his militia between the parties, visited both, and required them to disperse. Lyman Wight submitted and his troops dispersed. However, Austin's men did not disperse. Instead, Austin reluctantly withdrew from Daviess County to move his forces to lay siege to the City of Dewitt.[10]

Siege at Dewitt

Dewitt is located in the southeast corner of Carroll County, about seventy miles southeast of Far West, near the point where the Grand River empties into the Missouri River. A number of Mormons had established homes there, and a branch of the Church had been established with George M. Hinkle as branch president.[11] John Murdock and George Hinkle, as trustees for the Mormons and by the direction of Joseph Smith, purchased 134 of 304 lots in the town on June 23, 1838, from Henry Root, a non-Mormon land developer of sorts.[12] From the Mormon's perspective, Dewitt was well-suited to be a steamboat landing and a point from which goods and immigrants could be transported to other Mormon settlements.

Tensions were already high in Dewitt even before Austin arrived from Diahman with his forces in September. On July 30, a citizens group had ordered the Mormons to leave by August 7. The Mormons refused to go, and the local non-Mormons voted overwhelmingly at an election on August 6 that the Mormons should not be permitted to settle in the county. Consequently, a committee of five men was appointed to determine what actions to take next, with Dr. Austin, the vigilante leader, as head of the committee. The citizens group argued that the Mormons had violated the implicit agreement to confine themselves to Caldwell County, and thus the group felt justified in excluding them from Carroll County. The citizens group also asked the residents of other nearby counties for assistance in expelling the Mormons because they feared the Mormons from Caldwell County might come to help the Dewitt Mormons.

On August 20, according to John Murdock, "a mob of more than a hundred men came, and ordered us off, but finally gave us ten days and threatened if we were not away in that time they would exterminate us without regard to age or sex and throw our property into the river."[13] Two Mormon men who lived outside of Dewitt were harassed or threatened by the vigilante forces and held as prisoners overnight (Smith Humphrey and Pierce Hawley). These forces then came into town and threatened and intimidated the Mormons.

From September 1 to September 19, 1838, Austin's forces left Dewitt to join against the Mormons in Daviess County, but they then returned to Dewitt and surrounded it, giving the Mormons ten days to evacuate. The Mormons refused to leave without a struggle. The non-Mormon forces held the town under siege for three weeks and received frequent reinforcements as they were joined by troops from Ray, Howard, and Clay counties. A local farmer provided the vigilante forces with corn and beef and allowed them to stay on his land. However, the Mormons were not as fortunate; they were confined by the vigilante forces to the town and could not get to their outlying farms. Thus, they had to live on what provisions they already had in store.

Since the Mormons did not leave during the ten-day grace period, the vigilante forces began to attack the community. On October 1, 1838, a vigilante force of possibly as many as two hundred assembled at a camp meeting ground about one mile from Dewitt, while another group assembled on the opposite side of the river to prevent the Mormons from crossing into Saline County to the east.

On the morning of Tuesday, October 2, the vigilante forces proceeded on the main road to the outskirts of town, where they were fired upon by Mormon guards secluded in the brush. The vigilante forces advanced further until they approached the main Mormon defense works, and the two sides, consisting of about 30 Mormons and 150 vigilantes, drew battle lines. The two opposing forces exchanged fire, but there were no serious casualties reported on either side. John Murdock recorded the battle:

> We exchanged shots with them about [one] hour, but a deep ravine and a good many tree tops lay between us and them, consequently, they were some 30-40 rods from us in the woods. The head of both lines were near a cornfield, besides the road they came in on, and about 30 of their men, at the head of their ranks, got scared at seeing some execution done in their ranks, ran in the woods to the other end of their line and came in contact with 10 of our men, under Captain Surley, who were in ambush, behind a big log, and that scared them again, and they

ran back swearing the Mormons were surrounding them, jumping over into the cornfield, and this scared the rest and they followed suit, and away went the whole 150, that were able to run from 30.[14]

The upshot of this encounter was that the vigilantes determined they needed additional forces and withdrew to await reinforcements. A ten-day standoff ensued, with the vigilantes essentially surrounding the Mormons. During this time there were several skirmishes. The Mormons had to remain on constant alert and never knew when they would be fired upon. John Murdock wrote: "The mob about Dewitt continued to harass us day and night by shooting at our people in the woods, in corn fields, and firing into town, and into our camps. George M. Hinkle took the command of our men; I of ten men; H. S. Sherwood of ten, Brother Surley ten. I was continually employed, day and night, guarding."[15]

Ultimately, however, the outnumbered Mormons were running out of food and supplies, and some were ill. Some of the Mormons' cattle were killed or stolen, and some of their houses burned. There were also a number of Mormons temporarily camped at Dewitt who were living in wagons or tents because vigilante activity had prevented them from journeying all the way to Far West. The vigilantes also procured a cannon for potential use against the Mormons, and were beginning to train on how to use it.[16]

General Parks, of Ray County, with two companies of militia, went to the scene of difficulty but did not have enough force to disperse the vigilantes.[17] The Mormons twice appealed to Governor Boggs for help, but he refused to intervene. He reportedly responded, "The quarrel was between the Mormons and the mob," and that they "might fight it out."[18]

When the Mormons in Far West got news of the attacks at Dewitt, they organized two companies to assist the Mormons at Dewitt. These left Far West on October 5, one under the direction of Seymour Brunson consisting of forty-two men, and the other under the direction of Joseph Smith consisting of about twenty men.[19] Both groups were able to safely reach the Mormons at Dewitt.

A committee of six men from Howard and Chariton Counties initiated a series of negotiations between parties, but the Mormons refused to accept the proposed terms, which would have required them to leave, and no agreement was reached. The vigilante forces therefore prepared to make a major offensive against the Mormons, who fortunately were apprised of the planned attack by Judge James Erickson of the negotiating committee from Howard County.[20] Recognizing the seriousness of the situation, the

Mormons agreed to surrender Dewitt on October 10, on the terms that they would be paid the appraised value of their land, although Mormon accounts indicate that ultimately, nothing was ever paid for it.[21]

On October 11, 1838, the Mormons left Dewitt for Far West, having nowhere else to go. The men who had come from Far West rode at the front and rear of the procession. There were approximately forty to fifty families involved in this exodus and from fifty to seventy wagons.[22] Even as they left, some shots were fired at them.[23] Most of the Dewitt company arrived in Far West on October 14.

The trip to Caldwell County was difficult. The Mormons were in dire conditions even before the trip began. One of the Dewitt Mormons, a woman named Downey, died during this exodus in consequence of exposure. She was traveling from Canada to join the Mormons at Far West and was buried without a coffin.[24]

It is possible that the deaths of Lorain Page, the wife of Elder John E. Page of the Twelve, and two of their small children were the result of exposure and lack of necessities during this siege and the forced exodus. The Page family had arrived in Dewitt in late September while bringing a group of thirty families to Far West from Canada, where Elder Page had been a very successful missionary, and were without a home of their own for quite some time. Sister Page was taken into the home of home of Charles C. and Sarah Rich south of Far West some time after the Battle of Crooked River, and she died there in January 1839. Two of her children also died there.[25]

Zadok Judd, an eleven-year old boy in 1838, later wrote the following account of the exodus from Dewitt:

> Our first days travel brought us to a beautiful grove of timber; here we camped for the night. Here we buried old Sister Downey. She had travelled with us all the way from Canada. She was old and feeble and so much rough usage was more than she could endure. She was buried without much ceremony— without any coffin—wrapped in a quilt and put in the grave. It was a cold, frosty morning but the company was not long in getting started on the road.
>
> I was a barefooted cowboy, having two or three cows to drive. When I supposed the company was ready I started the cows out on the road. The whole country outside the thickest timber was covered with grass, which this morning was covered with white frost. I had not gone far until I found my feet very cold. The cows were anxious to eat but with whip and rocks I kept them moving until I found I was way ahead of the company; suffering with cold feet, I still plodded on, and in this condition the brethren from Far West on horseback overtook me.

One of them kindly offered to drive the cows and to take me up behind him on his horse. He told me to put my feet up on the horse's back and sit or squat on them and hold to him. I did so and soon became quite comfortable. To this day my heart swells with gratitude for his kindness. I never knew his name and perhaps never shall. I believe that was the most uncomfortable cow drive I remember of.

I think we were four or five days getting to Far West, where we found our brethren under arms. All the outer settlements and ranchers had moved to Far West on account of mob threats and violence. We camped here, living in our wagons and tents or such shelter as we could make with poles and brush; no house room could be had. We remained here several weeks, during which time much stormy weather occurred with a good deal of snow—quite disagreeable—and to make it worse our provisions consisted of corn-meal and Missouri pumpkins. The pumpkin johnny-cake gave me diarrhea as long as I ate it.[26]

News followed the Dewitt Mormons to Far West that the vigilante group was heading next to Daviess County with a cannon, used during the siege of Dewitt, for the purpose of driving the Mormons from there. The vigilantes took two Mormon prisoners along their way and told them they meant to "drive the Mormons from Daviess to Caldwell, and from Caldwell to hell."[27]

All of this led the Church members to believe they had to fend for themselves and could not rely upon the government for assistance in maintaining their homes and freedoms. John Corrill described these feelings:

> They (the Church) had been driven from place to place; their property destroyed; their rights as citizens taken from them; abuse upon abuse practiced upon them from time to time; they had sought for redress through the medium of the law, but never could get it; the state of Missouri refused to protect them in their rights; the executive had been petitioned many times, but never would do anything for them. This, in substance, had been their talk for months: "And the Governor," they said, "while they were at DeWitt, refused to do anything for them, but said that they must take care of themselves." Now they meant to do it, for they found that they must take care of themselves, as they could get help from no other quarter.[28]

Austin's Forces Return to Daviess County

After the Mormons evacuated Dewitt in mid-October, Dr. Austin's forces were encouraged by their success and returned to Daviess County to confront the Mormons there. The vigilantes commenced to burn the houses of the Mormons who lived outside of Adam-ondi-Ahman and drive them from their homes into the midst of a snowstorm in mid-October 1838. They burned cabins, stole animals, and harassed families. Several men were tied to trees, whipped, and left for their wives to cut them free. The Mormons fled into the city for safety, and the community's population swelled from about four hundred to more than a thousand in a few short days. These now home-less members were forced to live in tents and wagons at this time.

On October 15, 1838, the militia from Far West marched to Adam-ondi-Ahman to protect the Mormons there. Joseph Smith went with the Far West militia, although he was not officially a member. He recorded:

> While I was there a number of houses belonging to our people were burned by the mob, who committed many other depredations, such as driving off horses, sheep cattle, hogs, etc. A number of those whose houses were burned down, as well as those who lived in scattered and lonely situations, fled into the town for safety, and for shelter from the inclemency of the weather, as a considerable snowstorm took place on the 17th and 18th. Women and children, some in the most delicate condition, were thus obliged to leave their homes and travel several miles in order to effect their escape. My feelings were such as I cannot describe when I saw them flock into the village, almost entirely desti-tute of clothes, and only escaping with their lives.[29]

One of the displaced members in Daviess County was Agnes M. Smith, the wife of Don Carlos Smith (the Prophet's brother), who was on a mission in Tennessee at the time. The Smiths' home was plundered and burned by the vigilantes, and Agnes Smith traveled three miles to Diah-man on foot with two helpless babies, having to wade a tributary of the Grand River in waist-deep water. With no clothing, homeless, and nearly exhausted, she arrived at Adam-ondi-Ahman seeking shelter and safety from the vigilantes at the home of Lyman Wight.[30]

Edward Stevenson was a member of the force that went from Far West to aid the Mormons in Adam-ondi-Ahman in October 1838. Years later, he wrote:

> I distinctly remember one night when the horn blew, which was a signal for all to gather to the public square, armed and equipped. I was there with my gun and blankets, and word was that the mob was gathering secretly to destroy the peace and lives of our brethren at Adam-ondi-Ahman.

Brother Joseph called for all who would stand by him to meet him on the public square the next morning [October 15, 1838] prepared to march to Adam-ondi-Ahman by sunrise. I shall never forget the circumstance for the impression was indelible. It was twenty-five miles and we had to go out there on foot, but baggage wagons were provided to carry our luggage. . . .

One night the snow fell four or five inches on us. . . . The Prophet seeing our forlorn condition, called on us to form into two parties in battle array—Lyman Wight at the head of one line and he, Joseph, heading the other line. Two lines were formed of about equal strength, and a charge made. We had a sham battle and the weapons to be used were snowballs. We set to with a will full of glee and fun. . . .

After drilling the inexperienced militia Joseph the Prophet on the camp grounds was to be seen cheering up the boys. Thus the Prophet was cheerful, often wrestling with Sidney Rigdon, and he had his pants torn badly, but a good laugh over it. In the state of Missouri snow does not last long, for the climate is very moderate, so that in about two days, it was all over and pretty weather again.[31]

The Mormons Retaliate—Accused of Burning Millport and Gallatin

By October 17, Daviess County was a war zone. Austin's forces roamed the countryside and had burned many Mormon homes. On October 18, two non-Mormon communities in Davies County—Millport and Gallatin—were burned. There is controversy in the historical accounts about who did the burnings. Many Missouri settlers testified in court (before Judge King in November 1838), or otherwise maintained, that the Mormons launched retaliatory attacks against Millport and Gallatin and proceeded to burn those communities.

According to Mormon accounts, however, General Parks of the state militia arrived at Diahman at this time and reportedly told Lyman Wight, an officer in the state militia, to call out his men and go and put the mob down. Accordingly Lyman Wight immediately raised a force for the purpose of quelling the mob, and in a short time began its march. According to the Church history account, "The mob, having learned the orders of General Parks, and likewise being aware of the determination of the oppressed, broke up the encampment and fled. The mob, seeing that they could not succeed by force, now resorted to stratagem; and after removing their property out of their houses, which were nothing but log cabins, they fired them, and then reported to the authorities of the state that the Mormons were burning and destroying all before them."[32] Some Mormon accounts indicate that several locals burned their own homes and blamed it on the Mormons to agitate the community against the Church.[33]

According to various other accounts, however, the Mormons allegedly organized into three forces to carry out selective retaliatory attacks on October 18, 1838. These groups consisted of men from both Caldwell and Daviess Counties and included some regular militia and non-militia volunteers.[34]

One Mormon force of about eighty men, led by Lyman Wight, allegedly went to Millport, south of Gallatin, where many of the vigilante leaders lived, and proceeded to burn the community and confiscate property. The residents had been forewarned of the attack and had evacuated, but many of the town's twelve to fifteen buildings were completely gutted. The main intended victims were the Penniston family.[35]

Another Mormon group, led by David Patten, allegedly went to Gallatin, the county seat, and burned most of its buildings and took a considerable amount of property. This group was the largest of the three and may have had over one hundred members.[36]

The third Mormon group was smaller (about twenty men) and was led by Seymour Brunson. This group went to the small Grindstone settlement west of Adam-ondi-Ahman and found weapons and ammunition stashed by the vigilantes. They also confiscated some property, but it is not clear if they burned any homes. On their way back to Adam-ondi-Ahman the Mormons came across a recently burned Mormon home with a mother and three small children hiding in the bushes, and after considerable efforts to persuade her they were friendly forces, they took the family back to Adam-ondi-Ahman.[37]

It also appears that Mormon forces conducted several raids in the county and brought into Adam-ondi-Ahman wagons loaded with confiscated furniture, household items, bedding, clothing, foodstuffs, bee stands, cattle, and other animals. The goods were turned over to Bishop Vincent Knight and were designated as "consecrated property" to be dealt out to those in need. The Mormons who were still living outside of the city were counseled to remove to Adam-ondi-Ahman for safety.[38]

John D. Lee wrote that during this time Daviess County was in complete disorder. "Armed men roamed in bands all over. . . Both Mormons and Gentiles were under arms, and doing injury to each other when occasion offered. The burning of houses, farms, and stacks of grain was generally indulged in by each party. Lawlessness prevailed, and pillage was the rule."[39] In addition, John Corrill, with respect to the Mormons, wrote, "The love of pillage grew upon them very fast, for they plundered every kind of property they could get hold of."⁴⁰

However, Benjamin Johnson, a member of the Church, expressed a different view in describing the attitude and intentions of the Mormons towards these raids:

> [W]e were being hemmed in on all sides by our enemies and were without food. All the grain, cattle, hogs, and supplies of every kind were left in the country, or so far from home they could not be obtained except with a strong guard. So our only possible chance was to go out in foraging companies and bring in what ever we could find, without regard to ownership; and in this way corn, beef, cattle, hogs, bee stands, chickens, etc., with anything and everything left in the country that would sustain a thousand people, we took wherever it was found. Thus we did our best, to obtain food, dividing it as was needed.
>
> Here let me say that it should not be supposed . . . that we were common robbers because we took by reprisal that with which to keep from starvation our women and children. Ours was a struggle for our lives and homes, and a more conscientious, noble, and patriotic spirit never enthused man than that which animated our leaders in this just defense of our rights.⁴¹

Notes

1. In fact, public records indicate that several of the leading anti-Mormons purchased 290 acres of land in the Diahman area within four days after the Saints left: Sashiel Woods, John Cravens, Thomas Calloway, George Houx, and Adam Black. See Baugh, *A Call to Arms*, 156.
2. See John Butler Autobiography, 11–12.
3. Ibid., 12–13.
4. *History of the Church*, 3:59–63 and 70–73.
5. Greene, *Expulsion of the Mormons, Mormon Redress Petitions*, 24–25.
6. Corrill, *History of the Mormons*, 35.
7. Ibid.
8. Ibid.
9. Corrill, *History of the Mormons*, 35; *History of the Church*, 3:78–81.
10. Corrill, *History of the Mormons*, 35.
11. John Murdock was the father of the two Murdock twins who were placed in the care of Joseph and Emma after Mrs. Murdock died in Ohio. One of the twins died in Hiram, Ohio, as a result of exposure when Joseph was tarred and feathered. The other twin, Julia Murdock Smith, lived to maturity.
12. *John Murdock Journal*, 18.
13. Ibid., 18.
14. Ibid., 20.
15. Ibid.

16. *History of the Church*, 3:157–60.
17. Corrill, *History of the Mormons*, 36; *History of the Church*, 3:155–56.
18. *History of the Church*, 3:157.
19. Baugh, *A Call to Arms*, 73.
20. Ibid., 73–74.
21. *History of the Church*, 3:159; Corrill, *History of the Mormons*, 36–37. *History of Caldwell County*, 129, indicates the Mormons were paid for their cost in purchasing the original town site but received nothing for buildings and other improvements.
22. *John Murdock Journal*, 20.
23. Smith, *Mormon Redress Petitions*, 347.
24. Although official LDS history indicates that the woman's name was Jensen, Zadok Judd, a young man in the group, wrote that the woman's name was Downey, which appears more likely (Judd Autobiography, 9; *History of the Church*, 3:159–60).
25. Other Saints arrived at Dewitt during the siege or shortly before it as well. One was John Taylor, who later became president of the Church. He arrived in late August on his way from Canada but was there only a few days. Another was Stephen Markham.
26. Zadok Judd Autobiography, 9–10.
27. Corrill, *History of the Mormons*, 36–37.
28. Ibid.
29. *History of the Church*, 3:163.
30. *Autobiography of Edward Stevenson*, 77.
31. Ibid.
32. *History of the Church*, 3:163–64.
33. See, "Hyrum Smith Testimony," in Johnson, *Mormon Redress Petitions*, 623–24; Warren Foote Autobiography, 25.
34. Baugh, *A Call to Arms*, 86–87.
35. Ibid.
36. Ibid.
37. Ibid., 86–88.
38. Ibid., 89.
39. Ibid., 86, quoting John D. Lee, *Mormonism Unveiled*, 70.
40. Corrill, *History of the Mormons*, 38.
41. Johnson, *My Life's Review*, 37, 42–43.

Chapter 11

THE BATTLE OF CROOKED RIVER

THE BATTLE OF CROOKED RIVER[1] was a key factor in leading Governor Boggs to issue his extermination order that "the Mormons must be treated as enemies and must be exterminated or driven from the State if necessary for the public peace."[2] In fighting the battle, the Mormon militia was called out under orders by Caldwell County Judge Elias Higbee. They believed action was necessary to free three Mormon men who had been taken prisoners and also to protect themselves against a group that was acting like a mob in harassing Mormon homes.[3] However, the group they fought was official state militia, and one member of the militia was killed in the battle.

The confrontation arose in response to actions taken by forces led by Samuel Bogart, a captain in the state militia from Ray County, who was also an itinerant Methodist minister. Bogart had been given permission under orders from General David Atchison to patrol the Ray-Caldwell County border in response to news that the Mormons had burnt Millport and Gallatin and some homes of non-Mormons in Daviess County. However, in the latter part of October 1838, Bogart, purportedly acting under these orders, led his forces from cabin to cabin to intimidate and harass the Mormon settlers. His forces killed some of the Mormons' cattle for food, destroyed other property, and ordered several Mormon families from their homes.[4] Arza Judd wrote that Bogart's forces came to his house and ordered his family off and said that "we should see thunder and lightning at Far West before tomorrow night."[5] Bogart's men also took three Mormon men as prisoners or hostages: Nathan Pinkham Jr., William Seely, and Addison Green.[6]

During the evening of October 24, 1838, news reached Far West by Joseph Holbrook and David Juda, a Mormon guard patrolling the southern part of Caldwell County, that Bogart's forces had threatened some Church members and burned several Mormon homes at settlements along the Crooked River south of Far West; taken three Mormon men as prisoners and intended to kill them; and intended to attack Far West the next day.[7]

In response, in the early morning hours of October 25, the Mormon militia of seventy-five men rode south from Far West to assist these members. Fifteen men were diverted along the way to a different area, and the remaining sixty arrived on the banks of the Crooked River, about twelve miles south of Far West, in the dark hours of early morning to search for the kidnapped Mormon men.

Near sunrise that morning, an open gun battle took place between the Mormons and Bogart's forces. The Mormons were able to rescue the three kidnapped men, but the cost was high. David Patten of the Twelve was killed along with Gideon Carter and Patrick O'Bannion,[8] and an additional seven Mormon men were wounded. One of fifty of Bogart's men was killed.

Upon arriving at the river, the Mormon "army" tied their horses and proceeded on foot, not knowing the location of Bogart's encampment. It was just at the dawning of light in the east, when they were marching near the top of the hill that descends to the river, that the report of a gun was heard, and young Patrick O'Bannion reeled out of the ranks and fell mortally wounded. Captain David Patten ordered a charge and rushed down the hill on a fast trot. When they were within about fifty yards of the camp, the men formed a line. Bogart's men formed a line under the bank of the river, below their tents. It was still so dark that the Mormon men facing west could see little, while Bogart's men were looking to the east and could see the Mormon men silhouetted against the dawning light. In fact, David Patten was wearing a white blanket coat, which also made him easier to see.[9]

Bogart's men fired their guns, and three or four of the Mormons fell. Captain David Patten ordered the fire returned, which was instantly obeyed but at a great disadvantage in the darkness. The fire was repeated by the mob and returned by Captain Patten's company, who gave the watchword "God and Liberty." Captain Patten then ordered a charge, which was also instantly obeyed. The parties almost immediately came in contact with their swords, and Bogart's men were soon put to flight and began retreating across the river. As the Mormons pursued, one of Bogart's men wheeled from behind a tree, and shot David Patten, who instantly fell, mortally wounded, having received a large ball in his bowels.[10]

© David O. Lloyd

The hill where David Patten, Gideon Carter, and Patrick O'Bannion were killed during the Battle of Crooked River.

The ground was soon cleared, and the Mormons gathered their wounded and took them back to Far West in wagons, lying on beds made of tents. One had his arm broken by a sword. Brother Gideon Carter was shot in the head, and left dead on the ground, so defaced that the other men did not recognize him.

David Patten was carried some of the way to Far West in a litter, but due to his pains he was left at the home of Brother Stephen Winchester, three miles south of Far West, where he died about an hour after his arrival. Of this situation, Heber C. Kimball wrote:

> When the shades of time were lowering, and eternity with all its realities were opening to his view, he bore a strong testimony to the truth of the work of the Lord, and the religion he had espoused. The principles of the Gospel, which were so precious to him before, were honorably maintained in nature's final hour, and afforded him that support and consolation at the time of his departure, which deprived death of its sting and horror. Speaking of those who had apostatized, he exclaimed, "O, that they were in my situation; for I feel I have kept the faith; I have finished my course; henceforth there is laid up for me a crown, which the Lord, the righteous Judge, shall give to me." Speaking to his beloved wife Ann, who was present, he said, "Whatever you do else, do not deny the faith!"[11]

Joseph Smith was not a participant in the battle, but upon hearing news of the event from a messenger, he went with Hyrum Smith, Heber C. Kimball, and Lyman Wight "to meet the brethren on their return, near Log creek, where I saw Captain Patten in a most distressing condition. His wound was incurable."[12]

James Hendricks was one of the Mormon men wounded in the Battle of Crooked River. He was shot in the neck and paralyzed from the waist down, and he remained crippled the rest of his life. His wife, Drusilla, received the news that her husband had been shot from "a Mr. T. Snider, he did not belong to the church, but was a good man," and went immediately to see him:

> We had four miles to ride and on reaching there we met nine of the brethren that were wounded and they were pale as death. They were just going to get into the wagon to be taken to their homes. I went into the house. Sister Patten had just reached the bed where my husband lay and I heard him say, "Ann don't weep. I have kept the faith and my work is done." My husband lay within three feet of Brother Patten, and I spoke to him. He could speak but could not move anymore than if he were dead. I tried to get him to move his feet but he could not.[13]
>
> There were three beds in the room where my husband lay, he in one, Brother David Patten in one, and Brother Hodge in the other. Brother Hodge was the one shot in the hip, Brother O'Bannion was on the floor begging for a bed and some of the sisters ran and got him one. My husband was shot in the neck where it cut off all feeling of the body. It is of no use for me to try and tell how I felt for that is impossible, but I could not have shed a tear if all had been dead before me. I went to work to try and get my husband warm but could not. I rubbed and steamed him but could get no circulation. He was dead from his neck down.
>
> One of the brethren told me how he fell for he was close to him. After he had fallen one of the brethren asked him which side he was on (for it was not yet light enough to see) and all the answer he made was the watchword "God and Liberty." On hearing this it melted me to tears and I felt better. Then I was told how many of the brethren were wounded and who they were and was shown the weapons used and they bore blood from hilt to point. It makes me chill to think of it.[14]

David Patten and Gideon Carter were buried at Far West on Saturday, October 27, 1838.[15] It is likely they were buried in the pioneer cemetery west of Far West, along present-day Kerr Road, although the graves are not marked.[16] A large burial procession took the bodies to the cemetery. John Rigdon described these events:

I was at Patten's house when his body was brought there. I looked into the wagon box and there lay David Patten's body silent in death; he lay on his back, his lips tightly closed and no indication of fear in his countenance... The next day we buried both David Patten and Gideon Carter in military order. Joseph Smith and Hyrum Smith and Sidney Rigdon rode at the head of the procession on horseback. Then came the martial band and after that the bodies of David Patten and Gideon Carter and then quite a little procession followed. After, we took them out to a little burying ground just outside of the village and there we buried them.[17]

In pointing to the lifeless body of David Patten the Prophet Joseph said, "There lies a man who has done just as he said he would: he has laid down his life for his friends. Brother David W. Patten was a very worthy man, beloved by all good men who knew him. He . . . died as he had lived, a man of God, and strong in the faith of a glorious resurrection, in a world where mobs will have no power or place. One of his last expressions to his wife was—Whatever you do else, do not deny the faith."[18] In Doctrine and Covenants 124, received in Nauvoo in 1841, the Lord referred to David Patten, indicating that "he is with me at this time" (verse 19) and "I have taken him unto myself" (verse 130).

The known or probable Mormon participants in this battle were Daniel Avery, Caleb Baldwin, Israel Barlow, George Beebe, Titus Billings, William Bosley, Seymour Brunson, John Carey, Wilbur J. Carl, Gideon Carter (killed), Darwin J. Chase, Eli Chase (wounded in knee), Benjamin Clap, Isaac Decker, Moses Daley, James Durphee, James Emmett, Freeburn H. Gardner, Morgan L. Gardner, Luman Gibbs, Daniel Graves, Addison Greene, John P. Greene, Benjamin Grouard, Charles H. Hales, Stephen Hales, Elias Higbee, Francis Higbee, Isaac Higbee, James Hendricks (wounded in neck and paralyzed), Amos [Abraham] Hodge, Curtis Hodge (wounded in hip), Ervin [Lilburn] Hodge, Joseph Holbrook (wounded in elbow), Jefferson Hunt, Dimick B. Huntington, K. Jay, Benjamin Jones, David Juda, Arthur Milliken (wounded), George Morey, Patrick O'Bannion (killed), David W. Patten (killed), Morris Phelps, Parley P. Pratt, Nathan Pinkham, William Redfield, Charles C. Rich, James H. Rollins, William Seely (one of the three prisoners was wounded in left shoulder), Norman Shearer (wounded), Samuel H,. Smith, Hosea Stout, Daniel S. Thomas, Robert Thompson, Moses Tracy, Ferdinand Van Dyke, Stephen Winchester (possible participant), Solomon Wixom, Gad Yale, Lorenzo Dow Young, and Phineas Young.[19]

The Governor's Extermination Order

After the battle, a great deal of excitement prevailed in the area, and exaggerated reports were sent to Governor Boggs in Jefferson City. One such report was an inflammatory and inaccurate letter sent by Judge Ryland of Lexington, dated October 25, 1838, advising Governor Boggs of the battle and indicating that the Mormons were planning to attack Richmond that night. However, the Mormons "had not thought of going to Richmond—it was a lie out of whole cloth."[20] The letter also incorrectly indicated that ten of Bogart's men had been killed in the battle and the remainder had been taken prisoner and many of them wounded. Some excerpts from the letter:

> One of the company (Bogart's) has come in and reported that there were ten of his comrades killed and the remainder were taken prisoners, after many of them had been severely wounded; he stated further that Richmond would be sacked and burned by the Mormon bandits tonight. Nothing can exceed the consternation which this news gave rise to. The women and children are flying from Richmond in every direction. . . . My impression is, that you had better send one of your number to Howard, Cooper and Boone counties, in order that volunteers may be getting ready and flocking to the scene of trouble as fast as possible. They must make haste and put a stop to the devastation which is menaced by these infuriated fanatics, and they must go prepared and with the full determination to exterminate or expel them from the state en masse. Nothing but this can give tranquility to the public mind, and re-establish the supremacy of the laws. There must be no further delaying with this question anywhere. The Mormons must leave the state, or we will, one and all, and to this complexion it must come at last.[21]

On October 26, 1838, Governor Boggs issued an order to General Clark of the state militia ordering them to gather a force of two thousand men and proceed against the Mormons. This letter was issued in response to application from the citizens of Daviess County for "protection, and to be restored to their homes and property, with intelligence that the Mormons, with an armed force, have expelled the inhabitants of that county from their homes, have pillaged and burnt their dwellings, driven off their stock, and were destroying their crops; that they (the Mormons) have burnt to ashes the towns of Gallatin and Millport in said county."[22]

The next day, however, on October 27, 1838, Governor Boggs modified those instructions and issued the Exterminating Order, addressed to General Clark. The text is as follows:

SIR,—Since the order of the morning to you, directing you to cause four hundred mounted men to be raised within your division, I have received by Amos Rees, Esq., and Wiley C. Williams, Esq., one of my aids, information of the most appalling character, which changes the whole face of things, and places the Mormons in the attitude of open and avowed defiance of the laws, and of having made open war upon the people of this state. Your orders are, therefore, to hasten your operations and endeavor to reach Richmond, in Ray county, with all possible speed. *The Mormons must be treated as enemies and must be exterminated or driven from the state, if necessary for the public good. Their outrages are beyond all description.* If you can increase your force, you are authorized to do so, to any extent you may think necessary. I have just issued orders to Major-General Wallock, of Marion county, to raise five hundred men, and to march them to the northern part of Daviess and there to unite with General Doniphan, of Clay, who has been ordered with five hundred men to proceed to the same point for the purpose of intercepting the retreat of the Mormons to the north. They have been directed to communicate with you by express; and you can also communicate with them if you find it necessary. Instead, therefore, of proceeding as at first directed, to reinstate the citizens of Daviess in their homes, you will proceed immediately to Richmond, and there operate against the Mormons. Brigadier-General Parks, of Ray, has been ordered to have four hundred men of his brigade in readiness to join You at Richmond. The whole force will be placed under your command. (emphasis added by the authors).[23]

When this extermination order was received by state militia forces gathered against the Mormons at Far West, they announced their intent to drive the Mormons from the state.[24]

Notes

1. This battle is sometimes referred to in early Church documents as the Bogart Battle.
2. *History of the Church*, 3:169–70.
3. Ibid.
4. These were the families of Thorit Parsons, Nathan Pinkham, Sr., Mary Eaton, and Arza Judd, Jr.
5. Judd, *Mormon Redress Petitions*, 473.
6. *History of the Church*, 3:169.
7. See, for example, Charles C. Rich, *Mormon Redress Petitions*, 707.
8. O'Bannion, who was only nineteen years old, had been recruited by David Patten to show the Mormons where Bogart's men were camped. It appears that he was not a member of the Church.

9. Ward, *History of Caldwell County*, 130.
10. *History of the Church*, 3:170.
11. Jenson, *Historical Record*, Feb. 1886, quoting Heber C. Kimball Journal, 24.
12. *History of the Church*, 3:171.
13. Drusilla Hendricks Autobiography in *Henry Hendricks Genealogy*, 20.
14. Ibid., 20–21.
15. Patrick O'Bannion's parents made separate arrangements for his burial.
16. This cemetery is currently the property of the Community of Christ.
17. Rigdon, *The Life and Testimony of Sidney Rigdon*, 32.
18. *History of the Church*, 3:171.
19. Baugh, *A Call to Arms*, Appendix H, 197–202.
20. *History of the Church*, 3:173.
21. Ibid., 172–73.
22. Ibid., 174.
23. Ibid., 175.
24. The Extermination Order issued by Governor Boggs in 1838 was rescinded in 1976 by Missouri Governor Christopher Bond. The text of the Rescinding Order is included in the Appendix.

Chapter 12

THE ATTACK AT HAUN'S MILL

O N OCTOBER 30, 1838, THE greatest tragedy of all occurred in the Missouri-Mormon War when a group of more than one hundred vigilantes from neighboring counties attacked the Mormon settlement at Haun's Mill and killed seventeen Mormons (including three young boys) and wounded another fourteen. As LDS historian Andrew Jenson wrote, notwithstanding the fact that since the organization of the Church, "a large number of Mormons have suffered martyrdom for the truth's sake, on no other occasion have so many of the faithful at one time been called to lay down their lives as at the Haun's Mill Massacre on the 30th of October, 1838."[1]

Haun's Mill was a small settlement on Shoal Creek, about twelve miles east of Far West. It was founded by Jacob Haun, a convert from Green Bay, Wisconsin. The settlement consisted of a mill, blacksmith shop, a few houses, and a population of twenty to thirty families at the mill itself and one hundred families in the greater neighborhood. Due to its location, it served as a stopping point for Mormons on their way to Far West.

On October 25, a group of twenty men led by Nehemiah Comstock rode into Haun's Mill and demanded that the Mormons surrender their guns. Most did so, but one Mormon, Hiram Abbot, refused to turn over his gun and ran. Comstock's men fired upon him, but he was not hit. Also, in the few days before the attack, anti-Mormon forces in the area accosted Mormon companies traveling through the area en route to Far West and confiscated their weapons. One example was the party of Joseph

Young, which included nine wagons, traveling from Kirtland. This group stopped to rest a few days at Haun's Mill before proceeding to Far West and were at the mill the day of the attack.

In view of the volatile situation that was developing, Jacob Haun went to Far West to seek counsel on whether the Mormons should remain at the mill site. John Killian, an officer in the Far West militia, reportedly advised him to move the families into Far West at once, and Haun then met with Joseph Smith, who also reportedly told him to abandon the mill. According to an account given years later, Haun supposedly replied that they were "strong enough to defend the mill and keep it in [their] own hands," and with that, he returned to the community and reported that Brother Joseph's instruction was for them to stay if they thought they were strong enough to protect and hold the mill.[2]

At that point, the Mormons at Haun's Mill decided to place themselves in an attitude of self-defense. Twenty-eight men armed themselves and began taking turns doing guard duty at the mill. On the evening of October 28, the local vigilantes sent one of their number to enter into a treaty with the Mormons at the mill. Each side agreed to mutual forbearance and to exert themselves to prevent any further hostilities.[3]

Notwithstanding this "truce," the attack took place on Tuesday, October 30, in the late afternoon of what had, until then, been a routine and pleasant fall day. The vigilantes divided into three lines for purposes of the attack and rode into the mill area and dismounted their horses. David Evans raised a white flag, hoping for peace, but the vigilantes began to fire. Many of the Mormon men ran into a blacksmith shop (eighteen square feet) hoping for safety. The women and children ran for the cornfields and woods, and a few hid in nearby cabins. The vigilantes purposely fired on the fleeing women and children, who hid themselves the best they could. Fortunately, nearly all of the fifty women and children living in the settlement made it to safety. The only woman who was wounded was Mary Stedwell, who was shot through her hand while fleeing from the vigilantes. After she was shot, she fainted and fell over a log, into which the vigilantes shot upward of twenty balls but did not hit her again.[4]

Thirty-two men and three boys were known to have entered the blacksmith shop.[5] The vigilantes began to fire volley after volley into the shop, which offered only little protection because the spaces between the logs were not filled. Thus, bullets could enter through the cracks between logs. Joseph Young wrote in a detailed account, recorded in the *History of the Church*:

David Evans, seeing the superiority of their numbers (there being two hundred and forty of them, according to their own account), swung his hat, and cried for peace. This not being heeded, they continued to advance, and their leader, Mr. Nehemiah Comstock, fired a gun, which was followed by a solemn pause of ten or twelve seconds, when, all at once, they discharged about one hundred rifles, aiming at a blacksmith shop into which our friends had fled for safety; and charged up to the shop, the cracks of which between the logs were sufficiently large to enable them to aim directly at the bodies of those who had there fled for refuge from the fire of their murderers. There were several families tented in the rear of the shop, whose lives were exposed, and amidst a shower of bullets fled to the woods in different directions.[6]

David Evans and Nathan Knight went out of the shop and pled for a cease-fire, but it was to no avail as the vigilantes continued their fire. The two men were able to run safely to the woods, although Knight was shot in the hand, leg, and back in doing so. The Mormon men in the blacksmith shop soon realized the peril of their situation and began to run from the shop one or two at a time, which appeared to be their only hope for escape. As they ran, they were fired at by the vigilantes. Of the nineteen men who fled from the shop, thirteen were wounded while attempting to escape, and three of them later died as a result of their wounds. Also, Thomas McBride was wounded and killed, and John Walker was wounded before he left the shop but managed to escape. Only four Mormon men managed to escape from the shop unharmed: Rial Ames, Ellis Eamut, David Evans, and David Lewis.[7]

When resistance from within the blacksmith shop subsided, the vigilantes entered the shop. Eight Mormon men lay dead, and four were severely wounded but had not died. The vigilantes began stripping the wounded men of their clothing and boots. One Mormon man (William Champlin) and three Mormon boys were hiding in the shop uninjured and had concealed themselves as best they could, hoping they would not be discovered. William Champlin hid himself under dead bodies to make it appear that he was dead, although he was taken prisoner and held for three days after the battle. However, the vigilantes shot each of the three boys, killing two of them. Following the fight, one of the vigilantes outside the shop could see where the boys were hiding and put his gun through a crack in the wall and shot Alma Smith (age seven) in the hip. Alma feigned death and was able to survive the ordeal. Nine-year old Charles Merrick tried to escape through the open door and was fired upon and wounded three times. He died from his wounds four weeks later. The final boy was ten-year old Sardius Smith (Alma's brother and the son of Warren Smith, who was also killed in the shop), who offered no resistance and was shot to death in the head at point blank range by a member of the vigilante group.[8]

After the attack, the surviving Mormons were fearful that the vigilantes might return at any moment, and only a few able bodied men were available to bury the dead. The Mormons therefore buried the bodies in the most expedient way possible by interring them in a nearby unfinished dry well, some twelve feet deep. The bodies of all but one who died in or shortly after the attack were buried in this well (two men died a few weeks later), under the direction of Joseph Young. The bodies were put on a plank, one at a time, and slid into the community grave.[9]

The seventeen men and boys killed or mortally wounded in the attack at Haun's Mill included:

Hiram Abbot	Elias Benner
John Byers	Alexander Campbell
Simon Cox	Josiah Fuller
Austin Hammer	John Lee
Benjamin Lewis	Thomas McBride
Charles Merrick	Levi N. Merrick
William Napier	George S. Richards
Warren Smith	Sardius Smith
John York	

The wounded who recovered, and the nature of their wounds, if known, included:

Jacob Foutz (thigh)
Jacob Haun (unknown)
Charles Jimison (unknown)
Nathan K. Knight (finger, leg, and back)
Isaac Laney (ten places)
Tarlton Lewis (shoulder)
Gilmon Merrill (not known)
Jacob Myers (leg—amputated)
George Myers (shoulder—never fully recovered)

© Sheli Cunningham

Haun's Mill today.

Jacob Potts (right leg)
Alma Smith (hip)
Ms. Mary Stedwell (hand)
John Walker (right arm)
William Yokum (face and leg, which was amputated)

One of the murdered Mormons was Thomas McBride, who was sixty-three years old at the time.[10] McBride had an eighty-acre farm about three-fourths of a mile from Haun's Mill on Shoal Creek and was on guard duty at the mill on October 30, 1838, in place of his twenty-year-old son, James, who was sick that day.

James McBride recorded that when his father left his home for the last time to head for the mill, "Father was in good spirits, and his countenance wore a cheerful expression. Having shaved himself in his usual style, leaving side beards—and taking with him his guns and blankets, started on his return to the mill to join the rest of the guard."[11] He believes it likely that his father "had but little more than got to the mill—in fact not more than thirty minutes had elapsed from the time he left the house, when a gun was heard—and another—followed by the deadly crack of musketry, which told too well the fate of all who fell a prey to the blood-thirsty mob. Perhaps not more than six minutes had passed from the firing of the first gun, 'till the massacre was accomplished—the bloody deed was done."[12]

Nathan K. Knight saw a vigilante cut down Father McBride with a corn-cutter, saw them stripping the dying, and heard the boys crying for mercy. Knight made his escape across the mill-dam after receiving wounds through his lungs and finger. After the massacre was over, a woman led him to a house, and while lying there wounded he heard Mr. Jesse Maupin say that he blew one of the boys' brains out. Some time later while walking the streets of Far West, Brother Knight was met by three Missourians who threatened to butcher him. One of them by the name of Rogers drew a butcher knife and said that he did not have the corn-cutter with him that he cut down McBride with, "but by —— I have got something that will do as well." However, Brother Knight made his escape from the men without being harmed.[13]

Isaac Laney was shot many times that day but survived. James McBride was well acquainted with Isaac Laney, and gave this account of his experience:

> Isaac Laney a young man that was baptized into the church at the same time that I was, was in the black-smith shop, when the mob began to fire on them. His gun stock was shot to pieces in his hands. He then escaped from the shop, ran to the mill, and climbed down one of the mill timbers into the creek, that being the quickest way for him to escape danger. From there he went into the house, where sister Catherine, Mrs. Haun, Mrs. Merril and some other women were. They administered to Isaac, and put him under the floor. He had received eleven bullet marks in his body. I was well acquainted with Isaac Laney, and helped to take care of him until he recovered. He told me that when trying to escape from the mob, the blood gushing from his mouth would almost strangle him. While he was under the floor he said he suffered a great deal for want of water. The women not daring to venture out to get water until they felt sure the mob was entirely gone. Isaac recovered, and lived thirty-five years from the day of the Haun's Mill Massacre.[14]

Aftermath

The day after the attack, the vigilantes proceeded to rob the houses and wagons of the Mormons at the mill. Joseph Young recounted the attack:

> To finish their work of destruction, this band of murderers, composed of men from Daviess, Livingston, Ray, Carroll, and Chariton counties, led by some of the principal men of that section of the upper country, . . . proceeded to rob the houses, wagons, and tents, of bedding and clothing; drove off horses and wagons, leaving widows and orphans destitute of the necessaries of life; and even stripped the clothing from the bodies of the slain. According to their own account, they

fired seven rounds in this awful butchery, making upwards of sixteen hundred shots at a little company of men, about thirty in number.[15]

Isaac Laney also recorded that a few days after the slaughter the vigilantes returned and tarried at the mill about three weeks, during which time they robbed the mill of about one hundred bushels of wheat and a similar amount of corn, shot a number of hogs, and stole some honey.[16]

Casualties and Motives of the Vigilantes

The attackers were composed of men from Daviess, Ray, Livingston, Carroll, and Chariton counties, and included some of the principal men of those counties. The vigilantes were led in the attack by Colonel Thomas Jennings, a long-time militia officer. Three of the vigilantes were wounded but none were killed.[17] John Hart from Livingston County was shot in the arm; John Renfrow had his thumb shot off; and Allen England from Daviess County was severely wounded in the thigh.[18]

Although the vigilantes were never called into account for their actions, some of them attempted to justify the attack as a form of precautionary self-defense. They allegedly feared that the Mormons would attack them in their homes, as had recently occurred in Daviess County at Gallatin and Millport. Also, there had been word throughout the countryside that the Mormons annihilated Bogart's militia in the Battle of Crooked River.[19] Although this information was incorrect, it served to increase fear in the community. Nevertheless, even if such fears were the actual motives for the attack, it is difficult to envision that they somehow justified the viciousness of the attack that took place. It is also known that some members of the vigilantes from Daviess County held grudges against the Mormons.[20]

Further, it is inconclusive and somewhat unlikely that the vigilantes acted in accordance with the governor's extermination order. That order was issued on October 27 from faraway Jefferson City, and it is unlikely that vigilante leader Jennings learned of the order before he attacked the Mormons at Haun's Mill on October 30. In fact, the two militia leaders near Far West did not learn of the order until the day of the attack at Haun's Mill, and they would have had to get word to Jennings on that same day, which is unlikely given the distances and travel times involved. In addition, the Mormons at Far West did not learn of the governor's order until it was read to them by the leaders of the militia on October 31, the day after the attack at Haun's Mill.

Account of Amanda Smith

Amanda Smith, a survivor of the Haun's Mill massacre, was twenty-nine years old in 1838. Her family had traveled from Kirtland to Missouri in a company of nine wagons, including that of Joseph Young. Two days before they arrived in Caldwell County, they were accosted by vigilantes who confiscated their weapons. The company then traveled a few more miles to Haun's Mill, where the Smith family pitched their tent by the blacksmith's shop. Her husband, Warren, and ten-year-old son, Sardius, were killed by the vigilantes, and another son, Alma, was shot in the hip. Miraculously, Amanda Smith was directed by the Lord through prayer and faith in how to heal the young man. A third son, Willard, was able to hide from the vigilantes and was not harmed.[21]

Amanda Smith wrote this account of the miraculous healing of her son Alma:

> The entire hip joint of my wounded boy had been shot away. Flesh, hip bone, joint and all had been ploughed out from the muzzle of the gun, which the ruffian placed to the child's hip through the logs of the shop and deliberately fired. We laid little Alma on a bed in our tent and I examined the wound. It was a ghastly sight. I knew not what to do. It was night now. There were none left from that terrible scene, throughout that long, dark night, but about half a dozen bereaved and lamenting women, and the children. Eighteen or nineteen, all grown men excepting my murdered boy and another about the same age, were dead or dying; several more of the men were wounded, hiding away, whose groans through the night too well disclosed their hiding places, while the rest of the men had fled, at the moment of the massacre, to save their lives. The women were sobbing, in the greatest anguish of spirit; the children were crying loudly with fear and grief at the loss of fathers and brothers; the dogs howled over their dead masters and the cattle were terrified with the scent of the blood of the murdered. Yet was I there, all that long, dreadful night, with my dead and my wounded, and none but God as our physician and help. 'Oh my Heavenly Father,' I cried, 'what shall I do? Thou seest my poor wounded boy and knowest my inexperience. Oh, Heavenly Father, direct me what to do!'
>
> And then I was directed as by a voice speaking to me. The ashes of our fire was still smoldering. We had been burning the bark of the shag-bark hickory. I was directed to take those ashes and make a lye and put a cloth saturated with it right into the wound. It hurt, but little Alma was too near dead to heed it much. Again and again I saturated

the cloth and put it into the hole from which the hip joint had been ploughed, and each time mashed flesh and splinters of bone came away with the cloth; and the wound became as white as chicken's flesh.

Having done as directed I again prayed to the Lord and was again instructed as distinctly as though a physician had been standing by speaking to me. Near by was a slippery-elm tree. From this I was told to make a slippery-elm poultice and fill the wound with it. My eldest boy was sent to get the slippery-elm from the roots, the poultice was made, and the wound, which took fully a quarter of a yard of linen to cover, so large was it, was properly dressed. . . .

I removed the wounded boy to a house, some distance off, the next day, and dressed his hip; the Lord directing me as before. I was reminded that in my husband's trunk there was a bottle of balsam. This I poured into the wound, greatly soothing Alma's pain. 'Alma, my child,' I said, 'you believe that the Lord made your hip?' 'Yes, mother.' 'Well, the Lord can make something there in the place of your hip, don't you believe he can, Alma?' 'Do you think that the Lord can, mother?' inquired the child, in his simplicity. 'Yes, my son,' I replied, 'he has showed it all to me in a vision.' Then I laid him comfortably on his face and said: 'Now you lay like that, and don't move, and the Lord will make you another hip.' So Alma laid on his face for five weeks, until he was entirely recovered—a flexible gristle having grown in place of the missing joint and socket, which remains to this day a marvel to physicians.

On the day that he walked again I was out of the house fetching a bucket of water, when I heard screams from the children. Running back, in affright, I entered, and there was Alma on the floor, dancing around, and the children screaming in astonishment and joy. It is now nearly forty years ago, but Alma has never been the least crippled during his life, and he has traveled quite a long period of the time as a missionary of the gospel and a living miracle of the power of God.[22]

Amanda Smith also wrote of opposition from the vigilante group during the five weeks she was caring for her wounded son near the scene of the massacre. Many of the Mormons had left the area, but a few of the bereaved women and children had gathered at the house of David Evans, two miles from the scene of the massacre. One day a mobber told the women that the captain of the militia had ordered them to stop praying, or else he would send down a posse and kill every one of them.

However, the women did not stop offering their prayers; they prayed in secret, and Sister Smith received strength in a miraculous manner:

Our prayers were hushed in terror. We dared not let our voices be heard in the house in supplication. I could pray in my bed or in silence, but I could not live thus long. This godless silence was more intolerable than had been that night of the massacre. I could bear it no longer. I pined to hear once more my own voice in petition to my Heaven Father. I stole down to a corn field, and crawled into a stalk of corn. It was as the temple of the Lord to me at that moment. I prayed aloud and most fervently. When I emerged from the corn a voice spoke to me. It was a voice as plain as I ever hear one. It was no silent, strong impression of the spirit, but a voice, repeating a verse of the Saint's hymn:

That soul who on Jesus hath leaned for repose,
I cannot, I will not, desert to its foes;
That soul, though all hell should endeavor to shake,
I'll never, no never, no never forsake![23]

From that moment I had no more fear. I felt that nothing could hurt me. Soon after this the mob sent us word that unless we were all out of the State by a certain day we should be killed. The day came, and at evening came fifty armed men to execute the sentence. I met them at the door. They demanded of me why I was not gone? I bade them enter and see their own work. They crowded into my room and I showed them my wounded boy. They came, party after party, until all had seen my excuse. Then they quarreled among themselves and came near fighting. At last they went away, all but two. These I thought were detailed to kill us. Then the two returned. 'Madam,' said one, 'have you any meat in the house?' 'No,' was my reply. 'Could you dress a fat hog if one was laid at your door?' 'I think we could!" was my answer. And then they went and caught a fat hog from a herd which had belonged to a now exiled brother, killed it and dragged it to my door, and departed. These men, who had come to murder us, left on the threshold of our door a meat offering to atone for their repented intention.[24]

Conclusion

As of this writing, the site of Haun's Mill is owned by the Community of Christ. A historical marker and interpretative sign are placed there. The location of the well where the bodies of the Mormons who were killed were buried has not been located. Perhaps it is fitting that they rest in peace, undisturbed by the living.

Notes

1. Jenson, *Historical Record*, December 1888, vol. 7, 684.
2. Daniel Tyler, Recollections of the Prophet Joseph Smith, *Juvenile Instructor* 27 (Feb. 1, 1892):94–95. See also Ward, *History of Caldwell County*, page 145–46 and Baugh, *A Call to Arms*, 118.
3. *History of the Church*, 3:184.
4. Ibid., 3:185.
5. Baugh, *A Call to Arms*, 120.
6. *History of the Church*, 3:183–186.
7. Baugh, *A Call to Arms*, 122–23.
8. *History of the Church*, 3:185.
9. Ward, *History of Caldwell County*, 150; James McBride Autobiography, 14. As of this writing the exact location of the well has not been determined. For more information on the site, see the discussion at Baugh, *A Call to Arms*, page 133, note 129.
10. Although some accounts indicate Thomas McBride was a Revolutionary War veteran, the son's account indicates he was born in 1776 (James McBride Autobiography, 5).
11. James McBride Autobiography, 9–10.
12. Ibid., 11.
13. *History of the Church*, 3:187.
14. James McBride Autobiography, 14.
15. *History of the Church*, 3:186.
16. Isaac Laney, *Mormon Redress Petitions*, 268. See also the account of David Lewis, *Mormon Redress Petitions*, 276–77.
17. *History of the Church*, 3:326, footnotes.
18. Ibid.
19. Baugh, *A Call to Arms*, 127.
20. Baugh, *A Call to Arms*, 115, citing Holcombe, *The Haun's Mill Massacre: An Incident of the "Mormon War" in Missouri*, St. Louis Globe-Democrat, 6 October 1887.
21. Jenson, *LDS Biographical Encyclopedia*, vol. 2, 792–94. After leaving Missouri in 1839, Amanda Smith established a home in Nauvoo and later went to Utah in 1850. She resided in Salt Lake City until a few months before her death, when she went to live with her daughter in Richmond. Sister Smith died June 30, 1886, at age 77, due to natural causes associated with old age. She was the mother of eight children, six of whom were living at the time of her death, sixty-seven grandchildren, and thirty-two great-grandchildren (Ibid., 796).
21. Ibid., 794–96.
23. *Hymn* no. 85, "How Firm a Foundation," verse 7.
24. Jenson, *LDS Biographical Encyclopedia*, 796–97.

Chapter 13

THE SIEGE AND SURRENDER
AT FAR WEST

A S NEWS OF THE BATTLE of Crooked River spread rapidly throughout the area, state militia forces began to march to confront the Mormons at Far West. By then, many Mormons from outlying areas had moved to Far West, and a final showdown appeared imminent. Many expected major hostilities between the Mormons and the state militia, but as events played out, the greatly outnumbered Mormons surrendered and agreed to leave the state without a significant loss of lives on either part.

On October 26, the day before Governor Boggs issued the extermination order, Boggs relieved General David Atchison of command of the state militia marching against the Mormons and appointed General John Clark as the commander.[1] Many Mormons suspected Boggs took this action because Atchison was too friendly (neutral) to the Mormons and would not be aggressive enough in driving them from the state. According to Philo Dibble, "The governor, thinking Atchison was too friendly towards the Mormons, took his command from him and placed General Clark in command of the militia."[2] Clark was from Howard County and needed a few days to travel to Far West. Until he arrived, the state forces were under the command of General Samuel Lucas, the commander of the Jackson County militia and a friend of Governor Boggs.

Lucas did not wait for Clark to arrive to take action and began to march his forces toward Far West from the south. Along the way, the advance guard came across two Mormon families, those of John Tanner and William Carey. Tanner was clubbed on his head with a pistol, which hurt him badly and exposed his skull, but he survived. Carey fared even worse from a vicious blow to his head by a pistol.[3] Tanner was allowed to take the severely wounded Carey to Far West, but Carey died there a few days later.

The Mormons heard reports that forces were coming against them and sent a force of 150 men to investigate under the direction of Colonel Hinkle, the commander of the Caldwell County militia. They saw Lucas's troops and managed to return to Far West by a circuitous route ahead of them. On October 30, Joseph Smith delivered a stirring address at the public square, encouraging the men to defend their families, homes, and property. At the conclusion of his remarks, the Mormons formed companies and prepared a defense line just south of town.

The state militia approaching Far West was led by General Alexander Doniphan, who was friendly to the Mormons and interested in maintaining peace. His troops advanced to within two hundred yards of the Mormon defense line. The Mormons hoisted a white flag, and Doniphan withdrew to camp for the night one mile south on Goose Creek.[4]

The militia sent a dispatch to Far West, ordered by Governor Boggs, requesting that two non-Mormon men, John Cleminson and Adam Lightner, be allowed to leave with their families. Mary Elizabeth Rollins Lightner, the wife of Adam Lightner, was a Mormon.[5] Both families chose to remain in Far West.

The Mormons sent Charles C. Rich, bearing a white flag, to meet with Doniphan. On the way, Samuel Bogart shot him at close range but missed. Rich instinctively wanted to shoot back but did not, explaining, "I drew my pistol to shoot him but the voice of the spirit plainly manifested to my mind, that if I did . . . it would be the means of exasperating our enemies, and of causing them to take revenge by killing my brethren."[6] Rich met briefly with Doniphan, who assured him that he did not intend to attack Far West but could not speak for other elements of the state militia.

Reed Peck, Colonel Hinkle's adjutant, offered to go to Doniphan's encampment to see if some peaceful arrangement could be reached. General Doniphan met with Peck and agreed to meet with several Mormon officers on the following morning at 8:00.[7]

During that night, the Mormon men built a barricade of approximately one mile in length along the southern edge of the city, with wagons and timber.[8] William Draper wrote: "We set to work with all our might and threw up a breastwork of such material as we could get, house logs, plies, wagons, boards slabs, and wagons boxes and other materials such as we could gather through the night, and when morning came we had about a half or three quarters of a mile of beautiful breastwork."[9] Some Missourians later charged that the Mormons were fortifying as an act of defiance to the laws of the state, but John Corrill's account to the state legislature countered this assertion by downplaying the effectiveness of the line, saying that "it was about as good a defence as a common fence would be."[10] Also, many of the Mormon men involved in the Battle of Crooked River left town for their safety. Edward Stevenson described the events of that evening:

> The camp fires of our enemies on the banks of Goose Creek were ablaze in the darkness. Brother Carey was brought in with his skull wounded badly, being laid bare, having been struck with a rifle over the head and thrown into a wagon in this mangled condition and uncared for. He was brought to his family and soon after died.. . . during the night a temporary breastwork of logs, wagons, and timbers were thrown up which the next morning looked like a wonderful night's work and considerably warlike. The sisters had gathered up many of their valuable and expected battle, and that they would have to flee. The Saints had gathered into the city, leaving their homes in the country.[11]

Some of the militia, particularly those under the command of Cornelius Gillium, "were painted like Indians; some more conspicuous than others, were designated by red spots; and he also was painted in a similar manner with red spots marked on his face, and styled himself the 'DELAWARE CHIEF.' They would hoop and halloo, and yell as nearly like Indians as they could, and continued to do so all that night."[12]

Early the morning of October 31, Lyman Wight arrived with one hundred mounted and armed Mormon men from Adam-ondi-Ahman. At 8:00, Doniphan and Lucas met with Colonel Hinkle, John Corrill, and Reed Peck, representing the Mormons. Joseph Smith instructed the Mormon men to seek peace on any terms short of battle. John Corrill said that Joseph told him to "beg like a dog for peace, and afterwards said he would rather go to States-prison for twenty years, or would rather die himself than have the people exterminated."[13]

However, the militia leaders indicated they were waiting for orders from the governor (which would prove to be the extermination order), and General Lucas was not willing to enter negotiations. By then, the Mormons in Far West saw the gravity of the situation and that they were greatly outnumbered. Accounts vary as to how many state militia were on hand, but there were likely about 2,500 militia at the initial siege of Far West, and another 1,400–1,600 arrived with General Clark shortly after the Mormons surrendered.[14] The Mormon militia probably numbered only five hundred men.[15] Also, news of the attack at Haun's Mill had reached Far West by this time, and the Mormons began to fear the worse—that the militia forces at Far West intended to massacre them.

After the governor's order arrived, the three Mormon men and two others, William W. Phelps and Arthur Morrison,[16] met with General Lucas and Doniphan on the eminence just south of Far West in the afternoon. General Lucas read the governor's extermination order, and the Mormons were shocked by its severity. John Corrill wrote:

> This order greatly agitated my mind. I expected we should be exterminated without fail. There lay three thousand men, highly excited and full of vengeance, and it was as much as the officers could do to keep them off from us anyhow; and they now had authority from the executive to exterminate, with orders to cut off our retreat, and the word Mormons, I thought, included innocent as well as guilty; so of course there was no escape for any. These were my first reflections on hearing the order.[17]

However, General Lucas said that he would be more mild than the extermination order required and that he would spare their lives on certain conditions. He made several specific written demands of the Mormons:

- First, to give up their leaders to be tried and punished.
- Second, to make an appropriation of their property, all who had taken up arms, to the payment of their debts, and indemnify for damage done by them.
- Third, that the balance should leave the State, and be protected while doing so by the militia, but to be permitted to remain under protection until further orders were received from the Commander-in-Chief.
- Fourth, to give up the arms of every description to be receipted for.[18]

General Lucas regarded Colonel Hinkle as the proper spokesman for the Mormons, rather than Joseph Smith, because Hinkle was the leader of the Caldwell militia. Accounts indicate that Hinkle protested the terms, but Lucas was not willing to negotiate or postpone his demands.[19] Lucas gave the Mormons about two hours until sunset to make up their minds and deliver the prisoners or his forces would commence an attack upon Far West. John Corrill explained:

> A gentleman of note told me that if these men were suffered to escape, or if they could not be found, nothing could save the place from destruction and the people from extermination. We knew that General Lucas had no authority, and his requirements were illegal; for he was out of the bounds of his division, and the Governor's order was to General Clark, and not to him; but there was no other way for the Mormons but to submit.

The Mormon men immediately returned to Far West and told Joseph Smith, Sidney Rigdon, Lyman Wight, Parley P. Pratt, and George W. Robinson what the governor's order and General Lucas required. There are conflicting accounts as to what the Mormon leaders understood the terms to be, but it appears they returned to meet with Lucas expecting to discuss the situation or to be held only temporarily. According to John Corrill, "Smith said if it was the Governor's order, they would submit, and the Lord would take care of them." Joseph and the others returned to see the militia. Upon arriving, Colonel Hinkle reportedly said, "Here general are the prisoners I agreed to deliver to you," but the Mormon leaders were shocked to hear this and to be retained as prisoners.[20] John Corrill's account continues:

> We met General Lucas, with his army, but a short distance from town. He had made every arrangement to surround and destroy the place; but the prisoners delivered themselves up, and General Lucas, with the army and prisoners, returned to their camp. These prisoners were to be retained as hostages till morning, and then, if they did not agree to the proposals, they were to be set at liberty again. I suppose they agreed to the proposals, for they were not set at liberty.[21]

However, Joseph Smith wrote the following account of being taken into the camp of Lucas's forces:

> Towards the evening I was waited upon by Colonel Hinkle, who stated that the officers of the militia desired to have an interview with me and some others, hoping that the difficulties might be settled without having occasion to carry into effect the exterminating orders which they had received from the governor. I immediately complied with the request, and in company with Elders Sidney Rigdon and Parley P.

Pratt, Colonel Wight and George W. Robinson, went into the camp of the militias. But judge of my surprise, when, instead of being treated with that respect which is due from one citizen to another, we were taken prisoners of war and treated with the utmost contempt. The officers would not converse with us, and the soldiers, almost to a man, insulted us as much as they felt disposed, breathing out threats against me and my companions. I cannot begin to tell the scene which I there witnessed. The loud cries and yells of more than one thousand voices, which rent the air and could be heard for miles, and the horrid and blasphemous threats and curses which were poured upon us in torrents, were enough to appall the stoutest heart. In the evening, we had to lie down on the cold ground, surrounded by a strong guard, who were only kept back by the power of God from depriving us of life. We petitioned the officers to know why we were thus treated, but they utterly refused to give us any answer, or to converse with us.[22]

Parley P. Pratt described the chaotic scene when the prisoners arrived at the camp:

The haughty general [Lucas] rode up, and without speaking to us, instantly ordered his guard to surround us. They did so very abruptly, and we were marched into camp surrounded by thousands of savage looking beings, many of whom were dressed and painted like Indian warriors. These all set up a constant yell, like so many bloodhounds let loose upon their prey, as if they had achieved one of the most miraculous victories that ever graced the annals of the world.[23]

Sidney Rigdon also recorded the "howling" of the militia and that he "could distinctly hear the guns as the locks were sprung, which appeared from the sound to be in every part of the army. General Doniphan came riding up where we were, and swore by his Maker that he would hew the first man down that cocked a gun. One or two other officers on horseback rode up, ordering those who had cocked their guns to uncock them, or they would be hewn down with their swords."[24]

Many Mormons blamed Colonel Hinkle for betraying the prophet into the militia's hands; even the Prophet accused Hinkle of being a traitor who had already agreed to the terms outlined by Lucas prior to his capture.[25] However, Hinkle explained that he had no intentions of betrayal. He wrote:

When the facts were laid before Joseph, did he not say, "I will go"; and did not the others go with him, and that, too, *voluntarily*, so far as you and I were concerned? My understanding was that those men were to be taken and kept until the next morning as hostages; and if they did not, upon reflection and consultation with the officers in the camp of the enemy, during the night, conclude to accept of the terms proposed to us, but choose to fight, then they were to be kept safely, and returned to us in the city next morning, unharmed and time given us to prepare for an attack by the militia.[26]

In any event, the shrieking of Lucas's forces continued throughout the night, terrorizing the citizens of Far West, who feared that their Prophet and the others might have been murdered. Many of the Mormons recorded that they could hear the yells and screams of the militia from their camp, even though it was miles away. Edward Stevenson wrote: "It seemed as though ten thousand kept up a constant yelling in the mob camp. The loud yells, cursing, and blasphemous language against the Mormons was enough to appall the stoutest hearts."[27] Phebe Hancock wrote: "I lived three miles from that camp, yet I could hear screams and yells as though some of the demons were let loose from the lower regions. I remember that I went out behind a mound and prayed to the God of Heaven that he would deliver his own Prophets."[28]

On November 1, the state militia held an illegal court martial, and General Lucas ordered the five men to be shot the next morning.[29] However, Alexander Doniphan, who was ordered to carry out the execution, refused to do so, saying, "It is cold-blooded murder. I will not obey our order. My brigade shall march for Liberty tomorrow, at 8 o'clock; and if you execute these men, I will hold you responsible before an earthly tribunal, so help me God."[30] Doniphan took his brigade and rode off as promised.[31] As a result, Lucas lost his nerve and the Mormon men were not executed. Joseph and the others were nevertheless retained as prisoners.[32]

Also that morning, General Lucas marched his army near Far West, and Colonel Hinkle marched out the Mormon militia, who gave up their arms, about six hundred guns, as well as swords and pistols, and surrendered themselves as prisoners. Then, under the pretense of searching for arms, the militia tore up floors, upset haystacks, purportedly raped some women, plundered many valuable effects, and wantonly wasted and destroyed a great amount of property.[33]

Several other Mormon men were arrested that day. One of them was Hyrum Smith, who described the experience as follows:

About twelve o-clock that day [November 1] Colonel Hinkle came to my house with an armed force, opened the door, and called me out of doors and delivered me up as a prisoner of that force. They surrounded me and commanded me to march into the camp. I told them that I could not go; my family were sick and I was sick myself, and could not leave home. They said they did not care for that—I must and should go. I asked when they would permit me to return. They made me no answer, but forced me along with the point of the bayonet into the camp, and put me under the same guard with my brother, Joseph; And within about half an hour afterwards Amasa Lyman was so brought and placed under the same guard. There we were compelled to stay all that night and lie on the ground.[34]

The next morning, Joseph and his fellow prisoners were taken to the Far West public square in a heavily guarded wagon and paraded before the Mormons. While kept under strong guard, the prisoners were allowed a few moments to go to their respective homes and gather additional clothing and personal items. Joseph Smith wrote this account:

I found my wife and children in tears, who feared we had been shot by those who had sworn to take our lives, and that they would see me no more. When I entered my house, they clung to my garments, their eyes streaming with tears, while mingled emotions of joy and sorrow were manifested in their countenances. I requested to have a private interview with them a few minutes, but this privilege was denied me by the guard. I was then obliged to take my departure. Who can realize the feelings which I experienced at that time, to be thus torn from my companion, and leave her surrounded with monsters in the shape of men, and my children, too, not knowing how their wants would be supplied; while I was to be taken far from them in order that my enemies might destroy me when they thought proper to do so. My partner wept, my children clung to me, until they were thrust from me by the swords of the guards. I felt overwhelmed while I witnessed the scene, and could only recommend them to the care of that God whose kindness had followed me to the present time, and who alone could protect them, and deliver me from the hands of my enemies, and restore me to my family.[35]

In his later years, Joseph Smith, III (the son of Joseph the Prophet), recounted in his memoirs:

I remember vividly the morning my father came to visit his family after the arrest that took place in the fall of 1838. When he was brought to the house by an armed guard I ran out of the gate to greet him, but was roughly pushed away from his side by a sword in the hand of the guard and not allowed to go near him. My mother, also, was not permitted to approach him and had to receive his farewell by word of lip only. The guard did not permit him to pass into the house nor her to pass out, either because he feared an attempt would be made to rescue his prisoner or because of some brutal instinct in his own breast. Who shall say?[36]

After the brief visit to Far West, the Mormon leaders were loaded into wagons and taken to Independence by Brigadier General Moses Wilson, along with confiscated weapons.

On November 2, the second day of the surrender, about five hundred Mormon men were then drawn up in a hollow square on the public square in Far West and forced to sign a deed of trust to convey their property in trust to certain appointed commissioners for the use of the creditors of the Church, and also to pay all the damages done by Mormons. David Pettigrew described the scene:

> A sorrowful scene issued—stealing, robbing, plundering and compelling us to deed away all our personal property, as well as the real estate. When we were marching up to the place prepared for us to sign our deeds of trust, for we were all prisoners and compelled at the point of bayonet to march forward, on my way one of the guards struck me on the head with his gun, which almost stunned me. When I approached the table a lawyer asked me if I acknowledged this to be my act and deed. I replied, "Yes, done at the point of the sword."[37]

General John B. Clark soon arrived in Far West and ratified what General Lucas had done. He acted vigorously to make the Mormons feel the hopelessness of the situation. He stationed guards around Far West and did not allow the inhabitants to leave for any errands or purpose whatsoever.[38] Fuel and food were scarce, and the hungry Mormons were forced to live on parched corn. The Mormons from Dewitt had also arrived in Far West and were in temporary shelter as best they could find. Meanwhile, the militia were foraging liberally upon the Mormons crops and livestock and destroying their property.[39]

After a few days, General Clark relaxed the restraints and allowed the Mormons to go out for wood and provisions. He then assembled the Mormons on the temple square and delivered a written speech. He told the suffering Mormons he would not force them out of the state in the depths of winter and emphasized how lenient he was being. He explained:

> For this [leniency] you are indebted to my clemency. I do not say that you shall go now, but you must not think of staying here another season, or of putting in crops. . . As for your leaders, do not once think—do not imagine for one moment—do not let it enter your mind that they will be delivered, or that you will see their faces again, for their fate is fixed—their die is cast—their doom is sealed.[40]

William Draper wrote this account of General Clark's advice:

> Now men, I will say that you have thus far complied the treaty as made with you leaders by giving up arms and deeding over your property to pay the expenses of this war which you have been the instigators of, and I think you must feel as though you have been dealt very leniently with, as our orders were to exterminate you all without discrimination. But as you have thus far complied with the treaty, you will now be let to go to carry out the rest of it's stipulations, which are to leave the state of Missouri by planting time in the spring or be exterminated or driven out at the point of the bayonet or rifle and one of the two things must and will be done. . . .
>
> I will now give you a piece of good advice; when you are discharged go to and provide for the wants of your families and make speedy preparations to leave this state and hunt a place wherever you can and scatter about like other people and never gather together again in companies not even of ten under presidents, prophets, or bishops and apostles, to govern you, if you do you will bring down the wrath of a just people upon you as you have heretofore done.[41]

Brigham Young sat nearby, and Clark's forces were not able to recognize him, even though they were looking for him. He spoke of the experience:

> I sat close by him, although I was the very particular one they wanted to get and were inquiring for; but as kind Providence would have it they could not tell whether it was Brigham Young they were looking at or somebody else. No matter how this was done, they could not tell. But, standing close by General Clark, I heard him say, "You are the best and most orderly people in this State, and have done more to improve it in three years than we have in fifteen. You have showed us how to improve, how to raise fruit and wheat, how to make gardens, orchards and so on; and on these accounts we want

you; but we have this to say to you, No more bishops, no more high councils, and as for your prophet," and he pointed down to where Joseph lay, right in the midst of the camp, "you will never see him again." Said I to myself, "May be so and may be not; but I do not believe a word of it."[42]

Far West Under Siege

The Mormons recorded many instances of misconduct by the militia during the siege of Far West. The militia searched the Mormons' homes and took property. There were many allegations of plunder and several of rape. The extent to which the militia acted under orders from the governor or their militia leaders is difficult to determine. Undoubtedly, there were some troops and officers who attempted to be impartial and conducted themselves in a fair manner. However, others appeared to use the situation to steal and plunder to any extent they could. John Corrill discussed the issue of misconduct in his account to the Missouri legislature:

> During this campaign, many reports were circulated concerning the misconduct of the soldiers, but how far they were true I am not able to say, but I thought at the time, the officers tried to keep good order among the troops, and that whatever abuse was practiced on the Mormons ought to have been charged on the individuals that did it, and not upon the officers or community at large. It was said that women were insulted and even ravished, but I doubt the truth of the latter. Some were insulted; yet, as soon as the officers were informed, they set guards to prevent further insult. Two men that were taken prisoners were struck on the head, one was badly hurt and the other killed. The man who killed him accused him of having abused his family and burned his house; but on returning home he found his house had not been burned at all. Why he was not committed for trial, I never knew. Many others were taken prisoners, but generally were well treated and set free without injury. There was much corn, cattle, fodder, etc., used for the army, but the officers said the state would pay for it. There were some instances of soldiers shooting cattle, hogs and sheep, merely for sport, when they did not want them for food, but this, I understood, was contrary to the officers orders. There were also several cases in which persons were plundered of horses and other property, even clothing and furniture out of houses, by the soldiers, but they alleged that they were looking after and getting their property back which had been taken from them. I have been told that the same has been practiced, more or less, by companies passing through the county, since the troops

have been withdrawn. Others, to whom they were indebted, have taken their property for debts, until they are literally stripped, and are at this time in a miserable, destitute situation.[43]

Many Mormons recorded their experiences during the siege of Far West. One such account, by Joseph Holbrook, typical of many, is included here:

> The mob or militia burned my house, stole a valuable horse from me, killed my fat hogs and drove off my stock. I had some 300 bushels of corn taken from the crib; they . . . destroyed my hay and left everything in a state of desolation from one side of the country to the other. [They] abused our sisters whenever they thought it best to suit their brutal and hellish desires.
>
> November 4, 1838, [we had] a severe snowstorm and some very cold weather for some three weeks, which drove the troops out of the county except some few companies who said they were left to see that the Mormons left the state and also to continue to take the brethren prisoners. Thus my freedom and my life for three months were in constant danger as one old resident by the name of "Snodgrass" came with eight soldiers at one time to the house where I had been stopping a few days and made diligent search for me in every house in the neighborhood from top to bottom and swore they would take me to the battle-ground on Crooked River and there shoot me.
>
> My wife had very poor health during the fall and winter by being exposed much to the inclement weather by having to remove from place to place as our house had been burned and we were yet left to seek a home wherever our friends could accommodate us and for my safety but as I cannot write one hundredth part of the suffering and destruction of this people who were in a flourishing condition a few months before but were now destitute. I could have commanded some $2,000.00 but now I had only one yoke of oxen and two cows left.[44]

The Mormons continued to endure many sufferings during the few months after the surrender of Far West. Michael Arthur, who resided in Clay County and had been a friend of the Mormons for several years, described the conditions in a letter to the delegation from Clay County in the Missouri General Assembly, then in session, dated November 29, 1838. Excerpts are as follows:

> Humanity to an injured people prompts me at present to address you this. You were aware of the treatment to some extent before you

left home, received by that unfortunate race of beings called Mormons, from devils in the form of human beings; inhabiting Daviess, Livingston and part of Ray Counties.

Not being satisfied with a relinquishment of their rights, as citizens and human beings, in the treaty forced upon them by General Lucas, of giving up their arms and throwing themselves upon the mercy of the State and their fellow citizens generally (hoping thereby to gain protection of their lives and property); they are now receiving treatment from those demons which makes humanity shudder, and the cold chills run over any man not entirely destitute of humanity.

These demons are now strolling up and down Caldwell County in small companies armed, insulting the women in any and every way, and plundering the Mormons of all the means of sustenance (scanty as it was) left them, driving off their cattle, horses, hogs, etc., and rifling their houses and farms of everything thereon; taking beds, bedding, wardrobes, and such things as they see they want—leaving the Mormons in a starving and naked condition. These are facts I have from authority that cannot be questioned, and can be maintained and substantiated at any time.[45]

During the siege of Far West, many of the Mormon women were left alone because their husbands had been arrested or had left the state for their personal safety. Nancy Tracy's account is typical of the suffering endured by so many:

I had my door open and looked out upon the scene as the army marched into the city. As I lay in my bed sick, I thought the end of them would never come. They stationed one company near my house and there camped. I was alone except for my little children. My husband had to leave, for all those who were in the Crooked River battle were being hunted for by the soldiers. So I was at their mercy. Still they assured me that I would not be molested. However, they searched the premises and put a double guard around my house. So I was a prisoner in my own home with no one to care for me but my little boy. Everyone had all he could do to look out for his own. It was a trying time indeed! The brethren that were in the battle of Crooked River had all left for parts unknown except my husband and Brother Holbrook. Brother Holbrook had been wounded in the fight, but he played he was a sick woman in bed so nicely that he was not detected although the house was searched well. My husband had, by a narrow escape, managed to evade the soldiers and was still hidden in the city.

When the General had everything fixed and had our people tied in every way, he called off the army and told them to go to their homes, but to hold themselves in readiness if they should be called again in case the Mormons did not comply with all the requirements asked. So they dispersed. Now there was nothing to do but go to work and prepare to leave after sacrificing everything. I had my last shake of the ague and fever which lasted two hours. After that I began to get better, but while the attack lasted it was severe. I thought that every bone in my body would come out. I was so thankful when it was over.

We soon moved back to our farm where wood was plentiful for the winter, but the Missourians, were prowling around. So we moved in with a neighbor close by and made what preparations we could in our poverty for our exit in the spring.[46]

In 1839, after they were somewhat settled in Illinois, several hundred Mormons prepared redress petitions or claims for the damages to person and property that they incurred in the state of Missouri, both at this time and earlier in Jackson County. The petitions were presented to the U.S. government in an attempt to obtain relief for the Missouri persecutions. However, the U.S. government never intervened on behalf of the Mormons. These various petitions and claims are generally referred to collectively as the Mormon Redress Petitions and are available from various sources for review.[47]

The Mormons Surrender and Evacuate Diahman

On November 7, General Clark sent General Wilson with militia forces to Adam-ondi-Ahman "to disarm the Mormon forces there."[48] On November 8, 1838, the Mormons there were forced to surrender their arms, and they were allowed ten days to move to Far West, and from there to leave the state. Thus, Adam-ondi-Ahman was abandoned.

One Church member, Daniel McArthur, recorded the surrender:

We were marched along side a fence and ten men of us were dropped in a corner of the fence in several places until we were all distributed, and then they placed six of the mob over each mess of us until all were supplied with a guard, and from this guard the Saints received all kinds of abuse, some had the guns of the mob cocked and muzzle placed at their breasts with a threat from the mob that they would make two holes through them quicker than God Almighty could make them.[49]

While they had us confined in this kind of a way, the balance of the mob was ransacking the Saints' houses, barns, stables and fields, stealing all they could lay their hands on. They would break locks to barns and take every horse they could find. After they had kept us under guard from noon until night, they then placed a guard around the city and released us to go to our homes after they had stolen all that they could lay their hands upon. The mob took up their camp quarters in the city and stayed several days, and while in camp they made it a practice to shoot down all the hogs that came by their camps, also oxen and cows. I saw them load their gun and shoot at a four-year-old steer and break his hind leg and then stand and shout and holler like so many savages, notwithstanding in the time they had made a bull pen and caused us to go into it and then had a platform made for us to go up one by one and sign away all our property to them to defray the expenses they might be put to by exterminating us from the state in case we were not out of the state in ninety days, for that was the set time for us to be out of the state, and at the same time, shooting down all the oxen they could get at and doing all they could to prevent us from getting out of the state at the set time.[50]

The Diahman Mormons evacuated that city and moved south twenty-five or so miles to Far West, waiting for spring to arrive, which was the appointed time they were to leave the state. Some lived in tents; others made temporary arrangements. William Cahoon made this affidavit of his experience, which was typical of many of the Mormons:

> I was residing in Daviess County, Missouri, and while away from home I was taken a prisoner in Far West by the Militia, and kept under guard for six or eight days, in which time I was forced to sign a Deed of Trust, after which I was permitted to return home to my family in Daviess County, and found them surrounded by an armed force, with the rest of my neighbors, who were much frightened. The order from the militia was to leave the county within ten days, in which time my house was broken open and many goods taken out by the militia. We were not permitted to go from place to place without a pass from the general, and on leaving the county, I received a pass . . . to pass from Daviess to Caldwell County, and there remain during the winter, and thence to pass out of the state of Missouri. . . During this time, both myself and my family suffered much on account of cold and hunger because we were not permitted to go outside of the guard to obtain wood and provisions.[51]

A committee of twenty-four men was established for the purpose of disposing of the property of the Mormons in Daviess County, including land, stock, and grain. Of this group twelve were Mormons and twelve were not. The Mormons were allowed three months, although it was winter, to collect their stock and grain and get out of the county. William Huntington, who was one of the Mormon committee members, wrote that "no other Mormon was to come into the county upon penalty of death."[52] He also recorded:

> We immediately organized, myself acting as foreman. We labored in the county four weeks, collected many of our cattle, horses, sheep, wagons and other property. Ascertained where the fields of corn were belonging to the brethren, the number of acres and the amount of bushels of corn, as near as we could calculate, which amounted to 29,465 bushels, we lost. We hauled some out in the four weeks we were permitted to do business in the county. Though we were by our permit allowed the privilege of doing business during the winter, at the expiration of one month, we were ordered out of the county as our lives would not be safe. Accordingly, we closed up all business and left at the expiration of the time. I saw the last Mormon out of Diahman the morning I left the county.[53]

Some Missourians Were Friendly to the Mormons

Many Missourians were either neutral in these battles or friendly to the Mormons. However, befriending the Mormons, or extending sympathies to them, potentially had its own perils. For instance, John Butler had a non-Mormon friend named Nathan who would not volunteer to fight the Mormons, so the militia drafted him. He said, "I have never done the Mormons any harm and they will not do me any harm. . . . They had forced him to come to fight them, but they could not force him to shoot and he was going home in the morning." Nathan left the militia and visited the Butlers in Far West, but the militia came after him three or four hours later. He refused to go with them and spent the night with the Butlers. He had his breakfast in the morning and told the Butlers that if the militia drove the Mormons away, his house would be a home for them as long as they had a mind to stay. He wished them good luck and started out, not back to the militia camp but back to his own home.[54]

Oliver Huntington wrote that a young man named Ezekiel Megin stood up for the Mormons before the surrender at Diahman:

> [D]ressed up as nice as possible, with white gloves and white hat; he made a fine appearance, which attracted some considerable attention from the mob (I say mob because I consider all their proceed-

ings according to mob law although, acting under executive authority) insomuch that they began to talk to him for being a Mormon and for not leaving them, that he was too [fine] a looking man to be there and already a home was provided for him; when to their astonishment they found he was not a member of the society; and . . . he must leave; but he stood for the Mormons declaring he never wished to live with better people. This little occurrence gave a great many quite favorable opinion the Mormons, and opened the eyes of others to look for themselves."[55]

Joseph Preaches a Sermon in Jackson County

Joseph Smith and the prisoners with him—Sidney Rigdon, Hyrum Smith, Parley P. Pratt, Lyman Wight, Amasa Lyman, and George W. Robinson—were first taken to the camp of the militia and then to Independence in Jackson County. While en route, they discovered that General Clark had sent an express to order General Lucas to bring the prisoners to him at Richmond. However, Lucas and his troops wanted to exhibit the Mormon prisoners in the streets of Independence, so they went ahead.

Upon reaching Independence on Sunday, November 4, some local citizens visited Joseph's group. One of the women asked the troops which of the prisoners was the Lord whom the Mormons worshiped. One of the guards pointed to Joseph. The woman then turned to Joseph Smith and inquired whether he professed to be the Lord and Savior. Joseph replied:

> I professed to be nothing but a man, and a minister of salvation, sent by Jesus Christ to preach the Gospel. This answer so surprised the woman that she began to inquire into our doctrine, and I preached a discourse, both to her and her companions, and to the wondering soldiers, who listened with almost breathless attention while I set forth the doctrine of faith in Jesus Christ, and repentance, and baptism for remission of sins, with the promise of the Holy Ghost, as recorded in the second chapter of the Acts of the Apostles. The woman was satisfied, and praised God in the hearing of the soldiers, and went away, praying that God would protect and deliver us. Thus was fulfilled a prophecy which had been spoken publicly by me, a few months previous—that a sermon should be preached in Jackson county by one of our Elders, before the close of 1838."[56]

Mormon Prisoners

At about the same time that Joseph Smith and other leaders were arrested, another forty-seven Mormon men were arrested at Far West and marched to the Richmond jail and put under guard.[57] Richmond was the county seat for Ray County, where the Battle of Crooked River occurred. At Richmond, they guarded the prisoners, put seven of them (the leaders) in irons, and held a court of inquiry before Judge King; after which they retained thirty-six for trial and let the rest go free. Those retained for trial were charged with various crimes—treason, murder, arson, burglary, and larceny.[58]

One night during this incarceration at Richmond, Joseph Smith powerfully rebuked the prison guards as recorded by fellow prisoner Parley P. Pratt:

> In one of those tedious nights we had lain as if in sleep till the hour of midnight had passed, and our ears and hearts had been pained. We had listened for hours to the obscene jests, the horrid oaths, the dreadful blasphemies and filthy language of our guards, Colonel Price at their head, as they recounted to each other their deeds of rapine, murder, robbery, etc., which they had committed among the Mormons while at Far West and vicinity. They even boasted of defiling by force wives, daughters and virgins, and of shooting or dashing out the brains of men, women and children.
>
> I had listened till I became so disgusted, shocked, horrified, and so filled with the spirit of indignant justice, that I could scarcely refrain from rising upon my feet and rebuking the guards, but I had said nothing to Joseph or anyone else, although I lay next to him, and knew he was awake. On a sudden he arose to his feet and spoke in a voice of thunder, or as the roaring lion, uttering, as near as I can recollect, the following words:
>
> "Silence! Ye fiends of the infernal pit! In the name of Jesus Christ I rebuke you, and command you to be still. I will not live another minute and hear such language. Cease such talk, or you or I die this instant!"
>
> He ceased to speak. He stood erect in terrible majesty. Chained, and without a Weapon, calm, unruffled, and dignified as an angel, he looked down upon his quailing guards, whose knees smote together, and who, shrinking into a corner, or crouching at his feet, begged his pardon, and remained quiet until an exchange of guards.
>
> I have seen ministers of justice, clothed in ministerial robes, and criminals arraigned before them, while life was suspended upon a breath in the courts of England; I have witnessed a congress in solemn

session to give laws to nations; I have tried to conceive of kings, of royal courts, of thrones and crowns; and of emperors assembled to decide the fate of kingdoms; but dignity and majesty have I seen but once, as it stood in chains, at midnight, in a dungeon, in an obscure village of Missouri.[59]

One of the arrested prisoners, Ebeneezer Robinson, recorded some of the experiences and sufferings of the prisoners:

> Tuesday November 6, we started for Richmond, under a strong guard mounted; we, the prisoners, walked about thirteen miles, when they camped for the night. Having had no dinner, we felt the want of food. The officers of the army having made no preparation for us, our only resort was to get ears of corn, which had been provided for the horses, and roast them in the fire, and eat, which the writer and others did, and we confess it proved a sweet and delicious repast.[60]

> [At Richmond] two three-pail iron kettles for boiling our meat, and two or more iron bake kettles, or Dutch ovens, for baking our corn bread in, were furnished us, together with sacks of cornmeal and meat in the bulk. We did our own cooking. This arrangement suited us very well, and we enjoyed ourselves as well as men could under similar circumstances. We spread our blankets upon the floor at night for our beds, and before retiring, we sang an hymn and had prayers, and practiced the same each morning before breakfast.

> The soldiers inside the building usually gave good attention during these devotions. Some of them were heard to tell other soldiers to come and hear these Mormons sing, for, said they: "They have composed some of the d——dst prettiest songs about Diahman [Adam-ondi-Ahman] you ever heard in your life."

> Some of the guards, however, at times, were very rude in speech and actions. One was heard to cry out to another: "Shoot your Mormon, I have shot mine." From this we concluded he helped compose the mob that committed that brutal, unhuman massacre at Haun's Mill.[61]

Court convened on November 13, with Austin A. King on the bench and Thomas C. Burch, the state's attorney. The Mormon prisoners were charged with high treason against the state, murder, burglary, arson, robbery, and larceny. The charge of murder was made on account of the militia member that was killed in the Battle of Crooked River. Fortunately, most of the Mormon men who had participated in that battle had left the state by then. Ebeneezer Robinson described this experience:

> After the trial had progressed a few days, we understood the judge to say that "nothing but hanging would answer the law," thinking perhaps, from the testimony, that we were all guilty of treason. On another occasion we understood him to say, speaking of the prisoners, that, "if they would deny the Book of Mormon they might go clear." These things were talked over among the prisoners, but not one of our number would accept of freedom upon such unholy terms, notwithstanding it might possibly save them from the gallows. In view of these things, when we were seriously contemplating the worst, judge of our happy surprise when, on Saturday, the 24th, the judge issued [an ordering freeing most of the brethren.][62]

The court continued in session for a few days, and then most of the prisoners were discharged on bail. They raised the bail money by bailing each other out. They were able to return to their homes in Far West and join their families to prepare to leave the state.

During the investigation, the Mormon prisoners "were mostly confined in chains and received much abuse."[63] Further, the legal proceedings before Judge King were a one-sided affair. Judge King had sat on the court martial with General Lucas at Far West when the decision was made to execute Joseph Smith and others, and the Mormon witnesses were generally treated badly and intimidated to such an extent it was considered useless to attempt to make an extended defense. Ebenezer Robinson wrote:

> The matter of driving away witnesses or casting them into prison, or chasing them out of the country, was carried to such a length, that our lawyers, General Doniphan and Amos Rees, told us not to bring our witnesses there at all; for if we did there would not be one of them left for final trial; for no sooner would Bogart and his men know who they were, than they would put them out of the country.
>
> As to making any impression on King, if a cohort of angels were to come down, and declared we were clear, Doniphan said it would all be the same; for he (King) had determined from the beginning to cast us into prison. We never got the privilege of introducing our witnesses at all; if we had, we could have disproved all they swore.[64]

As a result of the preliminary hearings before Judge King, eleven men were retained in prison, without bail, to stand trial. Six of them—Joseph Smith, Lyman Wight, Caleb Baldwin, Hyrum Smith, Alexander McRae, and Sidney Rigdon—were sent to jail at Liberty, Clay County, to stand trial for the alleged retaliatory actions allegedly taken by Mormon men in

Daviess County. Since Daviess County did not have a jail, the prisoners were held in the jail at Liberty, Clay County. In addition, Parley P. Pratt, Morris Phelps, Luman Gibbs, Darwin Chase, and Norman Shearer were put into Richmond Jail to stand trial for alleged crimes committed at the Battle of Crooked River.

None of the men ever stood trial, although they were held in prison for several months. Of the five held in Richmond, a grand jury dismissed the charges against Darwin Chase and Norman Shearer on April 24, 1839. King Follett was then arrested, however, and taken to the jail with the others. The four prisoners were granted a change of venue and taken to Columbia, Boone County, on May 22, 1839, in a grueling trip that took five days in heavy rain. From the jail in Boone County, Phelps and Pratt escaped on July 4, 1839, and made their way to Illinois. King Follett was recaptured and the last to be released. Luman Gibbs denied the faith and was released.[65]

Of the men held at Liberty Jail, Sidney Rigdon was first released due to poor health in January 1839. Joseph Smith, Hyrum Smith, Lyman Wight, Alexander McRae, and Caleb Baldwin were held prisoners for several months until April 1839. More is written of their experience in the next chapter.

Notes

1. Ward, *History of Caldwell County*, 133.
2. Philo Dibble Autobiography, in *Faith Promoting Classics*, 89.
3. William Cary and his family had arrived in the Far West area from Ohio just a few days previous to this incident. He had a wife and several small children. See "Hyrum Smith Testimony Sworn Before Nauvoo Municipal Court," in Johnson, *Mormon Redress Petitions*, 626.
4. Ward, *History of Caldwell County*, 133–34.
5. Governor Boggs was personally acquainted with Mary Elizabeth Rollins Lightner, who had worked as his seamstress when the Mormons were in Independence.
6. Baugh, *A Call to Arms*, 139, quoting *Items* from Charles C. Rich, LDS Archives, Salt Lake City, Utah, Box 3, manuscript. Also, Charles C. Rich, *Mormon Redress Petitions*, 328.
7. Baugh, *A Call to Arms*, 139.
8. Corrill, *History of the Mormons*, 40.
9. Draper Autobiography, 10.
10. Corrill, *History of the Mormons*, 40.
11. Autobiography of Edward Stevenson, 102–103.
12. Ward, *History of Caldwell County*, 134; "Hyrum Smith Testimony," in Johnson, *Mormon Redress Petitions*, 626–27.
13. Corrill, *History of the Mormons*, 40–41.
14. Baugh, *A Call to Arms*, 135.

15. *History of the Church*, vol. 3, 201.

16. Baugh, *A Call to Arms*, 140. Four of the five Mormon men were members of the Caldwell militia. John Corrill was not but was the elected representative to the state legislature from Caldwell County.

17. Corrill, *History of the Mormons*, 42.

18. *History of the Church*, 3:188.

19. Baugh, *A Call to Arms*, 141.

20. Lyman Wight petition in Johnson, *Mormon Redress Petitions*, 660; also in *History of the Church*, 3:445.

21. Corrill, *History of the Mormons*, 42.

22. *History of the Church*, 3:188–90.

23. *Autobiography of Parley P. Pratt*, 186–87.

24. Sidney Rigdon, *Mormon Redress Petitions*, 675.

25. Jesse, *Personal Writings of Joseph Smith*, letter to Emma Smith, 4 Nov. 1838, 399.

26. Baugh, *A Call to Arms*, 149, quoting George M. Hinkle letter to W. W. Phelps, 14 August 1844, published in *Journal History* 13:451 (Oct. 1920).

27. *Autobiography of Edward Stevenson*, 104–05.

28. Letter from Phebe Adams Hancock, typescript, family resources.

29. *History of the Church*, vol. 3, 190. Some accounts indicate that seventeen preachers sat on the court martial and approved the decision to execute the men. See Johnson, *Mormon Redress Petitions*, 407.

30. *History of the Church*, vol. 3, 190–91.

31. Ibid., 414.

32. Ibid., 190–91.

33. Ibid., 192.

34. Ibid., 414.

35. Ibid.,193–95.

36. "The Memoirs of President Joseph Smith," *The Saints Herald*, Nov. 6, 1884.

37. Pettigrew, *An Enduring Legacy*, 3:205.

38. Ward, *History of Caldwell County*, 140; Corrill, *History of the Mormons*, 43.

39. Ward, *History of Caldwell County*, 140; *History of the Church*, vol. 3, 202.

40. *History of the Church*, 3:203.

41. William Draper Autobiography, 15–16.

42. *Journal of Discourses*, 14:206–207.

43. Corrill, *History of the Mormons*, 43–44.

44. Joseph Holbrook Autobiography, 46.

45. See *Parley P. Pratt Autobiography* (1985 ed), 244.

46. Nancy Tracy Autobiography, 20–22.

47. Johnson, *Mormon Redress Petitions*.

48. *History of the Church*, 3:204.

49. Daniel McArthur Autobiography, 9–10.

50. Ibid.

51. Autobiography, in *Reynolds Cahoon and Sons*, 86.

52. William Huntington Autobiography, 6–7. The Mormons appointed to this committee in addition to William Huntington were William Earl, Elijah Gaylor, William Hale, Henry Herriman, Mayhew Hillman, Henry Humphrey, John Reed, Oliver Snow, Daniel Stanton, Benjamin Wilbur, and Z. Wilson (*History of the Church*, 3:210).

53. William Huntington Autobiography, 7.

54. John Butler Autobiography, 14–15.

55. Oliver Huntington Autobiography, 36.

56. *History of the Church*, 3:201.

57. *History of the Church*, 3:209. In addition to the Prophet and others who had previously been arrested, the *History of the Church* lists the following men as having been arrested at this time: Caleb Baldwin, Alanson Ripley, Washington Voorhees, Sidney Tanner, John Buchanan, Jacob Gates, Chandler Holbrook, George W. Harris, Jesse D. Hunter, Andrew Whitlock, Martin C. Allred, William Allred, George D. Grant, Darwin Chase, Elijah Newman, Alvin G. Tippets, Zedekiah Owens, Isaac Morley, Thomas Beck, Moses Clawson, John T. Tanner, Daniel Shearer, Daniel S. Thomas, Alexander McRea, Elisha Edwards, John S. Higbee, Ebenezer Page, Benjamin Covey, Ebenezer Robinson, Luman Gibbs, James M. Henderson, David Pettigrew, Edward Partridge, Francis Higbee, David Frampton, George Kimball, Joseph W. Younger, Henry Zabriski, Allen J. Stout, Sheffield Daniels, Silas Maynard, Anthony Head, Benjamin Jones, Daniel Carn, John T. Earl, and Norman Shearer. (See also Ebeneezer Robinson, *The Return 2*, 234).

58. Corrill, *History of the Mormons*, 43.

59. *Autobiography of Parley P. Pratt*, 210–11. (Spelling and grammar have been modernized.)

60. Ebenezer Robinson, *The Return* (February 1890), 212.

61. Ibid. (March 1890), 234.

62. Ibid.

63. Ibid., 236.

64. Ibid.

65. *Autobiography of Parley P. Pratt*, 201.

Chapter 14

LIBERTY JAIL

THE IMPRISONMENT OF JOSEPH SMITH, Hyrum Smith, Sidney Rigdon, Lyman Wight, Alexander McRae, and Caleb Baldwin in Liberty Jail from November 1838 to April 1839 forever marks Liberty, Missouri, as a significant place in Church history.

The outer walls of Liberty Jail were constructed of stone two feet thick, and the inner walls and ceilings were hewn oak logs, about a square foot. There was about a foot of space between the outside masonry walls and the inside oak walls, and this space and the space above the ceiling was filled with loose rock to make escape virtually impossible. The only openings in the lower level were two iron barred windows, two feet wide and six inches high, and an opening in the ceiling to the upper room with a heavy wooden door.

Elder Lyman O. Littlefield, who at that time was learning the trade of a printer in the town of Liberty, witnessed the arrival of the prisoners:

> It was the privilege of the writer—if it may be called such—to witness their entrance into the place. They, of course, traveled upon the main road leading from Richmond, and entered the town of Liberty on the east. They were all in one large, heavy wagon with a high box, which, as they were seated, hid from view all of their forms, except from a little below the shoulders. They passed through the centre of the town, across the public square, in the centre of which stood the court-house. After crossing this square the wagon containing them was driven up the street northward about the distance of two blocks, where, at the left hand side of the street, was a vacant piece of ground, upon which, close to the street, stood the Liberty jail, ever to be rendered

famous by the entrance into it of these illustrious prisoners. * * * The inhabitants of Liberty, and many from the surrounding country, were out to witness the entrance of the prisoners into the place, and many, on that occasion, in my hearing, expressed their disappointment that the strangers should so much resemble all other men of prepossessing appearance.

This large, clumsy built wagon—the box of which was highest at each end—finally halted close to the platform in front of the jail, which platform had to be reached by means of about a half a dozen steps, constructed on the south and north sides of the same. The jail fronted the street at the east.

The prisoners left the wagon and immediately ascended the south steps to the platform, around which no banisters were constructed. The door was open and, one by one, the tall and well proportioned forms of the prisoners entered. The Prophet Joseph was the last of the number who lingered behind. He turned partly around, with a slow and dignified movement, and looked upon the multitude. Then turning away, and lifting his hat, he said, in a distinct voice, 'Good afternoon, gentlemen.' The next moment he had passed out of sight. The heavy door swung upon its strong hinges, and the Prophet was hid from the gaze of the curious populace who had so eagerly watched.

Because Joseph used the term 'good afternoon,' some of the people became excited and made various threats. The custom of a Missourian would have been to say 'good evening.' They thought his expression implied a covert meaning that he should make his escape before morning. Joseph being an eastern man, expressed himself after the custom of the eastern people. Finally the excitement subsided, the people dispersed and the prisoners were left to seek the best rest their hard, dark, and cheerless prison quarters might afford them."[1]

Food was scanty, of poor quality, and, at times, poisoned. Some of the prisoners suspected that they were sometimes fed human flesh. Fortunately, several Church members were able to bring them wholesome food in spite of the many persecutions the Church was facing during the time. The prisoners were incarcerated during the coldest Missouri months, and they were forced to sleep on the cold stone floor with only a bit of loose straw for comfort. They suffered from the intense cold and exposure because the "windows" did not have glass, only bars that let in the cold air.

Prescindia Huntington described a visit she took with her father, Heber C. Kimball, and Alanson Ripley to Liberty Jail in February 1839:

When we arrived at the jail we found a heavy guard outside and inside the door. We were watched very closely, lest we should leave tools to help the prisoners escape. I took dinner with the brethren in prison; they were much pleased to see the faces of true friends; but I cannot describe my feelings on seeing that man of God there confined in such a trying time for the Saints, when his counsel was so much needed. And we were obliged to leave them in that horrid prison, surrounded by a wicked mob.[2]

Alexander MacRae, one of the prisoners, wrote about his experience in Liberty Jail:

During our imprisonment, we had many visitors, both friends and enemies. Among the latter, many were angry with Brother Joseph, and accused him of killing a son, a brother, or some relative of theirs, at what was called the Crooked River Battle. This looked rather strange to me, that so many should claim a son, or a brother killed there, when they reported only one man killed.[3]

Among our friends who visited us, were Presidents Brigham Young and Heber C. Kimball . . . , George A. Smith . . . , Don C. Smith, brother of Joseph, came several times, and brought some of our families to see us. Benjamin Covey . . . brought each of us a new pair of boots, and made us a present of them. James Sloan, his wife and daughter, came several times. Alanson Ripley also visited us, and many others, whom to name would be too tedious. Orin P. Rockwell brought us refreshments many times; and Jane Bleven and her daughter brought cakes, pies, etc., and handed them in at the window. These things helped us much, as our food was very coarse, and so filthy that we could not eat it until we were driven to it by hunger...

Sometime during our stay in Liberty jail an attempt was made to destroy us by poison. I supposed it was administered in either tea or coffee, but as I did not use either, I escaped unhurt, while all who did were sorely afflicted, some being blind two or three days, and it was only by much faith and prayer that the effect was overcome.[4]

With her husband imprisoned in Liberty Jail, Emma Smith and her children were among the Latter-day Saints who made their way across northern Missouri to Quincy, Illinois, in the winter of 1839. This experience was vivid in her mind when she wrote to Joseph on March 7, 1839:

I shall not attempt to write my feelings altogether, for the situation in which you are, the walls, bars, and bolts, rolling rivers, running streams, rising hills, sinking valleys and spreading prairies that separate us, and the cruel injustice that first cast you into prison and still holds you there, with many other considerations, places my feelings far beyond description. Was it not for conscious innocence, and the direct interposition of divine mercy, I am very sure I never should have been able to have endured the scenes of suffering that I have passed through, since what is called the Militia, came into Far West, under the ever to be remembered Governor's notable order.

We are all well at present, except Frederick, who is quite sick. Little Alexander who is now in my arms is one of the finest little fellows you ever saw in your life, he is so strong that with the assistance of a chair he will run all round the room. . . . No one but God, knows the reflections of my mind and the feelings of my heart when I left our house and home, and almost all of every thing that we possessed excepting our little children, and took my journey out of the State of Missouri, leaving you shut up in that lonesome prison. But the recollection is more than human nature ought to bear. . . .[5]

In response, Joseph wrote to Emma from Liberty Jail in a letter dated March 21, 1839:

Affectionate wife. . . . I want to be with you very much but the powers of mobocracy is too many for me at [present]. . . . I shall have a little money left when I come. My dear Emma, I very well know your toils and sympathize with you. If God will spare my life once more to have the privilege of taking care of you I will ease your care and endeavor to comfort your heart. I want you to take the best care of the family you can which I believe you will do. I was sorry to learn that Frederick was sick but I trust he is well again and that you are all well. I want you to try to gain time and write to me a long letter and tell me all you can and if the old major [their dog] is alive yet and what those little prattlers say that cling around your neck. Do you tell them I am in prison that their lives might be spared?

I want all the church to make a bill of damages and apply to the United States court if possible. However, they will find out what can be done themselves. You expressed feelings concerning the order and I believe that there is a way to get redress for such things but God ruleth all things after the council of his own will. My trust is in him. The salvation of my soul is of the most importance to me, for as much as I know for a certainty of eternal things, if the heavens linger, it is nothing to me. I must steer my bark safe, which I intend to do. I want you to do the same.

Yours forever,

Joseph Smith

P.S. I want you to have the epistle copied immediately and let it go to the brethren, first into the hands of father, for I want the production for my record. If you lack money for bread do let me know it as soon as possible. My nerves tremble from long confinement but if you feel as I do you don't care for the imperfections of my writing. For my part a word of consolation from any source is cordially received by me. I feel like Joseph in Egypt. "Doth my friends yet live, "if they live do they remember me, have they regard for me? If so, let me know it in time of trouble. My dear Emma, do you think my being cast into prison by the mob renders me less worthy of your friendship. No, I do not think so, but when I was in prison ye visited me."[6]

Presinda Buell visited the inmates, and Joseph Smith wrote a letter thanking her for her kindness. Excerpts are as follows:

I was glad to see you. No tongue can tell what inexpressible Joy it gives a man to see the face of one who has been a friend after having been enclosed in the walls of a prison for five months it seems to me that my heart will always be more tender after this than ever it was before my heart bleeds continually when I contemplate the distress of the Church. Oh that I could be with them I would not shrink at toil and hardship to render them comfort and consolation I want the blessing once more to lift my voice in the midst of the Saints. I would pour out my soul to God for their instruction it has been the plan of the Devil to hamper me and distress me from the beginning to keep me from explaining Myself to them and I never have had opportunity to give them the plan that God has revealed to me—for many have run without being sent, crying tidings my Lord and have done much injury to the Church, giving the Devil more power over those that walk by sight and not by faith.

But trials will only give us that knowledge to understand the minds of the Ancients. For my part I think I never could have felt as I now do if I had not suffered the wrongs that I have suffered; all things shall work together for good to them that love.[7]

While confined and suffering in Liberty Jail, Joseph Smith received answers to his heartfelt prayers and was comforted and instructed. He wrote a letter in March of 1839 to the "Church of the Latter-day Saints at Quincy, Illinois, and Scattered Abroad, and to Bishop Partridge in Particular." By that time, Far West was nearly abandoned and many Mormons had relocated to the vicinity of Quincy, Illinois. Portions of these letters are incorporated into the Doctrine and Covenants sections 121–23, as discussed in more detail in the chapter entitled "Church Governance and Revelations."

Sometime during April 1839, the prisoners, except for Sidney Rigdon, who was released because of ill health, were transported to Gallatin, Daviess County, for trial. The prisoners were weak because of their long confinement but glad to breathe fresh air again. Hyrum Smith described the difficult experiences the prisoners had there:

> Some time in April we were taken to Daviess county, as they said, to have a trial. But when we arrived at that place, instead of finding a court or jury, we found another inquisition; and Birch, who was the district attorney, the same man who had been one of the court-martial when we were sentenced to death, was now the circuit judge of that pretended court; and the grand jury that were empanelled were all at the massacre at Haun's Mills and lively actors in that awful, solemn, disgraceful, cool-blooded murder; and all the pretense they made of excuse was, they had done it because the governor ordered them to do it.
>
> The same men sat as a jury in the day time, and were placed over us as a guard in the night time. They tantalized us and boasted of their great achievements at Haun's Mills and at other places, telling us how many houses they had burned, and how many sheep, cattle, and hogs they had driven off belonging to the "Mormons," and how many rapes they had committed, and what squealing and kicking there was among the d—— b——s, saying that they lashed one woman upon one of the damned "Mormon" meeting benches, tying her hands and her feet fast, and sixteen of them abused her as much as they had a mind to, and then left her bound and exposed in that distressed condition. These fiends of the lower regions boasted of these acts of barbarity, and tantalized our feelings with them for ten days. We had heard of these acts of cruelty previous to this time, but we were slow to believe that such acts had been perpetrated. The lady who was the subject of this brutality did not recover her health to be able to help herself for more than three months afterwards."[8]

The prisoners asked for a change of venue to Marion County but were denied; however, they were given one to Boone County. As the prisoners journeyed toward Boone, the guards got drunk and the brethren thought the Lord had presented to them an opportunity to escape. The story of this escape was afterward told by Hyrum Smith as follows:

> They gave us a change of venue from Daviess to Boone county, and a mittimus was made out by the pretended Judge Birch, without date,

name, or place. They (the court officials at Gallatin) fitted us out with a two horse wagon, a horse and four men, besides the sheriff, to be our guard. There were five of us that started from Gallatin, the sun about two hours high, and went as far as Diahman that evening, and stayed till morning. There we bought two horses of the guard, and paid for one of them in our clothing which we had with us, and for the other we gave our note. We went down that day as far as Judge Morin's, a distance of some four or five miles. There we stayed until the next morning, when we started on our journey to Boone county, and traveled on the road about twenty miles distance. There we bought a jug of whisky, with which we treated the company, and while there the sheriff showed us the mittimus before referred to, without date or signature, and said that Judge Birch told him to carry us to Boone county, and never to show the mittimus; and, said he, I shall take a good drink of grog, and go to bed, and you may do as you have a mind to. Three others of the guards drank pretty freely of the whisky, sweetened with honey. They also went to bed, and were soon asleep and the other guard went along with us, and helped to saddle the horses. Two of us mounted the horses, and the others started on foot, and we took our change of venue for the State of Illinois; and in the course of nine or ten days arrived safely at Quincy, Adams County, where we found our families in a state of poverty, although in good health.[9]

Notes

1. Lyman Littlefield Reminiscences, 79–80.
2. Prescindia Huntington Autobiography, in *Women of Mormondom*, 209.
3. It is also noteworthy that Joseph was not a participant in the Battle of Crooked River.
4. Letters of Alexander McRae to the *Deseret News*, Salt Lake City, UT, Oct. 9 and Nov. 1, 1854.
5. Jesse, *Personal Writings of Joseph Smith*, 399.
6. Ibid., 448–49.
7. Ibid., letter to Presendia Buell, 15 Mar 1839, 426–28.
8. Hyrum Smith Testimony, in Johnson, *Mormon Redress Petitions*, 636–37.
9. Ibid., 638.

Chapter 15

THE EXODUS FROM FAR WEST

THE LATTER MONTHS OF 1838 and first few months of 1839 comprised one of the darkest periods in the history of the Church. At this time, Joseph Smith and a number of other Mormon men were imprisoned, and the Prophet was being criticized by some members, as well as apostates. The city of Far West had been plundered by militia-mobs. The Mormons from outlying settlements at Dewitt and Daviess County were in Far West mostly without homes and were living in temporary quarters. The Mormons had been subjected to much abuse and had lost much of their property, and their lives were filled with turmoil as they were compelled to leave within a few months.

The leadership of the Church fell upon Brigham Young and Heber C. Kimball as the senior apostles still in Missouri. Thomas B. Marsh had left the Church, David W. Patten had been killed in October 1838 in the Battle of Crooked River, and the First Presidency was in jail.

Under these difficult circumstances, the Far West High Council met on December 13, 1838, with several apostles. Brigham Young, who was presiding, had called the meeting. One of the purposes of the meeting was to replace brethren who had to flee for their lives and to ordain two new apostles, John E. Page and John Taylor.[1]

During the meeting, the brethren had occasion to stand up for the Prophet Joseph Smith. They expressed their continuing faith in the truthfulness of the gospel and in Joseph as the Prophet and leader of the Church. For example, one high councilor, Solomon Hancock, said, "He is a firm believer in the Book of Mormon and Doctrine and Covenants. . . .

Br. Joseph is not a fallen Prophet, but will yet be exalted and become very high."[2]

Covenant to Assist the Poor

One of the Mormons' concerns was that it was impossible for many of them to leave the state because of their poverty. They simply did not have the necessary means to travel. In many cases, this poverty was caused by the persecution and loss of property they had suffered. To this end, a public meeting was held on January 26, 1839, to discuss these circumstances and how to assist the poor. As a result, 380 people entered a mutual covenant to assist the poor in relocating from the state of Missouri. The covenant was as follows:

> We, whose names are hereunder written, do for ourselves individu-
> ally hereby covenant to stand by and assist one another, to the utmost
> of our abilities, in removing from this state in compliance with the
> authority of the state; and we do hereby acknowledge ourselves firmly
> bound to the extent of all our available property, to be disposed of
> by a committee who shall be appointed for the purpose of providing
> means for the removing from this state of the poor and destitute who
> shall be considered worthy, till there shall not be one left who desires
> to remove from the state: with this proviso, that no individual shall
> be deprived of the right of the disposal of his own property from the
> above purpose, or of having the control of it, or so much of it as shall be
> necessary for the removing of his own family, and to be entitled to the
> over-plus, after the work is effected; and furthermore, said committee
> shall give receipts for all property, and an account of the expenditures
> of the same. Far West Missouri, January 29, 1836.[3]

A committee of seven was appointed to head this initiative. The Church then carried out this directive, and all of the Mormons who wished to go were able to leave the state. "The Church therefore put into the hands of the committee, all their best furniture [and] farming utensils. Many sold their farms, put in the avails in part; others put in money and in consequence of the sale of lands in Jackson County, we were enabled to remove all the poor who had a desire to leave the state of Missouri into the state of Illinois."[4]

The Exodus

The exodus from Far West began in mid-February 1839, during a brief break in the weather. This was earlier than required by General

Clark of the state militia, who was enforcing the governor's extermination order, but the Mormons hoped that once they left, Joseph and the others would be freed from prison. The Mormons traveled east and crossed the Mississippi River into Illinois, near Quincy. It was a journey of more than two hundred miles. The break in the weather was slight, however, and the Mississippi River was frozen and icy by the time many of the Mormons arrived there. The last of the Mormons left Far West on April 20, 1839.[5]

Brigham Young had not been arrested, possibly because of his relatively low profile among the Missourians compared to other leaders, but he soon became a "wanted" Mormon, and, for a time, had to be secretive until he left Missouri in mid-February.[6] Once Brigham Young left, Heber C. Kimball, who was less well known among the locals, remained behind to finish the removal, but before he left in April, Elder Kimball was also forced into hiding during the day and would counsel with other Church leaders only at night.[7]

Brigham Young departed Far West on February 14, 1839, in company with his family and the families of Heber C. Kimball and several others. The journey from Missouri was slow, difficult, and cold. Several times Brigham left his family in camp or at the house of a friendly family and returned with his teams to help others. During one absence their infant daughter was thrown from a wagon and run over. She nevertheless survived. The Young family finally gained refuge in Atlas, Pike County, Illinois, where they remained for several weeks. Before arriving at the temporary Mormon settlement in Quincy in the spring of 1839, Mary Ann Young had kept house in eleven different places.[8]

The other Mormons had similar difficulties in their journeys and experienced great hardships. Anson Call left Far West with his family in the middle of February 1839. He recalled: "The snow was about a foot thick and the weather cold and severe. The first night the wagon tipped over and went into the creek. The next day it was cold and blustering and when night came we were cold and wet. We raised the wagon tongue and put some clothes over it and made our bed underneath. After this, we found tent poles and campfires all the way. We arrived in Palmyra [Missouri] the 3rd day of March."[9]

Daniel McArthur wrote:

> In the month of February, I left the state of Missouri in company with Perry Green Session and family, and were also in company with several other families. When we left Far West, the mob would not give

us but five cents for a bushel of corn, but when we got away a few miles, they charged us 75 cents for a bushel of corn. At this time I was quite destitute for clothing. I was obliged to wear summer clothing through the winter on the account of being on the tramp from the state of Ohio to the state of Missouri, and after arriving in this state, the mob was so hostile I could not get any work to do to earn any clothing, and when I got to Quincy, Illinois, I was almost naked, but when I got here I soon got work and rigged myself out with comfortable clothing.[10]

Warren Foote wrote this account of how they passed the winter and how the Church helped him move from Far West:

> There not being any work going on this winter, my nephew Franklin Allen and myself concluded to build us a hut, and live by ourselves. My niece, Caroline Allen, did our cooking. We had a great many spelling matches and parties in the neighborhood during the winter, and all enjoyed themselves, as well as they could under the circumstances. The mobbers did not allow the Saints to hold meetings but the young would have their amusements. There had been a committee appointed by the Church to gather means from those who had to spare, to assist those who were not able to move themselves out of the state. Stephen Markham was one of that committee. Having lost all of our goods that we sent by water, we had nothing to help ourselves with. Mr. Markham succeeded in getting a team for us, and on the first day of April 1839, my father, George Gates, and wife, and my sister Almira, and myself started for Illinois in company with Mr. Markham's family, and one or two other families. We arrived in Quincy on the 14th.[11]

Some of the Mormons had to leave on short notice out of fear for their personal safety. For instance, David Pettigrew and Edward Partridge left together on news that the Sheriff of Davies County was looking to arrest Mormons who had been released on bail at hearings in Richmond:

> [On] the 19th of January, 1839, . . . we heard the sheriff of Daviess County was about to pay us another visit and we be brought again into greater difficulties perhaps. The counsel, therefore, was for us to leave the state of Missouri immediately. Bishop Partridge sent me word about eleven o'clock at night, informing me that we must be twelve miles from Far West by daylight. I sprang from my bed, put on my clothes, soon had my horses geared up and made ready as fast as I could. I bid my family farewell, commending them to the care of the Almighty God. It was hard parting with them whom I loved so dearly,

but I was forced. I went to Brother Partridge; he was nearly ready and a few minutes after we were under way. It was a cold night, hailing and raining, but we were prospered on our way, and on the next evening found ourselves in Carroll County, sixty-five miles from Far West, and arrived at Quincy, Illinois, in safety, though the weather was extremely cold.[12]

The experience of Nancy Tracy was also difficult, and unfortunately was typical of many. She wrote:

> We started in March, about the middle, I think. Imagine our feelings in leaving our homes and starting out not knowing where we were going and leaving our Prophet and leaders in prison at the mercy of those bold fiends of human shape. Notwithstanding our afflictions, the hand of the Lord was over His people, and they found a place of rest for the season.
>
> . . . We took our march toward the rising sun. It stormed continually. Our outfit for the journey was a meager one. It consisted of one horse attached to the two wheels of a wagon with bed sheets for a cover. The box was seven feet long; so sometimes at night we could make a bed in the cart by taking things out. But we would make our bed outside when the weather would permit. It was tedious traveling. When we got on the Mississippi bottom, it was terrible. It was 9 miles across and took two days to cross. At last we landed in Quincy, Illinois, and found the people very hospitable.[13]

Phebe Hancock wrote of her experience, "I left the State of Missouri in the Spring. I had eight in my family to cook for: Father and Mother Hancock lived with us. Father Hancock [Thomas] was seventy-five years old. We had only one small wagon. I walked every mile to the State of Illinois."[14]

When some of the Mormons arrived at the Mississippi River, it was frozen and difficult to cross. Levi Hancock's family walked on ice across the river but barely made it safely when the ice began to break up close to the shore.[15]

As the ice melted, the ferry began to run again, and most Mormons crossed the river in that manner. However, this was time-consuming since there was only one boat. An account by Elizabeth Haven indicates that in late February, "about 12 families cross the river into Quincy every day and about 30 are constantly at the other side waiting to cross; it is slow and grimy; there is only one ferry boat to cross in."[16]

The Mormons from Missouri settled temporarily in Quincy, Illinois. They began to search for another more permanent place to settle and soon discovered the area known as Commerce, Illinois, which later became Nauvoo.

Thus, Far West and Adam-ondi-Ahman were left abandoned.

Notes

1. *Far West Record*, 221. The men selected for the high council for the meeting were Simeon Carter, Jared Carter, Thomas Grover, David Dort, Levi Jackman, Solomon Hancock, John Badger, John Murdock, John E. Page, George W. Harris, John Taylor, and Samuel Bent.
2. *Far West Record*, 222.
3. *History of the Church*, 3:249–54.
4. William Huntington Autobiography, 8.
5. *History of the Church*, 3:326.
6. Arrington, *Brigham Young: American Moses*, 69.
7. Ibid., 70.
8. Ibid., 70–71.
9. Anson Call Autobiography, 17.
10. Daniel McArthur Autobiography, 10–11.
11. Warren Foote Autobiography, 27–28.
12. David Pettigrew, *An Enduring Legacy*, vol. 3, 207.
13. Nancy Tracy Autobiography, 22–23.
14. History of Phebe Adams Hancock.
15. Mosiah Hancock Autobiography, 17.
16. Letter from Elizabeth Haven (later Barlow) to Elizabeth Howe Bullard, 24 Feb. 1839, quoted in *Church History in the Fulness of Times* (LDS Institute manual), 214.

Chapter 16

THE APOSTLES RETURN
TO FAR WEST

O N APRIL 17, 1839, JUST as the last of the Mormons were leaving Far West, Brigham Young presided over a conference in Quincy, Illinois, at which twenty-one-year-old George A. Smith was sustained as one of the Twelve Apostles. Five of the Twelve then held a council with other Church officials to discuss the question of whether they should return briefly to Missouri to fulfill the revelation directing them to depart for their mission to England from Far West, given in July of 1838. In the revelation, the Lord commanded the Twelve to travel over the "great waters" to preach the gospel. They were to depart for this mission "on the twenty-sixth day of April [1839], on the building spot of my house [the Far West Temple site]" (D&C 118:4–5).

It was potentially dangerous for the men to return to Far West, and some believed that the Lord would not require them to go under the circumstances. However, the Twelve concluded that the Lord had spoken and would take care of them if they obeyed, so they agreed to return to the Far West temple site and fulfill the revelation.

This was one prophecy that some apostates and enemies of the Church believed would never be fulfilled since the Church had been forced to leave Far West and were settling in Illinois. Ignoring the potential risks, the available members of the Twelve returned to Far West to fulfill this prophecy.[1]

On April 18, 1839, five of the Twelve Apostles began the two-hundred-mile trip back to Far West: Brigham Young, Orson Pratt, John Taylor, Wilford Woodruff, and George A. Smith. They were unaware that Joseph and Hyrum Smith and the other Liberty Jail prisoners had recently been allowed to escape and were already on their way to Illinois. The apostles were accompanied by Alpheus Cutler, who was intended to be the master builder for the Far West Temple.[2]

On their way to Far West, the five apostles encountered another apostle, John E. Page, who was traveling with his family from Far West toward Quincy. The Page wagon had just tipped over on a hillside, and many of the contents had spilled, out, including soft soap that Elder Page was scooping up with his hands.[3] Brigham Young requested that he leave his family immediately and return to Far West with the other apostles. At first, Elder Page objected because he needed to take his family to Quincy, but Brigham Young insisted that he go with them and that his family would be all right without him. When Page asked how much time he could have to get ready, Brigham Young replied, "Five minutes." The apostles helped him reload his wagon, and Page returned to Far West with the others.[4]

During the night of April 25, 1839, the six apostles traveling together from Illinois arrived at Far West, along with about twenty members, all at risk for their personal safety. They were joined by Heber C. Kimball, who had arrived secretly during the night from a special assignment to visit Joseph Smith in Liberty Jail.

In the predawn light on the morning of April 26, 1839, the apostles rode into the public square of Far West and held a small meeting at the temple site.[5] They voted to excommunicate nearly three dozen members who had not remained loyal during the difficulties of the fall and winter. Elder Cutler, the master workman of the house, then recommenced laying the foundation of the temple by rolling up a large stone near the southeast corner. This was pursuant to the commandment given in Doctrine and Covenants 115:10–11 that the Mormons were to commence laying the foundation of the temple on July 4, 1838, and recommence laying the foundation on April 26, 1839.

The members of the Twelve then proceeded to ordain Wilford Woodruff and George A. Smith as apostles while standing on the chief cornerstone of the building. Darwin Chase and Norman Shearer (who had just been liberated from Richmond Prison) were then ordained to the office of seventy. Each of the seven apostles prayed in turn, according to their order in the quorum, after which they sang the hymn "Adam-ondi-Ahman." Elder Cutler then placed the cornerstone in position, after which the meeting adjourned and the Twelve began their return trip to Nauvoo.[6] Wilford Woodruff described the scene:

> The Twelve then gave the parting hand to the following Saints, agreeable to revelation: A. Butler, Elias Smith, Norman Shearer, William Burton, Stephen Markham, Shadrach Roundy, William O. Clark, John W. Clark, Hezekiah Peck, Darwin Chase, Richard Howard, Mary Ann Peck, Artimesia Granger, Martha Peck, Sarah Granger, Theodore Turley, Hiram Clark, and Daniel Shearer.
>
> Bidding good-by to this small remnant of the Saints who remained on the Temple ground to see us fulfill the revelation and commandment of God, we turned our backs on Far West, Missouri, and returned to Illinois. We had accomplished the mission without a dog moving his tongue at us, or any man saying, "Why do ye so?" We crossed the Mississippi river on the steam ferry, entered Quincy on the 2nd of May, and all of us had the joy of reaching our families once more in peace and safety. Thus the word of God was complied with.[7]

Not all of the Twelve were available to attend this event. The following seven of the Twelve were present: Brigham Young, Heber C. Kimball, Orson Pratt, John E. Page, John Taylor, Wilford Woodruff, and George A. Smith. However, five other members were not available. There was controversy at the time over Orson Hyde and William Smith; the former was eventually reinstated, but the latter left the Church all together. Parley Pratt was languishing in the Richmond Jail; Lyman Sherman had been sustained but died before his ordination; and Willard Richards was in England serving a mission.

Before departing from Far West, several of the men wandered the now deserted streets that had been their home just a few months before, and they also visited the home of Isaac Russell, a former member who had apostatized and remained in the area. Brigham Young related the story.

> As the Saints were passing away from the meeting, Brother Turley said to Page and Woodruff, "Stop a bit, while I bid Isaac Russell good-bye"; and knocking at the door called Brother Russell. His wife answered, "Come in, it is Brother Turley." Russell replied, "It is not; he left here two weeks ago," and appeared quite alarmed; but on finding it was Turley, asked him to sit down; but he replied, "I cannot; I shall lose my company." "Who is your company?" inquired Russell. "The Twelve." "The Twelve!" "Yes. Don't you know that this is the twenty-sixth, and the day the Twelve were to take leave of their friends

on the foundation of the Lord's House, to go to the islands of the sea? The revelation is now fulfilled, and I am going with them." Russell was speechless, and Turley bid him farewell. Thus was this revelation fulfilled, concerning which our enemies said, if all the other revelations of Joseph Smith were fulfilled, that one should not, as it had day and date to it.[8]

After the trip to Far West, the Twelve returned to Quincy for a brief period of time to prepare for the departure to England. A week later, four miles outside Quincy, the Twelve had a happy reunion with Joseph and Hyrum Smith, who had escaped from their imprisonment in Missouri. Said Brigham of the occasion, "It was one of the most joyful scenes of my life to once more strike hands with the Prophets, and behold them free from the hands of their enemies: Joseph conversed with us like a man who had just escaped from a thousand oppressions, and was now free in the midst of his children."[9]

Joseph resumed leadership of the Church, and arrangements were made to obtain lands in Commerce (Nauvoo), Illinois. On July 7, the Twelve Apostles gave their farewell address to the Mormons in Nauvoo in an emotion-filled meeting to begin their missionary trip to England.

Notes

1. See *History of the Church,* 3:306–307.
2. Ibid., 3:337.
3. John Page Autobiography in *Millennial Star,* 103–104.
4. Arrington, *Brigham Young: American Moses,* 71–72.
5. *History of the Church,* 3:336–39.
6. Ibid.
7. Cowley, *Wilford Woodruff: His Life and Labors,* 102.
8. *History of the Church,* 3:339–40.
9. Arrington, ibid., 72.

Epilogue

AFTER MOST OF THE MORMONS had left Far West for Illinois, Lyman Littlefield, an early Church member, returned to see the area because "[he] was uneasy in mind concerning the condition of my remaining friends in Caldwell and Daviess Counties, and obtained leave of absence from the printing office located in Lexington, Missouri, in order to take a trip there and see for myself their true condition."[1] His account of his visit is a fitting epilogue for the Far West era, for it exemplifies the rapid abandonment of the city and the feelings of many of the Mormons who left:

> At Far West the principal buildings stood intact, but many of the private dwellings were not occupied by their owners and builders. Those of the inhabitants still there were preparing to go upon their forced exit, as the gubernatorial mob edict had fixed the time when they must depart.
>
> I contemplated, with sadness, the change that had taken place in such a brief period of time. Those residences where I had passed happy hours and months, with the friends of my youthful prime, were deserted and desolate. My feet, as I stepped towards the thresholds where once I met with friendly greetings, awoke no responsive echoes. The voices of my young associates pronounced no word of tender recognition. The hand of affection was not there to grasp mine, as in the past. Those smiling faces that once beamed with gladness at my coming, while the eye sparkled with brightness and bosoms heaved with emotions of fidelity—alas, where were they all? My God! Why were they not there? The cruel truth full well I knew and my spirit was crushed! They were

gone to hunt an asylum from oppression! Was not that the new city our parents had built? Had they not acquired lawful titles to the soil? Was not that their country and rightful place of abode? Yes, but they were what the world call "Mormons," and such, in the estimation of a cruel, wicked populace, had no rights that should be regarded.

That townsite—Far West—and as far as the eye could extend over the rolling prairie towards the four points of the compass—was not marked by a single habitation for the abode of man, when our people halted their wagons and pitched their tents there in 1836. But within the short period of their residence, the scene had been transformed, as if by the hand of magic, and small towns, settlements and farm houses with their accompanying improvements, heightened the broad and dappled beauty of the undulating landscape, exhibiting evidences of the industry and skill of the hunted and ever-toiling Mormon people.

A short time previous I had looked over this romantic region with pride, hope and inspiring joy, but now with emotions of sadness, despondence and grief. Wherever I turned, loneliness and desolation were unbroken by any feature calculated to awaken cheerfulness or mollify the tendency to despondence. My people were not there! They had left their homes empty and desolate—all save a few, and they were struggling to prepare for the dreary journey. The houses, nearly all, were in the midst of stillness—save the sweet melody of birds, which fell upon my ear like a requiem dirge. No axmen were in the enclosures or groves; no curling smoke arose from the chimneys, indicative of bright firesides and tempting repasts; the voices of bleating lambs and lowing herds sent forth no echoes upon the ambient air. No, not even the barking of the faithful watchdog broke the monotonous silence.

At that time, what was missed more than all else were the voices of the loved ones which had saluted me in the past. Their cheerful music was hushed and the melody of their Sabbath orisons no more sent up anthems of praise into the ears of the God of Sabbaoth. Alas, where were they all? The forms of those early associates, those trustworthy young men, and the rosy-cheeked bevies of happy girls—once so vivacious and merry-hearted—indeed, where were they? Once we mingled there, in life's halcyon prime; but now I walked alone and the happy past lived but in memory. The aged, also, with gray heads and bent forms, the mother with the suckling babe and the father with his group of plodding boys—all, all had left, and at that hour were on the weary march, exiled and cast out from the homes their hands had built, and from the streets they had surveyed and converted into thoroughfares for enterprise and traffic. In the midst of those scenes, endeared by so many tender memories, I felt as a stranger, and almost as an intruder; for why should I be there, and they, the owners, ejected and driven away? That hour, though peculiar, was full of interest as the past and future were contemplated.

To me, that was an interesting spot. A great future awaits it. Twenty-five miles to the north, on the north side of Grand River, was Adam-ondi-Ahman, the place where Adam built an altar, offered sacrifice, and blessed his posterity. Also, that "is the place where Adam shall come to visit his people, or the Ancient of days shall sit, as spoken of by Daniel the prophet." (D&C 116) "I beheld till the thrones were cast down, and the Ancient of days did sit, whose garment was white as snow, and the hair of his head like the pure wool: his throne was like the fiery flame, and his wheels as the burning fire. A fiery stream issued and came forth from before him: thousand thousands ministered unto him, and ten thousand times ten thousand stood before him: the judgment was set, and the books were opened." (Daniel 7:9-10)

About fifty miles from there, in a southerly direction, the center stake of Zion is yet to be organized and a magnificent city and temple built, by command of the Almighty, at Independence, Jackson County. Far West will then cast off its gloomy aspect, for it will be rebuilt by the Saints and a temple erected there, the cornerstone for which is already laid. Concerning the erection of this house unto the Lord, and also the building up of Far West, the reader will please read Section 115, Doctrine and Covenants. Let the reader especially note this language made use of in the sacred revelation: "Let this city, Far West, be a holy and consecrated land unto me, and it shall be called most holy, for the ground upon which thou standest is holy."

Yes, I have looked upon that land when it was the peaceful abode of the Saints, who had found refuge there from Jackson and Clay Counties, from Kirtland and many other places. It was a delightsome country to look upon. It had been but little inhabited for hundreds of years, perhaps ever since the Jaredite and Nephite nations dwelt there. The chances favor the idea that its soil had not been stained with human blood, at least since the era just alluded to, unless the "red men of the forest" have since that early period, made that the scene of some bloody strife. But when Joseph stood there, on April 6, 1838, the Lord said, "the land" on which he stood was "holy." We may hope from this that the delightful region had escaped much of the pollutions of all the races that have dwelt upon it since Father Adam offered sacrifice upon the time-ruined altars of Adam-ondi-Ahman.

While the Latter-day Saints dwelt there, a great majority of them, at least, tried to walk circumspectly before the Lord and serve Him. Lucifer, the arch enemy of Christ, was not pleased that this should continue, and so inflamed the hearts of the people against them that the strength of the wicked were marshaled and drove them from their inheritances. Inasmuch as this was the case, the Lord, so far as the Saints are concerned, will not hold them responsible, because His house is not built at Far West and the residue of His people are not gathered there, and because that beautiful country is not filled with cities and those sanctuaries of worship which He is ever pleased to accept at the hands of a sanctified people. But there is a most glorious future in store for that and other portions of the Land of Zion, to be revealed at the appointed times, when the Saints shall return with strength and wisdom sufficient to obey His laws and build up the waste places, that Zion may arise and put on her beautiful garments.[2]

In 1838, the Lord declared that the land of Far West and Adam-ondi-Ahman was "most holy." This significance may relate to its past, to the events of the 1830s, and to its future importance. One reason this region is sacred is that it was the land where Adam and Eve and their posterity dwelt, and possibly where the righteous City of Enoch was located. The sacrifices, loss of life, and hardships endured by the early Saints in the 1830's also makes this "hallowed" ground. The marvelous promises of the future City of Zion also makes this a special and sacred area in the hearts of those who believe in the restored gospel.

Notes
1. Lyman Littlefield Reminiscences, 97.
2. Ibid., 97–102

APPENDIX A

MINUTES OF FAR WEST HIGH COUNCIL MEETING OF FEBRUARY 5, 1838, REGARDING STATUS OF MISSOURI PRESIDENCY

The following are the minutes of the proceedings of a general assembly of The Church of Jesus Christ of Latter-day Saints, assembled at the following places, to transact the business of said Church.

Thomas B Marsh was chosen Moderator, and John Cleminson Clerk. The Moderator addressed the throne of grace in prayer, after which he laid before the assembly the object of the meeting, giving a relation of the recent organization of the Church here, and in Kirtland. He also read a certain revelation given in Kirtland, Sept 4th, 1837; which made known that John Whitmer and William W. Phelps were in transgression, and if they repented not, they should be removed out of their places. Also, read a certain clause contained in the appeal, published in the old *Star*, under the 183rd page, as follows:— "And to sell our lands would amount to a denial of our faith, as that is the place where the Zion of God shall stand according to our faith and belief in the revelations of God.'"

Elder John Murdock then took the stand, and showed to the congregation why the High Council proceeded thus, was, that the Church might have a voice in the matter; and that he considered it perfectly legal, according to the instructions of President Joseph Smith Jr.

Elder G. M. Hinkle then set forth the way in which the Presidency of Far West had been labored with, that a committee of three, of whom he was one, had labored with them. He then read a written document containing a number of accusations against the three Presidents. He spake many things against them, setting forth in a plain and energetic manner, the iniquity of Phelps & Whitmer, in using the moneys which were loaned for the Church. Also D. Whitmer's wrong, in persisting in the use of tea, coffee, and tobacco.

Bishop Partridge then arose, and endeavored to rectify some mistakes of minor importance made by Elder Hinkle. Also, the Bishop spake against the proceedings of the meeting, as being hasty and illegal, for he thought they ought to be had before the common council: and said, that he could not lift his hand against the presidency at present: he then read a letter from President Joseph Smith, Jr.

A letter was then read by Thomas B. Marsh from William Smith, who made some comments on the same, and also on the letter read by Edward Partridge.

Elder George Morey (who was one of the committee sent to labor with the Presidency), then spake, setting forth in a very energetic manner, the proceedings of the Presidency as being iniquitous. Also, Elder Grover, one of the committee, spake against the conduct of the Presidency and Oliver Cowdery on their visit to labor with them.

Elder David W. Patten, then spake with much zeal against this Presidency, and in favor of Br. Joseph Smith and that the wolf alluded to in his letter, was the dissenters in Kirtland.

Elder Lyman Wight next stated that he considered that all other accusations were of minor importance compared to their selling their lands in Jackson County, that they (Phelps & Whitmer) had set an example which all the members were liable to follow: he said that it was a hellish principle, and that they had flatly denied the faith in so doing. Elder Elias Higbee then sanctioned what had been done by the council speaking against the Presidency.

Elder Murdock again took the stand, and stated that sufficient had been said to substantiate the accusations against them.

Elder Solomon Hancock plead in favor of the Presidency, stating that he could not raise his hand against them.

Elder John Corrill then spake against the High Council in regard to their proceedings, and labored hard to show that the meeting was illegal, and that the Presidency ought to be had before a proper tribunal, which he considered to be a Bishop and twelve High Priests: he labored in favor of the Presidency, and said that he should not raise his hands against them at present, although he did not uphold them in their iniquity

Elder Simeon Carter, next arose and spake against the meeting as being hasty.

Elder Groves followed brother Carter, in like observations and of like nature.

Elder Patten again took the stand in vindication of the cause of the meeting.

Elder Morley then spake against the Presidency, at the same time pleading mercy.

Titus Billings said that he could not vote until they had a hearing in the common council.

Elder Marsh said that the meeting was according to the directions of Br Joseph. He, therefore, considered it legal.

Elder Moses Martin then took the stand & with great energy spake in favor of the legality of the meeting and against the conduct of the Presidency of Zion, alleging that the present corruptions of the church here, were owing to the wickedness and mismanagement of her leaders.

The Moderator then called the vote in favor of the present Presidency. The negative was then called, and the vote against David Whitmer, John Whitmer, and William W. Phelps was unanimous, excepting eight or ten and this minority only wished them to continue in office a little longer, or until Joseph Smith came up.

APPENDIX B

Joseph Smith had asked Levi Hancock to write a song the day before the Fourth of July celebration in 1838. When singing this song, Solomon stood at the southeast cornerstone of the temple. These are the words, but the tune is unknown:

Song of Freedom

1. Come lovers of freedom to gather,
   And hear what we now have to say.
   For surely we ought to remember
   The cause that produced this great day.
   Oh, may we remember while singing
   The pains and distresses once born
   By those who have fought for our freedom
   And often for friends called to mourn.

2. The lives and the fortunes together
   And honors all sacred and dear
   Were solemnly all pledged forever
   By our honored Forefathers here.
   Including the great and the noble
   Who in our behalf were so brave
   They offered their lives for our freedom
   When called for our country to save.
   Oh, May we remember while singing
   The pains and distresses once born
   By those who have fought for our freedom
   And often for friends called to mourn.

3. The parliament lords and the commons
   To gather their soldiers prepare
   And placed at their heads men to lead them
   Then over the ocean did steer.
   To fight with their foes? Oh no, never!
   To deal with their enemies? No!
   But for some few fancied offenses
   Across the Atlantic did go.

4. T'was then a pardon was offered
    To all who would willingly yield,
    Excepting John Hancock and Adams,
    The fate of these men had been sealed.
    Thank God then, for good Patrick Henry
    And other men who with him dared
    To come out with heart rending speeches
    Against what these war lords declared.

5. The Tories were all crying "treason"
    Against those who called for their right,
    And they would not listen to reason
    But called their forces to fight
    To gain for the lords and the commons,
    Who called for a tax without right
    Then often from morning to morning
    Contended for it with their might.

6. God armed our forefathers with power
    And Washington came to their aid;
    In wisdom he lead the great battle
    And soon made the Tories afraid.
    He raised up the Standard of Freedom
    And called for his brave volunteers
    Who gathered quickly around him
    And from their bold enemy steered.

7. Hark! How the great battle rages
    Behold! He undauntedly stands.
    The great cause for hereafter ages,
    He pleads with his sword in his hands.
    Behold, English lords then came bending,
    And from their high chairs soon fell down.
    And Tories and tyrants lay bleeding
    Before this great Man of Renown.

8   Great love then filled every bosom,
    And joy beamed upon every face
    Where lingered the true seed of freedom,
    All willingly gave God the praise.
    They told the sad tale to their children,
    And told them the same to hand down

To their children's children forever
Until the great trumpet should sound.

9.   To celebrate this day of freedom
Don't let it ever be lost.
Remembers the wars of our Fathers
And also the blood they have cost.
Go children, and tell the same story
To your children's children unborn,
How English lords, tyrants, and Tories,
Have once caused your fathers to mourn.

10. T'was honor that nerved up your Fathers
And caused them to go forth and fight
To gain us this great day of freedom
In which we can now take delight,
Yes, daughters, you too have your freedom
You too have your country most dear,
You love well your own Independence,
Your Forefathers gained for you here.

11. Exalt the standard of Freedom,
And don't leave upon it a stain.
Be firm and determined forever
Your freedom and rights to maintain.
Remember the God of your Fathers.
Ye Sons and ye Daughters give ear;
Then with you t'wil be well hereafter,
And nothing you'll then have to fear.

12. Farewell, ye old venerable Fathers'
Who have stood for many a year.
Ye, like the aged trees have fallen,
Except just a few there and here.
White locks plainly show they're soon going
To earth-dust from whence we all came,
To rest in the mansion of glory
Beyond all the trials and pain.

Appendix C

The Executive Order signed in 1976 by Missouri Governor Christopher Bond, rescinding the extermination order issued in 1838 by Governor Boggs, provides as follows:

Executive Order

Whereas, on Oct. 27, 1838, the governor of the state of Missouri, Lilburn W. Boggs, issued an order calling for the extermination or expulsion of the Mormons form the State of Missouri;

And whereas, Gov. Boggs' order clearly contravened the rights of life, liberty, property, and religious freedom as guaranteed by the Constitution of the United States, as well the Constitution of the State of Missouri;

And whereas, in the Bicentennial year, as we reflect upon our nation's heritage, the exercise of religious freedom is without question one of the basic tenets of our free democratic republic,

Now therefore, I, Christopher S. Bond, governor of the state of Missouri, by virtue of the authority vested in me by the constitution and laws of Missouri, do hereby order the following:

Expressing on behalf of all Missourians our deep regret for the injuries and undue suffering which was caused by this 1838 order, I hereby rescind Executive Order No,. 44, dated Oct. 27, 1883, issued by Gov. Lilburn W. Boggs.

In testimony thereof I have heretofore set my hand and caused to be affixed the Great Seal of the State of Missouri in the City of Jefferson this 25th day of June 1976.

Signed, Christopher S. Bond, Governor
James C. Kirkpatrick, Secretary of State

SOURCES

AUTOBIOGRAPHIES

Butler, John. "Autobiography of John Lowe Butler I," typescript, HBLL; http://www.boap.org/LDS/Early-Saints/JButler.html.

Shurtleff, Stella Cahoon and Cahoon, Brent Farrington. *Reynolds Cahoon and His Stalwart Sons.* Salt Lake City: Paragon Press, Inc., 1960.

Call, Anson. "Autobiography of Anson Call," typescript HBLL; http://www.boap.org/LDS/Early-Saints/ACall.html.

Gunn, Stanley R. *Oliver Cowdery, Second Elder and Scribe.* Salt Lake City: Bookcraft, 1962.

Dibble, Philo. Autobiography. *Early Scenes in Church History: Four Faith Promoting Classics.* Salt Lake City: Bookcraft, 1968.

Draper, William. "Autobiography of William Draper," typescript, HBLL; http://www.boap.org/LDS/Early-Saints/WDraper.html.

Duncan, Chapman. "Autobiography of Chapman Duncan," typescript, HBLL; http://www.boap.org/LDS/Early-Saints/CDuncan.html.

Foot, Warren. "Autobiography of Warren Foote," typescript, LDS Archives; http://www.boap.org/LDS/Early-Saints/WFoote.html.

Groves, Elisha Hurd. Autobiography (1797–1868). LDS Archives (Ms d 2050, 11, 13, #11)

Hancock, Levi. "The Life of Levi Hancock," typescript, HBLL; http://www.boap.org/LDS/Early-Saints/LHancock.html.

Hancock, Mosiah. "Autobiography of Mosiah Hancock," typescript, HBLL; http://www.boap.org/LDS/Early-Saints/MHancock.html.

Hancock, Phebe. Personal letter, typescript, from author's family resources.

Hendricks, Drusilla Dorris. Autobiography (1810–1847). LDS Archives (Ms d 2050 bx 4 fd 9 #2)

Holbrook, Joseph. "The Life of Joseph Holbrook," typescript, HBLL; http://www.boap.org/LDS/Early-Saints/JHolbrook.html.

Huntington, Dimick Baker. Journal (1808–1859). LDS Archives (Ms d 1419)

Huntington, Oliver B. "History of the Life of Oliver B. Huntington Also His travels and Troubles Written by Himself," typescript, HBLL; http://www.boap.org/LDS/Early-Saints/OBHuntington.html.

Huntington, William. "A Brief Sketch of the Life of WIlliam Huntington, Sr.," typescript, HBLL; http://www.boap.org/LDS/Early-Saints/WHuntington.html.

Jackman, Levi. "A Short Sketch of the Life of Levi Jackman," typescript, HBLL; http://www.boap.org/LDS/Early-Saints/LJackman.html.

Johnson, Benjamin F. *My Lief's Review.* Independence, MO: Zion's Printing and Publishing Co., 1947.

Judd, Zadok Knapp. Autobiography (1827–1848). Typescript, BYU Special Collections Library.

Kimball, Heber Chase, in *Women's Exponent* (1880–1883). Salt Lake City: Vol. 9–11.

Littlefield, Lyman Omer Littlefield. *Reminiscences of Latter-day Saints.* Logan, UT: The Utah Journal Co., 1888.

Lymana, Amasa. *Millennial Star* (1865). London: Vol. 27.

Lyman, Eliza. "Life and Journal of Eliza Maire Partridge (Smith) Lyman," typescript, HBLL; http://www.boap.org/LDS/Early-Saints/EMPSLyman.html.

Marsh, Thomas. "History of Thomas Baldwin Marsh," *The Latter-day Saints' Millennial Star* (1864). London: Vol. 26.

McArthur, Daniel. "Autobiography of Daniel D. McArthur," typescript, HBLL; http://www.boap.org/LDS/Early-Saints/DMcArthur.html.

McBride, James. "Autobiography of James McBride," typescript, HBLL; http://www.boap.org/LDS/Early-Saints/JMcbride.html.

Miles, Samuel. Journal (1826–1881). LDS Church Archives (Ms d 2050, 25, 1, #1–2).

Miles, Samuel. "Recollections of the Prophet Joseph Smith," *Juvenile Instructor* 27 (1892), typescript, HBLL; http://www.boap.org/LDS/Early-Saints/REC-JS.html.

Murdock, John. "An Abridged Record of the Life of John Murdock," typescript, HBLL; http://www.boap.org/LDS/Early-Saints/JMurdock.html.

Osborn, David. "Autobiography of David Osborn, Senior," typescript, HBLL; http://www.boap.org/LDS/Early-Saints/DOsborn.html.

Partridge, Edward. Journal (1793–1836). Holograph, 2 vols. LDS Archives (Ms d 892).

Pettigrew, David. *An Enduring Legacy.* Vol. 3. Salt Lake City: Deseret Book, 1980.

Pratt, Parley P. *Autobiography of Parley P. Pratt.* Parley P. Pratt Jr., ed. Salt Lake City: Deseret Book, 1938.

Phelps, Morris. Autobiography (1831–1833). LDS Archives (Ms d 271).

Phelps, William W. "The Versatile W. W. Phelps, Mormon Writer, Educator and Pioneer." Thesis by Walter Bowen, BYU 1958.

Pulsipher, John. "Autobiography of John Pulsipher," typescript, HBLL; http://www.boap.org/LDS/Early-Saints/JPulsipher.html.

Rich, Sara. "Journal of Sarah DeArmon Pea Rich," typescript, HBLL; http://www.boap.org/LDS/Early-Saints/SRich.html.

Rigdon, John. "The Life of Sidney Rigdon. *Dialogue Magazine,* 1:4.

Robinson, Ebenezer. *The Return.* Davis City, IA, Sept. 1889.

Rogers, Samuel Hollister. Journal. BYU Harold B. Lee Library, 2 vols. (MSS 1134).

Stevenson, Edward. Journal (1820–1896), 46 vols. LDS Church Archives (Ms f 103).

Shurtliff, Luman. "Biographical Sketch of the Life of Luman Andros Shurtliff," typescript, HBLL; http://www.boap.org/LDS/Early-Saints/LShurtliff.html

Smith, Bathsheba Bigler. Autobiography (1822–1906). Holograph, BYU Harold B. Lee Library (MSS 920).

Smith, George. "My Journal," *The Instructor* 82:14.

Smith, Joseph F. *Life of Joseph F. Smith*. Salt Lake: Deseret Book, 1938.

Snow, Erastus. Autobiography. LDS Church Archives (Ms d 1329).

Stout, Allen. "Journal of Allen Stout," typescript, HBLL; http://www.boap.org/LDS/Early-Saints/AStout.html.

Thomas, Martha. Autobiography in "Daniel Stilwell Thomas Family History (non-published), LDS Church Archives.

Tracy, Nancy. "Life History of Nancy Naomi Alexander Tracy," typescript, HBLL; http://www.boap.org/LDS/Early-Saints/NTracy.html.

Woodruff, Wilford. *Wilford Woodruff, Fourth President of the Church of Jesus Christ of Latter-Day Saints: History of His Life and Labors as Recorded in His Daily Journals.* Matthias F. Cowley, ed. Salt Lake City: Bookcraft, 1964.

Young, Emily Partridge. Journal (1824–1899). LDS Church Archives (Ms d 2845).

BOOKS AND PUBLICATIONS

Baugh, Alexander L. "A Call to Arms: The 1838 Mormon Defense of Northern Missouri." PhD diss., Brigham Young University, 1971.

Black, Susan Easton and Porter, Larry. "Biographies of the Mormon Battallion," manuscript at LDS Visitors' Center at Nauvoo.

Arrington, Lenoard J. *Brigham Young: American Moses.* Chicago: University of Illinois Press, 1986.

Autobiography of Parley Parker Pratt. Edited by his son Parley P. Pratt. 3d ed. Salt Lake: Deseret Book, 1938.

Roberts. B. H. *A Comprehensive History of The Church of Jesus Christ of Latter-day Saints.* Salt Lake City: Bookcraft, 1970.

Smith, Joseph Field. *Essentials in Church History.* Salt Lake City: Deseret Book, 1946.

Far West Record: Minutes of The Church of Jesus Christ of Latter-day Saints, 1830–1834. Edited by Donald Q. Cannon and Lyndon W. Cook. Salt Lake City: Deseret Book, 1983.

Robison, Elwin C. *The First Mormon Temple: Design, Construction, and Historic Context of the Kirtland Temple.* Provo, UT: Brigham Young University Press, 1997.

Joseph Smith, *History of The Church of Jesus Christ of Latter-day Saints.* Edited by B. H. Roberts. Salt Lake City: The Church of Jesus Christ of Latter-day Saints, 1968.

Corrill, John. *A Brief History of the Church of Christ of Latter Day Saints.* St. Louis: Printed for the Author, 1839.

Whitney, Orson F. *History of Utah.* 4 vols. George Q. Cannon and Sons Co., 1896.

Mormon Redress Petitions: Documents of the 1833–1838 Missouri Conflict. Edited by Clark V. Johnson. Provo, UT: Religious Studies Center Brigham Young University, 1992.

Anderson, Mary Audentia Smith. "The Memories of President Joseph Smith III," *The Saints Herald*, Nov. 6, 1934.

Lisonbee, Janet and Curtis, Annette. *Missouri Mormon Burials: Obituaries and Life Sketches of the Early Saints Who Died and are Buried in Missouri.* Independence, MO: Missouri Mormon Frontier Foundation, 2008.

McConkie, Bruce R. *Mormon Doctrine.* 2d ed. Salt Lake City: Bookcraft, 1966.

Church Educational System, *Church History in the Fulness of Times.* 2d ed. Salt Lake City: The Church of Jesus Christ of Latter-day Saints, 2000.

Dyer, Alvin R. *The Refiner's Fire: The Significance of Events Transpiring in Missouri.* Salt Lake City: Deseret Book, 1968.

Dewey, Richard Lloyd. *Porter Rockwell: The Definitive Biography.* New York: Paramount Books, 986.

Bushman, Richard Lyman with Woodworth, Jed. *Joseph Smith: Rough Stone Rolling.* New York: Alfred A. Knopf, 2005.

Personal Writings of Joseph Smith. Compiled and edited by Dean C. Jessee. Salt Lake City: Deseret Book, 2002.

History of Caldwell and Livingston Counties, Missouri. St. Louis: National Historical Company, 1886.

Ward, Charlene. "A Brief History of Caldwell County." http://www.caldwellcountymissouri.com.

Journal of Discourses. 26 vols. London: Latter-day Saints' Book Depot, 1854–86.

Black, Susan Easton. *Who's Who in the Doctrine and Covenants?* Salt Lake City: Bookcraft, 1997.

PERIODICALS AND MISCELLANEOUS

Daniel Tyler, "Recollections of the Prophet Joseph Smith," *Juvenile Instructor* 27 (February 1892): 94-95; spelling standardized.

Elder's Journal of the Church of Latter Day Saints, 1837–38. Edited by Joseph Smith. 4 eds. Published at Kirtland, Ohio, and Far West, Missouri.

The Utah Genealogical and Historical Magazine. Edited by Andrew H. Lund. Salt Lake City, UT: Deseret News Press, 1923–1940.

The Saints Herald. Published by the Reorganized Church of Jesus Christ of Latter-day Saints (Community of Christ). Independence, MO: Herald House Publishers, Jan. 1860 to present.

Millennial Star (1840–1970), vol. 27 and 40.

Journal History of the Church (1839–1846). Salt Lake City, UT: The Church of Jesus Christ of Latter-day Saints.

The Utah Journal (1882–1889). Edited by John E. Carlisle. Logan, UT.

Kansas City Journal (1854–1942). Kansas City, MO.

Jenson, Andrew. *The Historical Record* (1886–1889). Salt Lake City, UT.

Women's Exponent (1872–1914). Salt Lake City, UT.

Hymns of The Church of Jesus Christ of Latter-day Saints (Salt Lake City: The Church of Jesus Christ of Latter-day Saints, 1985), 49.

ABOUT THE AUTHORS

Dan and Janet Lisonbee are natives of Mesa, Arizona, and are the parents of ten children. They currently reside in Brighton, Colorado. Dan received his law degree from Arizona State University and was a tax consultant for twenty years for TRW, a multi-national corporation headquartered in Cleveland, Ohio. He has written another book soon to be published, *The Laws of Nauvoo.*

Dan and Janet lived in Kirtland, Ohio, for several years and were involved in Church history there. Janet worked closely with the Community of Christ to develop and present tours of the North Kirtland Cemetery, where many early Church members are buried. She also developed an LDS Church history exhibit for the Lake County Historical Society and contributed historical articles for the *Kirtland Gazette.*

Janet is the author of *Mormon Graves in Kirtland* and *Missouri Mormon Burials* and has also researched the deaths of the early LDS members who died in the Nauvoo area. She was also a contributor to *Meridian Magazine* for two years.

Dan and Janet are lifetime members of the Church and have served in a number of capacities. Both have taught early morning seminary and served extensively in the youth programs of the Church. Dan has served as a bishop, bishop's counselor, high councilor, and counselor in a stake presidency.

0 26575 53344 6

186